ADVANCE PRAISE FOR

Africa's Incomplete Cycles of Development

"Deftly combining optimism with pessimism, this book sees both the future possibilities and challenges of development in Africa. Older ideas and voices merge with newer ones to navigate the throes of globalization, dynamic internal energies, and the synergies of new technologies with African cultural resources."

—Toyin Falola, The Jacob and Frances Sanger Mossiker Chair, Distinguished Teaching Professor, Humanities, University of Texas, Austin

"This is a dense, scintillating, elegant and thought-provoking book on Africa's development coming from a generation of millennials. To the authors, Africa's epic journey to sustainable development is one filled with gloom and doom. Despite the vast pessimism in the narrative, the authors also see a modicum of hope for their continent, through proffering an assortment of alternatives which are set to address contemporary Africa's development conundrum."

—Emmanuel Dumbu, Doctor of Philosophy in Business Management, Regional Programme Coordinator, Zimbabwe Open University

"This pioneering book comes at the most appropriate stage where the global divide of Africa and the developed world needs to be urgently addressed. It lays bare the prescription of reducing poverty and unlocking development in Africa by exploring a wide scope of strategies. The book is a well-researched and incisive account of modern-day Africa and its development challenges which if not attended to, the continent's dream of development will remain an illusion."

—Calvin Mudzingiri, Department of Economics, University of the Free State, South Africa

Africa's Incomplete Cycles of Development

Africa in the Global Space

Edward Shizha
Series Editor

Vol. 1

The Africa in the Global Space series is part of the Peter Lang
Political Science, Economics, and Law list.
Every volume is peer reviewed and meets
the highest quality standards for content and production.

PETER LANG
New York • Bern • Berlin
Brussels • Vienna • Oxford • Warsaw

Kenneth Mahuni, Josiah Taru,
and Wellington G. Bonga

Africa's Incomplete Cycles of Development

PETER LANG
New York • Bern • Berlin
Brussels • Vienna • Oxford • Warsaw

Library of Congress Cataloging-in-Publication Data

Names: Mahuni, Kenneth, author. | Taru, Josiah, author. |
Bonga, Wellington G., author.
Title: Africa's incomplete cycles of development / Kenneth Mahuni,
Josiah Taru, and Wellington G. Bonga.
Other titles: Africa in the global space; v. 1.
Description: New York: Peter Lang, 2020.
Series: Africa in the global space; v. 1
ISSN 2576-358X (print) | ISSN 2576-3598 (online)
Includes bibliographical references and index.
Identifiers: LCCN 2019017990 | ISBN 978-1-4331-6821-5 (hardback: alk. paper)
ISBN 978-1-4331-6818-5 (ebook pdf)
ISBN 978-1-4331-6819-2 (epub) | ISBN 978-1-4331-6820-8 (mobi)
Subjects: LCSH: Economic development—Africa. | Africa—Economic
conditions—21st century. | Africa—Foreign economic relations.
Classification: LCC HC800 .M337 | DDC 338.96009051—dc23
LC record available at https://lccn.loc.gov/2019017990
DOI 10.3726/b16093

Bibliographic information published by **Die Deutsche Nationalbibliothek**.
Die Deutsche Nationalbibliothek lists this publication in the "Deutsche
Nationalbibliografie"; detailed bibliographic data are available
on the Internet at http://dnb.d-nb.de/.

80 Broad Street, 5th floor, New York, NY 10004
www.peterlang.com

To my lovely wife Rachel,
I affectionately dedicate this book. Also to Cathrine, Marko and Tompson, my greatest inspirations and true embodiments of what sheer hard work can achieve, you made me believe and pursue this project to its accomplishment.

Kenneth Mahuni

To *Grace*,
Praise and Prominence Bonga, with affection and admiration.

Wellington Garikai Bonga

For my family.

Josiah Taru

"Progress is more plausible judged by the reduction of deprivation than further enrichment of the opulent" **Amatya Sen**

"What separates developing countries from developed countries is as much a gap in knowledge as a gap in resources."—**Joseph Stiglitz**

"Compared to developed countries, or even to some major emerging countries, burdened by aging populations, financial crises, widening budget deficits, faltering faith in politics and growing social demands, Africa has become the world's last 'New Frontier': a kind of 'it-continent'."—**Mo Ibrahim**

"Developed countries and advanced developing countries must open their markets for products from the developing world, and support in developing their export and import capacity."—**Anna Lindh**

"Knowing that an economy is in decline is not enough. We must know why the economy is failing to achieve economic growth if we are to take steps to establish or re-establish it."—**Jeffrey D. Sachs**

"The more corrupt the state, the more numerous the laws."—**Tacitus**

TABLE OF CONTENTS

FOREWORD

Africa continues to swim in a sea of unprecedented challenges which continue to militate against the continent's smooth progress. Despite the fact that the continent's leadership is now considered to be in the driving seat in terms of dictating its development trajectory, the continent and its leadership still has got a long way to go in order for it to fully unleash and realize its development potential as correctly highlighted by the authors of this pioneering book. Going back to as early as the 1940s and 1950s the story of Africa's underdevelopment has been told by several scholars notably early ones like Walter Rodney and most recently Dambisa Moyo—the latter in a powerful book which has forced some constituencies to rethink the efficacy of some of Africa's development strategies whilst at the same time ruffling many feathers especially amongst leading development practitioners and members of the donor community. The authors of this book have added a new and insightful dimension and explanations to the causes behind Africa's sluggish development pace.

The academic diversity of the authors makes the book unique. The total sum of their experiences and skills amassed over the years coupled with a powerful sense of observation of the development environment across the broad spectrum of the continent over the years equipped them with a paraphernalia of tools to intricately weave a vivid narrative of the sorry state of Africa's development affairs. Indeed in *Africa's Incomplete Cycles of Development* as you flip through the pages, the reader can sense that the authors are emotionally attached to the development story of their mother continent. Throughout the text, the authors continuously ask the reader, 'If Africa's time is not now, then when?' Obviously they are referring to nothing other than the development of Africa, their mother continent. This question they pause also makes the reader wonder if ever there shall be a time period in which we will one day talk of a progressive and developed Africa.

A very commendable aspect of the book is that the authors, throughout show a profound and deep knowledge of Africa, the environment from which they launch their narrative. As such the book is laced with witty metaphors, which besides adding humour to the text, they also help to open the eyes of the reader to the socio-political, institutional and economic dynamics of contemporary Africa, in particular how they all interplay to shape Africa's development trajectory. For instance, the authors tackle what they term 'electioneering mode' in the domain of African politics in which they take the reader through a number of issues which have a close link to electioneering mode, specifically how these have become and will remain a nemesis to the continent's good governance and its effective development for a long period to come.

The authors also correctly observed that the attainment of political independence was supposed to be viewed as synonymous to seeing light, light that was supposed to shine to everyone. As such African states which were pioneers of independence were supposed to be the flagship of the continent's transformation. But the reality on the ground turned to be the opposite. However, no hope is lost, according to the authors. Africa can turn a leaf from its current state of affairs. The authors are very positive of a better Africa if some of the pertinent challenges raised in the book are religiously addressed by current crop of leaders emerging on the continent.

To conclude, this book is a masterpiece coming from a generation of millennials punching above their weight, who are very much concerned by their continent's current poor state of development and have a deep understanding of what needs to be done for it to achieve the desired transformation. Not only do they bring to the fore contemporary issues besetting the continent, but they also see hope. In their words, 'There is hope for Africa and for that matter, plenty of it.' This makes the book a very insightful and useful piece to both those interested in understanding Africa's past, present and future development trajectory in particular and students of development studies in general!

Dr. T Mumvuma
Department of Economics
University of Zimbabwe

PREFACE

Our interest in seeing things done differently in African nation-states sparked the conversation on 'what needs to be done' by and for Africans to enjoy the same lifestyle and the fruits of development that are enjoyed in other parts of the globe. As we followed current affairs on Africa, we got the conviction that we need to understand and explain what is happening in African states that stifles development. We sought answers for the following questions: what has got Africa to where it is today? Who is to blame for Africa's current woes and regression? What can be done to change Africa's vicissitudes? Is prosperity attainable in the near future? Colonialism can no longer suffice alone as a scapegoat to point a finger at for our stagnation. Greater parts of the continent are now enjoying a modicum of peace. To this end we sought to give both historical events and current obtaining situations that explain our circumstances. As we searched for explanations, initially we thought of writing a discussion paper giving an overview of the challenges that constrain Africa's development processes. The proposed article and discussion paper never saw the light of day, but conversations and discussions around the issue continued for long.

After nearly three years of scanning the development landscape of our beloved continent, we mooted an idea of coming up with a book that captures the current state of Africa's development processes. Several discussions and debates drew us closer and closer to the idea of putting together insights and ideas that we had agreed on. Despite several overlapping ideas and lines of thought, we never quite jellied together on the approaches, methodologies and scope of the book. This was due to differences in academic fields and disciplines. Kenneth and Wellington's economics background made them opt for macro-level analysis in which huge chunks of economic statistics and quantitative data were handy in explaining and elucidating the state of development across Africa. On the other hand, Josiah opined that micro-level and localized every-day economic practice of people must be the focus of the book. Concomitantly, qualitative and ethnography were Josiah's chosen approaches against quantitative national data sets that Wellington and Kenneth proposed. We worked out our disciplinary differences and took the middle of the road approach in which we triangulated our approaches firstly as a way of adding rigour to our analysis and of capturing different facets of the development trajectory in Africa. Secondly, triangulation allowed us to find common ground, and to look at the poverty of our chosen and disciplinary methods and approaches.

Putting together a rich and well thought manuscript, is not so easy a task. The process is taxing and draining, intellectually, emotionally, financially and in terms of time that is expended doing background research, in libraries and sitting before a computer. The process requires a lot of rethinking and intellectual analysis together with concept binding and linkages. The writing up process was further complicated by several issues and factors. The geographical distance that separated the three of us as authors had its toll on us. Much of the coordination and discussions were done through emails and numerous telephonic conversations, kudos to this age of technology we now live in! As this was not enough, there were a host of other commitments that equally demanded the time and attention of the authors. Work, personal and family commitments were drawbacks that we had to incessantly deal with as we gingerly tied together pieces of this book. Wellington worked through the book as he traversed the breadth and length of Zimbabwe on work assignments. The same can equally be said for Kenneth as he burnt the middle-night oil, putting hours after hours sifting through documents, revising and adding pages to our project. His work took him away from home several times during the writing up process. Josiah had to juggle and balance between work, studies and this project. We persevered and at the end we managed to give our best and produce this book.

Africa's Incomplete Cycles of Development is a book that seeks to add a voice to growing concerns over Africa's prolonged stagnation which is not showing much signs of improvement. Pre-independence Africa was stuck in the mud, weighed down by the colonial yoke. Hope of a better continent was neither here nor there. Sadly however, post-colonial Africa is trying to transform the continent, albeit at a lacklustre pace. Fresh challenges keep on mounting, further complicating the transformation process. We explain a number of these challenges. For instance, in the book we explain how the residual economies most African states inherited gradually became an albatross to the development process of the continent. Instead of upgrading and revamping the residual economies to address demands of modern day Africa, greed was allowed to take precedence, hence most economies were run down dislocating the development process.

On the other hand, elections, ought to be an insignia of progression of a society as they give people unfettered access to leaders of their own choice which then outlines the roadmap of progress or demise of their nation state. A closer look at electoral processes in the continent will unearth interesting developments. A thorough exegesis of most of these will point to a development train slowly coming to a halt. A grinding halt! Not to be outdone on the global stage is China. Her 'invasion' of nearly every corner of the global village has brought interesting outcomes to the development discourse of Africa also, the book examines this. Not only do we show the numerous links to the continent's regression and underdevelopment in contemporary times, we also proffer a solution set befitting to the current problems. We construct strong arguments from the perspective of inhabitants who not only live and experience happenings in the continent but also have livelihoods which are affected directly on a day to day basis. In a nutshell, this text addresses the basic concepts of economics governing Africa's development or lack thereof. It is a combined product of our experiences. Leveraging off these experiences informed key themes of the book.

Hopefully, this book will raise the level of awareness among the general public, academic institutions, policy makers, development institutes, among others. The book will offer answers to many development and economic growth questions that have remained unanswered before or whose answers have failed to stand the path. The beneficiaries of the project will be all of us—ourselves, our children, our beloved ones, our societies and the continent as a whole—who will live to see a better Africa.

We hope this book is widely read and referenced for a better Africa. Many books have been written to help educate others about development and prosperity. This book is not designed to be exhaustive in its coverage of issues underpinning Africa's growth aspirations, but has in its ability managed to explore the uneasy areas worth addressed, areas that have remained in the fringes and areas that require greater concern for the betterment of Africa. Assured, in this project is the depth of analysis and areas covered together with identified solutions to contemporary Africa's problems.

If Africa's time is not now, then when?

ACKNOWLEDGEMENTS

The blessings of the Lord made the project a success. This book is in no way our own efforts. There are many people who contributed to its success. Some read earlier versions of this book, some gave advice, insights and constructive criticisms that helped us shape and refine our arguments. We wish to acknowledge and thank the following individuals and institutions for their contributions and assistance we received:

Kristin Purdy, a former Peter Lang Acquisitions Editor whose early contributions to this project will forever be cherished. **Michelle Smith**, the Acquisitions Editor who was later assigned to take us through the rest of this book consistently gave us feedbacks and updates on the progress of our book to its completion, every single effort you made to this beautiful project is invaluable. **Jackie Pavlovic**, the Production Manager at Peter Lang for ensuring that our manuscript conforms with the high standards of Peter Lang, we will remain grateful to your patience and long hours you had to put on this project to ensure every standard is maintained. The entire Peter Lang team for having faith in our project, all your contributions remain priceless!

Thabani Nyoni, MSc Economics student with the University of Zimbabwe, and an author of various research articles in international journals, devoted his time to proofread the project, and gave his honest opinion on many areas that required clarity and a second thought; and all was addressed accordingly. The strategy used by Thabani Nyoni of rating each chapter contents proved to be very critical to the success of the project. **Marshal Nyachuru**, MSc Economics graduate, provided his development knowledge by thoroughly going through our manuscript and highlighting areas of concern. **I.M Mavesere**, Monetary Economics and Development Economics lecturer at the University of Zimbabwe, offered his opinion on the addressed issues in the book. **Dr. Takawira Mumvuma**, a senior lecturer at the University of Zimbabwe, teaching Social economics and Development economics at undergraduate and post-graduate level, an author of various development manuscripts, managed to dedicate his precious time, and chose to go through our project and offered his side of the contents, of which the suggestions and highlights were factored in the final product.

Dr Garikai Makuyana, a Senior Economics lecturer at Great Zimbabwe University, made this dream project come true. In spite of his busy schedules, he always shared his honest views on the directions of this project, we will remain grateful for every piece of advice.

This project also could not have seen the light of day without the constant encouragements, powerful insights and nuggets of wisdom from **Dr. Robert Jeyakumar Nathan** from Multimedia University.

We are also greatly indebted to **Marko Mahuni**, who despite the busy schedule at Oxford University with studies always came on board. His patience while reviewing numerous sections of this manuscript and candid advice and comments are greatly appreciated.

There are many people who made this project possible through blind reviewing, typing, editing and reading through the manuscript, we thank you.

A special note of thanks is also extended to our dear families who managed to sacrifice to donate some time belonging to them for the success of the project. Their devotions, unconditional love, support, patience, optimism and advice is indispensable, we salute you guys!

ABBREVIATIONS

AFTZ	Africa Free Trade Zone
AGOA	African Growth and Opportunity Act
AMA	Arab Maghreb Union
AU	African Union
AUCPCC	African Union Convention to Prevent and Combat Corruption
BRI	Belt and Road Initiative
BRICS	Brazil, Russia, India, China and South Africa
CAADP	Comprehensive Africa Agriculture Development Programme
CEN-SAD	Community of Sahel-Saharan States CEN-SAD
COMESA	Common Market for Eastern and Southern Africa
CRPI	Corruption Perception Index
DRC	Democratic Republic of Congo
EAC	East African Community
EACJ	East African Court of Justice
EALA	East African Legislative Assembly
ECCAS	Economic Community of Central African States
ECOWAS	Economic Community of West African States
ESAP	Economic Structure Adjustment Program

FDI	Foreign Direct Investment
FTA	Free Trade Area
GDP	Gross Domestic Product
GVCs	Global Value Chains
HDI	Human Development Index
ICTs	Information and Communication Technology (ICTs)
IGAD	Intergovernmental Authority on Development
IMF	International Monetary Fund
IOC	Indian Ocean Commission (IOC)
MDGs	Millennium Development Goals
MRU	Mano River Union
NEPAD	New Partnership for Africa's Development
NGOs	Non-Governmental Organizations
OAU	Organization for African Unity
ODA	Official Development Assistance
PHLs	Post Harvest Losses
PIDA	Programme for Infrastructural Development in Africa
RECs	Regional Economic Communities
SACU	Southern African Customs Union
SADC	Southern African Development Community
SAPS	Structural Adjustment Programs
SDGs	Sustainable Development Goals
SSA	Sub-Saharan Africa
TNCs	Transnational Corporations
UN	United Nations
UNCTAD	United Nations Conference on Trade and Development
US	United States (of America)
USD	United States Dollar
WAEMU	West African Economic and Monetary Union
WFP	World Food Program

· 1 ·

WILL AFRICA EVER CATCH UP WITH THE REST OF THE WORLD?

Where Are the Majority? Positioning Africa

In the words of Collier (2007: 3) "the real challenge of development is that there is a group of countries at the bottom that are falling behind and often falling apart." A closer look at conditions of most African states and the rest of the world in present times vindicates this statement to a greater extent. Africa is undoubtedly among the bottom. Daron and Robinson (2012: 58) corroborates this:

> If you instead make a list of the poorest thirty countries in the world today, you will find almost all of them in Sub-Saharan Africa (SSA). They are joined by countries such as Afghanistan, Haiti, and Nepal, which, though not in Africa, all share something critical with African nations…

Developed states are savoring saccharine fruits of prosperity and advancement. Africa is still struggling at the deep end. When will the continent crawl out of the black hole? Positioning of Africa in the global economic and political space requires a brief historical analysis of the development trajectories so far. Africa for long has been considered the periphery whose development trajectories are guided by the auspices of the west. Shizha and Makuvaza (2017: 1) capture this:

> In place of colonialism as the main instrument of imperialism, we have today neo colonialism whereby the independent nation state proclaims international sovereignty but its economic system and thus its political policy is directed from outside, particularly from former colonisers.

The paternalistic stance adopted by Western nations as well as international institutions continue to portray Africa as a weaker actor in global development processes (Murithi, 2011). For Africa, most African initiatives to develop have external origins and are hegemonic in nature (El Bouhali and Rwiza, 2017: 15–16). The Berlin Conference of 1885 and the ensuing colonial occupation that followed are some of the cases in history in which Europeans reduce Africa to an inactive continent that requires shepherding from Europeans. Colonial imperialism incorporated Africa into the global capitalism system as an appendage of the western countries. African states economies are oriented as feeders for former colonial imperialist states in the North. Up to date the effects of colonialism are clear in most African states, the most enduring being the dynamic interaction between race and development (Hart, 2010: 2). The paternalistic stance has continued to reinforce the idea that Africa cannot achieve most without external assistance. True this maybe, the paternalistic and external influence are partly to blame for the state in which Africa finds itself in. These are coupled by self-inflicted problems embedded in the feeble economies of the continent which include corruption, selective application of law, human rights violations, electoral fraud, militarization of economies etc.

Africa has continued to be participant in historical processes that at times do not further her own goals and interests. The Cold War is one such event. The ideological war between the United States of America and Russia involved swaying African nation-states to either sides of the conflict. American government supported some African dictators in its bid to outdo the spread of Russia's ideological position. Post-colonial Africa has continued to be an arena of external assistance and paternalism. Bretton Woods institutions have prescribed several strategies to African nation-states. Of note are the Structural Adjustment Programmes (SAPs) rolled out in the 1980s and 1990s. SAPs dismally failed, increasing vulnerability and poverty among Africans. Furthermore, SAPs have weakened nation-states through the "rolling back of the state" which adversely affected the capacity of the state to spearhead the development processes (Khadiagala, 2011: 331; Tofa and Tofa, 2011: 334).

Multinational institutions have advanced development packages that do not take cognisance of the obtaining realities in Africa. The Sustainable Development Goals have come on the heels of Millennium Development Goals. The ever-changing goals and targets overburden African states as they fail to achieve the set targets. These approaches are external and foisted on Africa by international organizations. The targets set are too high for most African states. New targets are set before the previous targets are sufficiently achieved (Tofa and Tofa, 2011).

Apart from paternalist efforts, there has been movement in the direction of partnerships. USA government's partnership with African states is characterized by a carrot and stick approach. African states are rewarded for reforms they promise to introduce. The Millennium Challenge Account introduced by George Bush is the USA partnership model that augments development efforts initiated by African states believed to be on course to reform. Obama administration followed the same model while the Donald Trump led government has prioritized "America First" ahead of other nations, a stance which is likely to continue for as long as he is in charge.

Brazil, Russia, India, China and South Africa (BRICS) have partnered Africa states. Of note is the Chinese which has invested U.S. $66.4 billion as FDI since 2005 (Chen and Nord, 2017: 2; Ernst and Young, 2017: 18). The Chinese are spearheading another "scramble for Africa," frantically forging relations with African states. The Chinese are at the forefront of establishing relationships that see them investing and aiding African nation-state to pull out of their current position. The Belt and Road Initiative launched in 2013 focus on infrastructure development, especially roads and power generation projects. BRI has the ability to develop the infrastructure needed in Africa and aid in the connectivity of African state. Agenda 2063 by the Africa Union already identifies infrastructural development as pivotal to changing the fortunes of the continent and its inhabitants. Furthermore, Chinese investments in Africa have opened up opportunities for trade for most African nations, more than 100 000 jobs for Africans across the continent have been created (Chen and Nord, 2017; Ernst and Young, 2017). Regardless of these noble goals which dovetail neatly into African Union's aspirations, the broader aim is to catapult China to the centre of the global economic system. Primarily, the BRI links Chinese domestic market to the global market (Li, 2017: 17). Thus, the relations of Africa to China and western states have largely been paternalistic, with the continent's need and voice silenced. Africa remains lagging behind on most indicators of development.

Furthermore, the relations with China presents some challenges. Chinese BRI approach takes less cognisance of the political situations in African countries. Most BRI are not affected by the obtaining political conditions in the nations that China invest in. If liberties and freedoms are indicators of development, then the Chinese model is far from it. The Chinese are not good role models when it comes to human rights, rule of law and democratization. In this regard, Africans cannot expect much. We will have a thorough exegesis of growing Chinese on the continent in Chapter 4 in light of development of the continent.

Urbanization

Africa lags behind in the "urban revolution," though it is slowly catching up with other continents. Hart (2010: 5) asserts that less than 2% of Africans resided in urban centres in 1900. In the last decade, half of Africa is urbanized, concomitantly increasing the number of urbanites in Africa. The increase in cities and towns is not met with an equal expansion in industries and economic growth. African urban centres are characterized by lack of social amenities, inferior infrastructures and an increase in the informal economy.

Demography

The United Nations 2017 Revised World Population Prospectus states that Africa's population is growing at a higher rate of 2.6%. With around 1.3 billion inhabitants, Africa is the second populous continent after Asia. Projections are that in 2050 Africa's population will grow to 2.4 billion, signalling the importance of Africa to the global economy, as either producers or consumers. While large population may be the main resource for Africa, the composition as it stands is disappointing. 41% of African's population is youthful below 15 years, lacking skills and access to opportunities to drive the economies ahead. If Africa fails to take advantage of this population growth, other countries such as China will reduce the continent to a market (Ernst and Young, 2017: 17–18). The industrial revolution in Britain occurred at the back of large population growth that Europe was going through. Apart from the youth population, African has a large base of people in the diaspora. The diaspora is highly educated and skilled making it highly useful in guiding the development process once corrective measures are put in place.

Industrialization and Machine Revolution

Several western countries have entered the fourth stage of industrial revolution dominated by machine learning and artificial intelligence. Africa is still grappling with the third stage. Steam engines and electric grids ushered out first industrial revolution that occurred between 1760–1840s in Europe. Building upon the momentum, the last parts of the 19th century focussed on mass production and increased access to commodities manufactured. The third revolution in the 1960s was built on mainframe computing and semiconductors that drove production in most economies. The bulk Africa's industries show the characteristic of the earlier two stages of industrialization. Western economies are moving into the fourth stage of industrialization heralded by a shift from manufacturing into service industries. Japan, Malaysia and most of the west have a head start. Telecommunication, financial and retail industries are growing on the back of the current digital revolution. Investment in Africa is aligning itself to the fourth revolution with more than a fifth of FDI into Africa is channelled to telecommunication industries (Ernst and Young, 2017).

Natural endowments that Africa has are slowly loosing tract. Recently, the World Economic Forum (2017) divided countries into "innovation rich" and "innovation poor" countries. The shift towards innovations and technological advances are in line with the fourth industrialization phase the world is experiencing. Resources are no longer the basis of categorizing or moving forward economic growth.

The shift towards the fourth industrialization adversely affects African economies still operating in the previous stages. Shift to service industries leads to premature deindustrialization that negatively affects the Africa population (Rodrik, 2015). The bulk of the population is either low or semi-skilled making them redundant to the service industries. Two thirds of Africa have precarious access to electricity and the industries have not been fully mechanized.

There are opportunities that the fourth industrial revolution offers to Africa. Africa will for long continue to be the hub of manufacturing, allowing for customized manufacturing of commodities. This may drive the momentum for growth of Africa.

Countries in continents like Europe, North America, and Australia have advanced and are perched high up. Strides continue to be made in various sectors such as artificial intelligence, quantum physics, robotics, nanotechnology, among others. These have enabled their inhabitants to live much longer, healthier, comfortable lives of material comfort and prosperity.

In emerging economies like China and India despite few setbacks in their own backyards have proven their mettle to the world by advancing at incredibly amazing speeds as shall be highlighted briefly. These countries have massive populations in the world compared to other countries, China with 1.42 billion followed by India at 1.28 billion (World Population Review, 2018), this has however not dampened the spirit to advance. With reference to the emergence of China, India and other former communist countries on the global stage, the then US Federal Reserve chairperson Ben Bernanke in 2006, cited in Feenstra and Taylor (2014) observed that:

> The emergence of China, India and the former communist bloc countries implies that the greater part of the earth's population is now engaged, at least potentially, in the global economy. There are no historical antecedents for this development. (p. 1)

A few examples attest to this remark. In 2017, China was able to successfully manufacture and fly its first commercial passenger jet C919, an amazing feat for a country which is transforming rapidly. This is set to compete with traditional manufacturers such as Airbus and Boeing (Phillips, 2017).

On the other hand, India is well known for powerful information and communication technology (ICTs) systems. Some advanced countries are now outsourcing for critical services such as medical services in these countries to show their growing significance on the global space. For instance, "nighthawk firms" in United States of America (US) are increasingly outsourcing medical services from faraway places like India, Barcelona, Tel Aviv etc. (Feenstra and Taylor, 2014).

Despite vast geographical distances which may be among continents of the world, the desire to do commerce, share information and connect only makes these countries even closer. This is much more convenient in the present times of technological breakthroughs. To fully benefit from these phenomena a continent should have something to offer, it should claim a strategic position on the global space. Failure to be part of the advancing countries bandwagon makes a continent backward, its inhabitants will enjoy less.

So where are the majority? The majority have since taken off and are enjoying sustained levels of development. Africa is lagging behind, stuck at the bottom in a cesspool of poverty. If we say that the African continent has not been so lucky and can thus be classified among the losers on the global stage, we may not be very far from the truth. Kofi Annan, the former secretary general of the United Nations had this to say on 12 February 2000 at an United Nations Conference on Trade and Development (UNCTAD) in Thailand with reference to nations lagging behind the globalization, "But the main losers in today's very unequal world are not those who are too much exposed to globalization. They are those who have been left out." If we posit that "*those who have been left out*" refers to nations such as those in Africa and others from other parts of the world we cannot be far from the truth.

This is not to say that Africa is completely not moving with the rest of the world, but other continents are galloping whereas Africa is moving at a snail's pace and occasionally limping. For instance transformation of Asian countries such as South Korea, Singapore Taiwan and Hong Kong has often been termed, "a miracle." The narrative of these countries is a marvel to the world. The countries have thus earned themselves the moniker "Asian Tigers." They attained phenomenal growth rates within short periods.

Others may argue that it may be unfair to compare these set of countries, however we find it convenient to mention them because these countries show us how sustainable development can be achieved even if all odds can be against you. For instance after the Korean War in 1950s, South Korea was reduced to ruins. By then countries such as Uganda, Ethiopia were relatively better. However, due to sheer determination and will power South Korea came out of the ashes and has since become a strong economic powerhouse, and contributes significantly Official Development Assistance (ODA) to other nations including to Uganda and Ethiopia, who ironically were better off before.

The purpose of this book is to trace the development trajectory of Africa and the position it has since claimed on the global map. Different countries in the continent are at different stages of development cycles. Development is a never-ending process which can be best explained in terms of cycles. However, using the concept and applying it with respect to Africa helps us a great deal to understand the nature and complexity of developing the continent of Africa. For instance, a country like South Sudan cannot be in the same phase/cycle as Tanzania or Burundi and cannot be in the same phase as Botswana. Whilst the categorization of the countries themselves into cycles may not be perfect given the complexity of the problem at hand, the conceptual framework we conjecture however enables us to appreciate how development of Africa has fared over the years and buttresses the argument of Africa's incomplete cycles of development. It gives us a vivid picture of how African countries are doing compared to the rest of the world.

Interestingly the cycles have something in common. The common denominator is that they make Africa far and isolated from the rest of the world. Thus Africa is far and further away not in physical geographic terms from the rest of the world, but in socio-political as well as economic terms. So are Africa's incomplete cycles of development an issue?

As will be shown in the next chapters, the fact that Africa still remains backwards despite its immense potential and resources matters to the world. Since the continent has numerous incomplete cycles of development reflected by the member states, the challenge is how then they can be pulled together towards a common direction. By currently assuming a mediocre position on the global space, how can Africa fit to the rest of the world?

Attempting to Develop: The Desire to Join the Majority

Africa is making efforts that enhance development through internal arrangements and processes. Efforts to fully develop by the continent like the rest of the world are commendable and milestones in individual countries are notable. Matsinhe (2015: 110) acknowledges a very important remark made at a regional conference in 2014 in Mozambique, by the IMF Director, Christine Lagarde with respect to strides by Sub-Saharan Africa towards development:

> Sub-Saharan Africa is clearly taking off—growing strongly and steadily for nearly two decades and showing a remarkable resilience in the face of the global financial crisis. Economic stability has paid off. More than two-thirds of the countries in the region have enjoyed ten or more years of uninterrupted growth. This growth has delivered a more educated population, with significant decline in infant mortality.

Positive overtures to development by the continent are witnessed in a number of fronts, notably the formation of New Partnership for Africa's Development (NEPAD), a home-grown solution aimed at triggering sustained development processes in African nation-states. It was coined in 2001 by three presidents, its overarching objectives are:

- Achievement of a growth rate of seven per cent GDP per annum in the next 15 years
- Achievement of all the United Nations (UN) -stipulated Millennium Development Goals (MDGs)
- Capacity building through infrastructure, especially
- ICT and energy, human resources, skills development and reversal of brain drain (NEPAD, 2001).

Furthermore, regional political and economic blocs galore in the continent promote the growth of economies and political liberties. However, despite their existence, Africa is patch of regional blocs that are self-containing and lack common coordination and linkages to synchronise activities, currencies, policies and laws. Chapter 5 will examine how this is impeding development.

Africa like other continents can also innovate. Innovations so as to help solve some modern day problems in the continent have been encouraging. Oranye (2016), an innovation enthusiast chronicles a number of critical innovations which resulted in the continent in sectors such as health, microfinance, education, arts, entertainment, transport, energy etc. over the years. Oranye gives a much more optimistic view about what Africa can offer to the world inasmuch as innovation is concerned.

Africa is making reasonable strides in improving business environments to show the readiness of the continent to also make giant steps towards development. Rwanda for instance has recorded numerous successes in the business atmosphere. Despite having a disturbing past of a genocide which occurred in 1994 in which over 800 000 Tutsis and moderate Hutus in a space of 100 days, the current prevailing atmosphere has allowed Rwanda to be a destination of choice for investors the world over. Mauritius on the other hand has vastly improved the business atmosphere resulting in huge investment flows. If all countries in the continent move at least with a similar pace, then the continent would catch up with the rest of the world. The thesis of this book is to show that whilst the continent is trying to also move with others, the efforts have often encountered numerous setbacks. In some cases little successes which will have been achieved may quickly be reversed as long as the development path followed is not sustainable.

Prospects and Challenges of Contemporary Africa

Can the incomplete cycles of development of Africa be completed? The continent displays immense potential to prosper amidst a sea of challenges. Most countries of the developed world like Japan, South Korea, Sweden etc. are battling with ageing populations for instance, whereas Africa boasts of a young population. This is potential for demand of consumer and industrial goods as well as labor force. For instance the mobile phone usage of Africa has grown tremendously overtime. Mobile phone revolution which the continent has positively embraced has given birth to mobile money revolution. It has spurred improvement of financial inclusion of once marginalized inhabitants in the continent, a development which was not easy through traditional banking systems only. Mobile phone has thus allowed bankability of previously marginalized sections at the same time partially plugging the gap left out by the traditional brick and mortar banks. In East Africa for example, M-Pesa of Kenya has had a resounding success, this was made possible by increase in usage of mobile phones in the country. In Zimbabwe, the giant mobile operator Econet has enabled this through its product Ecocash.

There is hope in the agricultural sector for the continent despite its fragility. Africa has plenty of arable land area compared to other continents after Asia. Currently the agrarian sector contributes much to livelihoods in terms of employment and food security. Share of agriculture to Gross Domestic Product (GDP) in the continent currently stands at 15%. So can the current status of agriculture for the continent be relied upon as a driver to a sustainable development path?

The main challenge then is of low productivity still obtaining in most states of Africa in this sector. Rudimentary and often wasteful agricultural practices still prevail. In economies of Africa, practices like shifting cultivation, also known as "slash and burn" method are still present. This involves clearing vast tracts of land for agriculture. The land is used for a few years. It is then abandoned to allow it to regenerate and regain its fertility, at the same time new forests will be cleared for new farming. This technique is still evident in parts of Western and Central Africa, for instance in Cameroon. Jepma (1995) and Myers (1992) cited in Ickowitz (2006) argue that this technique is responsible for deforestation which has in turn contributed to climate change. By nature, these practices are for subsistence. Nevertheless, they inflict much harm to the environment with only, little output being realised.

Further, most agriculture for the continent is rain fed, this has however been made unsustainable by climate change which the world is grappling with. To compound the situation is that the continent frequently faces droughts. World Food Programme (WFP), in 2016 declared Southern Africa as emergency level 3. This was in reference to the drought, which the region faced attributable to El Nino. According to WFP countries which were hard hit included Malawi, Swaziland, Zimbabwe, Zambia and Madagascar. Droughts are now recurring in Sub-Saharan Africa of late.

Countries in the Horn of Africa, during the 2011–2012 rain season received below average rains due to climate change. As a result Oxfam estimated that about 12 million people were in need of assistance. Ethiopia and Somalia were the hardest hit states.

On the other hand, the continent loses quite substantial amounts of produce from agriculture, the mainstay of the continent, i.e. Post-Harvest Loses (PHLs). World Bank (2011) report on PHLs shows that PHLs on grain particularly in Sub-Saharan Africa were estimated to be around USD 4 billion. This is disturbing, since grains are an integral part of diet for most African inhabitants. PHLs in a country like Zimbabwe alone are around 30%, a figure which is too high for a country heavily anchored on agriculture.

The Democratic Republic of Congo (DRC) has a rich fish farming sector with over 686 species of fish, 80% of them are not found elsewhere. Of late farmers in this region have been bemoaning decreased fish harvests. These are attributed to poor preservation techniques, climate change etc. thus threatening livelihoods of a lot of people. In short, most PHLs in Africa are attributable to use of inadequate storage infrastructure, transport and expertise.

Related to the above, Bostan (2011: 15, 937) in Bamgbose (2015) at a policy dialogue contribution summarises the major impediments of the current structure of agriculture in the continent:

> According to Comprehensive Africa Agriculture Development Programme (CAADP) the reasons of agricultural underdevelopment are various. Some are continuing dependence on uncertain rainfall, nutritional deficiencies in Africa's soils, small and dispersed domestic markets the instability and decline of world prices for African agricultural exports, the small size of most farms, farmers' frequent lack of organisation, the lack of rural roads, neglect of the particular needs of women farmers (who produce most of the continent's food), and the spread of HIV/AIDS, poor government agricultural policies, low investment in farming sector and lack of technological apparatus.

Furthermore despite immense potential exhibited by agriculture in the continent, there is still underinvestment in the sector in the continent. In the 2003 Maputo Declaration, African countries undertook to commit 10% of their national budgets to agriculture development. Very few countries have reached this milestone. Nigeria and Egypt have significantly tried to meet this threshold.

Given the centrality of agriculture in the continent, there is therefore the need to come up with robust agriculture models which can drive and leverage sustainable development throughout the continent. This can then lay the bedrock for the continent to prosper. Thus sound policies both technical and financial should be designed to allow sustained growth and development in the sector.

There is immense potential for Africa in the mining sector. Thirty percent of the world's mineral resources are found in Africa yet only 8% of global minerals production comes from the continent. In an article entitled "*African mining opportunities and challenges*." Professor Mthuli Ncube noted a number of factors which still haunt mining sector in the continent. He opines that there is under investment in the sector, for instance expenditure on exploration activity per square kilometer for Africa stands at USD 5 compared to those of Canada, Australia for instance which average USD 65. Given that there is underinvestment of appropriate technology and infrastructure in the sector, then realizing much becomes a big challenge.

Furthermore, Ncube points also that the continent over depends on mining proceeds, which on its own has created a number of challenges including environmental as well as social problems. For instance, pollution, environmental degradation are some of the challenges. The economies of most African states are exposed to external shocks due to this overdependence. Thus leveraging sustainable growth and development by the continent cannot be guaranteed under these circumstances.

Due to advancement of technology the world over, Global Value Chains (GVCs) are increasingly integrating. This presents Africa with opportunities by virtue of having numerous resources at its disposal, at least as a starting point. The continent however still faces shortcomings such as skills and infrastructure deficits. It can reap huge rewards, however without such critical enablers, the continent will not benefit much. Globalization has mainly rewarded those economies which have advanced in skills, technology, business environments and infrastructure and punishing those without.

Africa sits on massive potential in the Ocean Economy as highlighted in Africa Union's Agenda 2063 (2015: 3):

> Africa's Blue/ocean economy, which is three times the size of its landmass, shall be a major contributor to continental transformation and growth, through knowledge on marine and aquatic biotechnology, the growth of an Africa-wide shipping industry, the development of sea, river and lake transport and fishing and exploitation and beneficiation of deep sea mineral and other resources.

Significant and sustainable gains can be reaped out of the ocean economy. In turn this can help to buttress other sectors in the continent. However, industries such as ship building, aquatic and marine biotechnology etc. (as indicated in Agenda 2063) are not fully developed. There is need for massive investments in such skills so as to enable the continent to derive maximum benefits from the hugely underutilized ocean economy.

Strides in emancipation of marginalized groups have been encouraging in the continent. Women empowerment is also slowly taking shape. This inspires hope for the continent. In 2016, the Africa Development Bank launched the "50 *Million Women Speak*" initiative worth USD 12.4 million. The facility targets urban and rural women entrepreneurs in the continent so that they network. The fund intends to address challenges faced by women such as lack of collateral, weak property rights etc.

In the field of politics, women are also taking up very influential leadership positions, which was not common earlier. For instance, Liberia was the first country to have a female president, Ellen Johnson from 2006 to 2018. On the other hand, Nkosazana Dlamini Zuma was the first female leader of the African Union, the powerful continental body. Thus women have to be part of the solution to advance the continent as their rights and concerns can also be championed by strategically positioning them in the society.

If Africa exhibits all the above potential, why then is it not catching up with the rest of the world? The continent is dogged with challenges. Largely, the thesis of this book aims to explore these setbacks. We show that once a country sets itself on a development path which is not firm, it can easily slide back. Some countries in Africa inherited economies from their colonial masters which were performing fairly well, years later they are progressing slowly with some even sliding back, hanging precariously on few residuals of prosperity from the colonial past. For some individual states development momentum has been difficult to maintain making the process unsustainable.

Sustainable development makes a nation resilient even in the face of adversities. Shaky and often half -baked development only makes a country vulnerable. A country like Japan has stood the test of time, despite numerous frequent disasters, they have always shown resilience. Earthquakes often hit Japan, resulting in severe damages to livelihoods. The earthquake of March 2011 for instance resulted in over 28,000 lives being lost and the economy was left severely crippled. The magnitude of challenges Japan occasionally faces, if they can be applied to other states in Africa, some would even be wiped from the face of the earth had it not been humanitarian aid which often comes to the rescue of the continent from the Global North. This is mainly because an economy on a sustainable platform of development has enough shock absorbers to cope with challenges. Social security systems, disaster preparedness, financial markets, labor markets etc. will be functional in an economy which has attained sound development, which is not easy in a poorly developed country.

Coping mechanisms will be abundant if a country is developing sustainably, should there be any threat to its development. In 2013 the South Western part of Madagascar was hit by cyclone Haruna which caused devastating floods. This affected livelihoods of a lot of people. Later on, the same region battled with a locust plague. It seriously affected agriculture, in particular rice and maize grain related crops further impoverishing people (Tropical Cyclone Haruna Situation Report, 2013). It will take time for this poor country to fully recover. In the first quarter of 2019, Southern African countries such as Zimbabwe, Zambia, and Malawi were hit by a powerful cyclone named Idai in which over 1000 people lost their lives. Most of those who survived lost their entire livelihoods. Given the weak governments for these countries shown by lack of disaster preparedness and early warning systems, it's the beginning of yet another cycle of poverty for the affected people.

References

Bamgbose, Ayo. "*The Language Factor in Development Goals:*" *The Cape Town Language and Development Conference: Looking Beyond 2015*. Edited by Hamish McIlwraith. 2015.

Chen, W., and R. Nord. *A Balance Act for China and Africa: The Effects of China's Rebalancing on Sub-Saharan Africa's Trade and Growth*. Washington, DC: IMF, 2017.

Collier, P. *The Bottom Billion: Why Poor Countries Are Failing and What Can Be Done About It*. New York: Oxford University Press, 2007.

Daron, A and Robinson A. J. *Why Nations Fail: The Origins of Power, Prosperity and Poverty*. New York: Crown, 2012.

El Bouhali, C., and Grace J. R. "Post-Millennium Development Goals in Sub-Saharan Africa: Reflections on Education and Development for All." In *Re-thinking Postcolonial Education in Sub-Saharan Africa in the 21st Century: Post-Millennium Development Goals*. Edited by E. Shizha and N. Makuvaza. Taipei: Sense Publishers, 2017.

Ernst and Young. *Attractiveness Program Africa: Connectivity Redefined*. Canada: Ernst and Young Publishing Services, 2017.

Feenstra, C. Robert, and Taylor M. Alan. *International Trade 3rd Edition*. New York: Worth Publishers, 2014.

Hart, K. "Africa's Urban Revolution and the Informal Economy." In *The Political Economy of Africa*. Edited by V. Padayachee. London: Routledge, 2010.

Ickowitz, A. "Shifting Cultivation and Deforestation in Tropical Africa: Critical Reflections." *Development and Change*. *Wiley Online Library* 37.3 (2006): 599–626. DOI:10.1111/j.0012-155x.2006.00492x

Khadiagala, G. M. "Introduction." In *Governance in the 21st Century*. Edited by K. Kondlo and C. Ejiogu. Cape Town: HSRC Press, 2011.

Lagarde, C. *Keynote address* at the Africa Raising Building to the Future conference, 29 May 2014, Maputo, Mozambique. http://www.imf.org/external/np/

Li, Y. "Belt and Road: A Logic Behind the Myth." In *China's Belt and Road: A Gamer Changer?* Edited by A. Amighini. Milano: ISPI, 2017.

Matsinhe, Franscisco. "African Languages: Towards an African Cultural Renaissance." *The Cape Town Language and Development Conference: Looking Beyond 2015*. Edited by Hamish McIlwraith, 2015.

Murithi, T. K. "The United Nations: Between Paternalism and Partnership." In *Africa in Focus: Governance in the 21st Century*. Edited by K. Kondlo and C. Ejiogu. Cape Town: HSRC Press, 2011.

Ncube, M. African Mining-Opportunities and Challenges. *Africa Business Insight*, 2012. https://www.howwemadeitinafrica.com/african-mining-%E2%80%93-opportunities-and-challenges/ Accessed on 23 May 2018.

Oranye, M. *Disrupting Africa: The Rise and Rise of African Innovation*. Johannesburg: ZuluBelle Publisher, 2016.

Phillips, T. "C-919: First Chinese-Built Passenger Jet Completes 'Beautiful' Maiden Flight." *The Guardian*, May 17, 2017. https://www.theguardian.com/world/2017/may/05/chinas-first-home-made-plane-makes-maiden-flight

Rodrik, D. "Premature Deindustrialization." *Economics Working Paper Number 107*. IAS School of Social Sciences. Princeton, NJ, 2015.

Tofa, M., and E. Tofa. "The Berlin Conference in Disguise: Revisiting the Interface Between Globalization and Imperialism in Contemporary Africa." In *Governance in the 21st Century*. Edited by K. Kondlo and C. Ejiogu. Cape Town: HSRC Press 2011.

"Tropical Cyclone Haruna Situation Report" No. 1." *reliefweb*, 22 February 2013. https://reliefweb.int/disaster/tc-2013-000022-mdg

United Nations Development Programmes. *World Population Prospects: The 2017 Revision*. New York: United Nations, 2017.

United Nations. Meetings Coverages and Press Releases. 2000 https://www.un.org/press/en/2000/20000211.sgsm7298.doc.html

World Economic Forum. *World Economic Forum Annual Meeting 2018 Overview*. Geneva: World Economic Forum, 2018.

· 2 ·

PERSPECTIVES ON DEVELOPMENT

Conceptualizing Development

The term development and the processes that the term stands for are elusive, contains value judgments and carry different meanings to different people. The elusive nature of defining development is highly subjective, based on theoretical and institutional perspectives of those defining the term. Different scholars and organizations propose different indicators of what it means to be developed and the procedures of reaching the state of being developed (Barnett, 2005: 175). The term and concept of development is further complicated by the kaleidoscopic meanings that the term carries.

Development, from one perspective, is a process to be undertaken by societies towards a higher state which is often considered to be desirable—a movement towards perfection. Evolutionary thinking lay the foundation of theories that portray development as a lineal progressive process of achieving perfection and realizing full potential inherent in a nation's resources (see Esteva, 2010: 3–6; Harrison, 1988). The modernization theory is illustrative of this understanding of development. Societies have to restructure their internal arrangements and operations by modernizing them so that they can be receptive to progress.

In literature, the term development has been used to denote "growth" which allows for the potential of any resource to be utilized for the benefit of humans to the maximum. Nkurunziza (2007) read the term development as denoting "progress" which implies a movement from an inferior state or stage to a higher and superior state. Development has also been discussed in terms of economic growth. Walt Rostow (1960) outlines the stages of economic growth that could deliver prosperity to non-communist societies. The growth of the economy was believed to trickle and cascade down to all persons in a given society. For long, development was thought of as a process of growing the economy. Development conceptualized as a process of growing the economy placed the state as the main driver of the process of development. This had its challenges as will be discussed later in the book.

On the other hand, development is an objective state, a stage and goal that has to be achieved. This last conceptualization is best illustrated by the pegging of Millennium Development Goals that were adopted by the United Nations General Assembly in 2000 (El Bouhali and Rwiza, 2017: 15). Nations choose developmental goals that they would prioritize and commit themselves to achieve the stated goals. The UN set the target and threshold that had to be achieved, for example ensuring that all children complete primary level education by year 2015. There were eight goals that were laid down. If all the goals were met, then the country that achieve such a feat would be rendered developed. The Agenda 2030 for Sustainable Development lays down seventeen Sustainable Development Goals (SDGs) for nations to pursue (Makuvaza and Shizha, 2017: 1–2). Nations concert their efforts to achieve the set thresholds with the stipulated timeframe. Sadly to most African states, attaining these benchmarks remains a big issue.

The term development exposes the geo-political power dynamics that structure the world. The existence of the term development inherently is indexical to the concept of underdevelopment. This latter term brings out the role of power in defining and parcelling the world casually into categories on the basis of development and lack of it. The majority of the Global South instantly became underdeveloped on Thursday 20 January 1949 when Harry Truman attributed the more than half of the world nations to be "underdeveloped areas." The usage of the term in the inauguration speech of the U.S president divided the world into laggers and leaders in development (Esteva, 2010: 2; Sachs, 2010: xvi). The term Third World has a French origin, as the "developed nations" tried to categorize the bulk of the world that was yet to reach the expected level of progress. The powerful nations, institutions and persons have the power to define themselves as developed and model-nations upon which other nations must follow their guide. The U.S.A. labelled the global South "underdeveloped" as a political strategy to sway away African states from Russian linkages. Development was the turf upon which political victory against Russia could be scored. It was a political tool for USA during the Cold War (Harrison, 1988: 8).

Development is elusive complicating both the process and meanings that are attributed to the concept (Mishra, 1987: 105). The term has multiple meanings that are structured by the power relations in the world. Pursuance of development projects is never value-free. It is a way of position a nation within relations that structure global power dynamics and organization.

The failure of African post-colonial states to drive the processes of development has led to a shift in attentions. There is radical shift from the statist approach to development through recognition of various actors in the processes of development. Non-Governmental Organizations, international institutions, religious organizations are identified as effective actors who can drive meaningful development processes and push for the goals associated with development. Scholars have unbundled the concept of development to bring out its multifaceted nature and to give development a human-face. Social scientists have called for development processes and goals that prioritize human rather than GDPs and economies. These different conceptualizations have been supported by several theoretical and conceptual frameworks that have informed the processes and goals that development practitioners pursued. We now turn to the history of development theories that emerged from the different epochs and conceptualization discussed above.

Despite many disagreements with regards to what constitutes development, most scholars and people believe that development is something desirable and ought to be sought after. Sen (1999) opines that development increases freedoms and choices that people can make within their context. Todaro (1994: 18) adds more components to Sen's (1999) conceptualization of development as freedom by adding the need for institutions that foster growth and improvement in peoples' well-being as well as promoting social networks that are beneficial to humans. Furthermore, Todaro (1994) notes that development involves raising people's standards of living and access to basic human needs and rights.

Development Trajectories and Approaches

Africa and the Development Discourse

El Bouhali and Rwiza (2017: 15–19) note that current development processes expose the hegemonic nature of development concept. Power relations structure development processes and conceptualizations. The global South's efforts to develop place them in lopsided interactions with the global North. The colonial enterprise by European imperial powers points to the power relations that have always structured development discourse. One of the main reasons for occupying the global South was to bring about "civilization" to the erstwhile lagging behind parts of the world.

Colonialism as a vehicle for modernization: The imperial states saw it as "The Whiteman's burden" to shepherd the other until he and his society look similar to the western world. Colonial era saw the inception of African societies into the global capitalist economy. Economies of African societies were organized as appendages and add-ons of the western economies. The colonial period allowed western nations to benefit from the resources and human capital that was abundant in African societies. Furthermore, the infrastructural development erected during the colonial era facilitated easy milking of resources from the African nations for the benefit of western nations. The development of African economies and humans was tangential.

It is worthy to note that colonialism is the earliest attempt to organize and assist African societies to model themselves along western imperial powers. The need to modernize the economy was imperative. To achieve modernization, Africans had to "break with the past" by adopting western values, family structures and worldview. The process of development was a direct assault of indigenous cultures and structure. The process of modernizing and developing African nations was synonymous with westernization. The process of modernizing and developing Africa nations had several challenges. Modernization failed to deliver the proceeds of development to the majority of Africans. Enclaves of modern societies existed in urban areas while rural areas remained unchanged. Race mediated access to the benefits and improvement associated with modernization. Europeans enjoyed the benefits derived from the modernized economic system and political machinery. Lastly, modernizing with the aim of reaching a state that existed in the global North had its own pitfalls. The western powers continued to progress and improve institutions. For African nations catching-up became difficult. The process of development proved to be an unending process that made it impossible to replicate conditions existing in the global North at any given time.

Decolonization and development ideologies: The 1950s was characterized by strong calls for decolonisation. African states were calling for political and economic independence from imperial powers that had occupied them. This period exposed the power dynamics that inform the interventions given in the name of development. The remarks by President Truman pointed to the need for America in guiding "underdeveloped areas" to simulate its level of progress. In the process, development was a tool used to recruit African nations to its side in the Cold War against Russian socialism. Liberation movements in African nations were supported ideologically, technically and financial by Marxist-Leninist states of Russia and China.

Modernization theorists identified the indigenous systems and values as the causes of underdevelopment in African nations. Marxist-Leninist pointed to external factors as the possible explanations for the underdevelopment of African states. Broadly, the Dependistas blame the unequal power relations between the *core* (global North) and the *periphery* (global South). Rodney (1972) blamed the underdevelopment of Africa on its relationship with Europe. Africa entered into the global political system as an inferior partner, as colonies whose economies were re-oriented to support and supply European industries with raw materials. Dependistas called for withdrawing from exploitative global systems that undermined the economic interest of the global South. Delinking from the global economic system was proposed as the solution to the lack of progress in Africa. Furthermore, the global South was encouraged to foster networks that promoted equal partnership and grow local economies. These ideas formed the basis of the ideological force that inspired liberation movements to fight against colonial dominations. African states that gained independence quickly followed the Marxist-Leninist ideologies to re-orient their economies and delink from exploitative global capitalist system.

African Socialism and the meaning of development: After leading his nation to the attainment of independence in 1961, Julius Nyerere proclaimed the future development trajectory for his nation-state. Nyerere called for African socialism as one of the approaches that can deliver development to the new nation-states. African Socialism as propounded by Nyerere aimed at bringing back humans to the core of the development process. African Socialism realized that infrastructure development in the form of railways, roads, industries and schools were empty as the development must focus on developing humans. African socialism developed people first.

Modernization theorists identified establishment of infrastructure as the hallmark of development, Nyerere (1973) argues that infrastructure aid the development process. Most African states inherited a partial modernized economic system from the colonial masters, despite this most of the modern infrastructure remained under-utilized. For development to take off, development needs not to be internally driven, people must develop themselves. Development has to be locally driven through capacitating humans. Once this is achieved people can effectively utilize the infrastructure to increase their potential. Nyerere broadens the concept of development to include freedom (see Sen, 1999). The vital component of development involves capacity building of individuals so that they are comfortable using the aids to development.

Post-colonial states and the development industry: As the colonial imperialism came to an end, former colonizers took it upon themselves to shepherd former colonies through the process of development and modernization. Bilateral agreements, direct involvement through transfer of experts and financial support between former colonies and colonizers emerged as part of decolonization settlements. The economies of the colonies remained as the feeders for western economies, providing raw material for latter economies. National economies of most African nations have failed and remained intricately linked to that of the former colonies. Senegal continues to supply timber, various nuts and legumes and cheap labour to the French economy.

The economy was structured in a way that benefited white settlers. For Africans across the continent, independence came with optimism for good and decent livelihoods, political participation and economic prosperity. Early years of the post-colonial states were marked with hope and high expectation that the post-colonial government would address issue of housing, education, wealth distribution and business ownership which had been lopsided to the advantage of white minorities (Mlambo, 2014: 206).

To a larger extent, the post-colonial governments made efforts to improve the lives of blacks through pegging of minimum wages, subsidies on staple food, free primary education and health for the poor (Mlambo, 2014: 194). In Zimbabwe, between 1980 and 1990 the government increased primary schools from 3358 to 6042 and doubled enrolment into primary schools. Private colleges aided the government in its effort to educate the blacks. Enrolment of

Africans into university rose fivefold in the same period. In the health sector, the government rehabilitated 161 clinics and constructed the same number of clinics across the country. Through the Primary Health Care, the government facilitated poor Africans' access to health service. The poor accessed health care services for free. Children were immunized and fed through government programmes. The post-colonial government managed to reduce infant mortality rate which was higher among Africans. Furthermore, life expectancy for Africans increased significantly (Mlambo, 2014: 209–210). The post-colonial government had the ability and the means to actively take a leading role in improving the lives of the citizens. This was possible due to a stable and booming economy that grew by 21% in the first two years of independence (Mlambo, 2014: 212). These efforts were short lived as the post-colonial government had inherited a debt of more than USD700 million, recurring droughts, financial mismanagement and corruption (Bond and Manyanya, 2003: 17). The government turned to IMF and World Bank for a quick fix to economic challenges gripping the nation.

African nations' engagement with international financial institutions such as World Bank and International Monetary Fund (IMF) has been less successful in spearheading economic growth and development. From the 1980s the Bretton Woods institutions pointed to existing structural set-ups in most African nations as inhibitive to development and progress. IMF through the Structural Adjustment Programme (SAPs) recommended the minimal role the government must play in driving both the economy and development. SAPs prescribed the rolling back of the state and allowing the market to deliver services, economic growth and development. SAPs failed in all nations across the continent. The prescribed SAP increased vulnerability and left-out many of the people. SAPs were accompanied with massive retrenchments of employees, removal of subsidies on food, education and health services. In Zimbabwe, SAPs were introduced under the policy framework called Economic Structural Adjustment Programme (ESAP). ESAP reversed the gains from the state in the health, labour and education services (Mlambo, 2014:194–210). During this period, as the state is "rolled-backed," new players in the form of the market and Non-Governmental Organizations take the centre stage in driving the development process. The market has its challenges, it recognizes those who have the money to access services and commodities. While NGOs offer piecemeal approaches that create enclaves of development. Development is still something that is external to Africa and needs to be introduced from outside.

Cycles of Development of Countries in Africa

The preceding sections have shown the different views and approaches on the concept of development and how it has evolved over time. It is worthy at this point noting also that some African countries are often praised through exhibiting encouraging figures of economic growth. It's not unusual to come across institutions such as IMF heaping praises on growth figures reflected by Africa compared to other countries in some platforms. Sadly, these seemingly "*healthy*" economic growth figures have not really translated much in terms of development of the general populace of the continent. For example countries such as Nigeria, Sudan, Algeria, when oil prices are high, they post healthy figures of growth and national accounts, but if oil prices take a nosedive, these economies normally catch a cold. Some of these countries have little to show for these *healthy* figures.

Thus to us growth and development is not about mere GDP figures. There is still a huge mismatch between economic growth figures and real development. This is corroborated by Sen (1983:5). He once observed that, "Growth is not the same thing as development … But it can scarcely be denied that economic growth is one aspect of the process of economic development." Thus although encouraging figures of economic growth about the continent can be encountered across different platforms, these should not be misconstrued as implying development of Africa. Rather, they should be understood as implying the potential the continent has, although more still needs to be done for that economic growth to be hammered into sustainable development.

Armed with the above background, we now want to look at how Africa has progressed over the years in its quest to also better the lives of its inhabitants. Different member states in the continent have had their own peculiar experiences of development.

Countries of Africa as they appear in the present vary in terms of the capacities to develop and development stages they have attained over the years. Some countries are well ahead, whilst others are far behind and exhibit few signs of catching up. At this juncture therefore in order for us to unpack the African narrative on development, we have tried to split the stages into convenient categories and decided to call them *cycles or phases of development*. Putting the countries into different phases dovetails with the aforementioned background. If only the countries were developing uniformly, then we would not conjecture the cycles of development thesis.

Each cycle of development has its unique features which makes it peculiar from the others. Countries in each phase/cycle are further subdivided into two groups, i.e., category (A) upper case and (B) lower case with the exception of those in the First Cycle. This is mainly because the states fitting into this category are too few, hence inconvenient to subdivide them. However, with succeeding cycles, the subdivision has much appeal and becomes more convenient to cement our thesis of cycles of development with respect to Africa.

In each cycle where we make subdivisions, category (B) (lower case) set of countries is for those countries relatively behind in terms of development than category (A) (upper case) set of countries in each respective cycle.

The Challenge of Classifying the Countries into the Respective Cycles

Africa is a mixed bag of countries with a rich diversity in terms of culture, values, politics, economics, governance systems etc. among its inhabitants. Moreover the countries have different historical experiences which in a way influenced and continue to shape their development trajectories. For instance, North African states like Egypt, Tunisia, Libya, Morocco and Sudan experienced a phenomenon which is now known as the Arab Spring starting on 18 December 2010 in Tunisia (Salih, 2013) which however was not experienced in the other parts of the continent. Similarly in 1994 Rwanda experienced a genocide in which many lives were lost, a historical event which other parts of the continent did not experience.

Just recently in Zimbabwe in November 2017, an operation code named "*Operation Restore Legacy*" ushered in a second republic. Such a peaceful transition of power is hard to come by in the continent, thus opening its own chapter of history. On the other hand, a country like Eswathini (formerly Swaziland) is the only remaining absolute monarch in the continent. Due to this set up, the country is traversing on its own development course which owes a lot to this status.

Given the few highlights above, we can appreciate that coming up with a homogenous criterion of putting each country in its respective phase is no easy task. However, the final classification we came up with helps the reader to understand the central argument of this book.

After a brief synopsis of salient features, we conjecture for each cycle, we profile selected countries in their respective cycles covering key regions of the continent, i.e., Central, East, North, Southern and West African countries. Focus will be on the nature of each state and as to why it qualifies into the respective cycle and not in others. Whilst the continent has 54 countries, we shall profile those which are distinct. The classification we come up with will also helps the reader to be able to easily put the remaining countries in their appropriate cycles. Table 2.1 below shows the countries and their respective cycles.

FIRST CYCLE	SECOND CYCLE			THIRD CYCLE
South Sudan	Nigeria	Uganda	Cote d'ivoire	South Africa
Somalia	Madagascar	Tanzania	Comoros	Egypt
Eritrea	Ghana	Angola	Djibouti	Morocco
Libya	Ethiopia	Mozambique	Namibia	Rwanda
	Seychelles	Sudan	Congo Brazzaville	Botswana
		Mali		
	Sao Tome and Principe	Cameroon	Liberia	Mauritius
			Equatorial Guinea	
		Tunisia	Algeria	
	Zimbabwe	Senegal		
	Zambia	Togo		
	Kenya	Benin		
	Burundi	Niger		
	DR Congo	Malawi		
	Gambia	Sierra Leon		
	Guinea Bissau	Burkina Faso		
	Guinea	Gabon		
	Lesotho	Cape Verde		
	Eswathini	Central Africa Republic		
	Chad	Mauritania		

Source: Compiled by Authors

Table 2.1: List of African Countries and Their Respective Cycles of Development.

- **First Cycle**

The first cycle is a regressive phase. Very fragile states are found in this. This is a phase with the fewest number of countries. We have the fewest number of countries in this cycle because this is the least desirable as it contains most challenges impinging on development. Being stuck in this phase brings much more despair than a sense of hope not only to the concerned nation's people but also to the entire continent. For the whole continent to move, everyone has to pull together in almost the same direction.

The nature of problems in countries that fit into this phase, are immense. For countries in this cycle advancing into other progressive phases is no easy task. From the observation we made, graduating into the second and subsequent phases is even a mammoth task. The state in its present form risks collapse than migrating into the second cycle. Conflict still hovers above for countries in this category such that the primary focus for the people is to have an end to conflict and let people come back then at list think of how to move forward with nation rebuilding. The conflict is mainly political by nature, which impairs and dislocates a nation. All this militates against any meaningful attempts at sustainable development.

In addition, in the first cycle, energy is expended much more in trying to bring conflict to an end rather than developing directly economically. So for any meaningful development to take place for states in this cycle, we opine that first things should come first. Politics has to be corrected, thereafter economics follows.

In the first cycle, the critical player, i.e., the government exists but is simply too weak and ineffective for things to start moving in a manner which can change fortunes for a nation, hence dreaming for sustainable development is still an illusion. In this book we consider the government a critical player, because in Africa given the current state of development, the government is still instrumental in ensuring that nations are steered forward in the right direction. If the government correctly plays its role, then it would be easier for the private sector to actively partake. In its fragile state, the government is not very much in control of the levers of the economy, for us to talk of meaningful development in the first cycle. As a result the role of the private sector also to steer forward development remains at painfully low levels so as to bring much needed transformation to people.

Sharing the same physical location with a country in this cycle will not spare you of their challenges. Problems in the countries in this cycle also spill into your own country resulting in dire consequences, distorting your development efforts in the process. Given that a country already has development issues to attend to, its connection with a country in the first cycle only makes its situation worse.

One other complication with the first cycle group of states is that of political uncertainty. It is much more pronounced in this group of countries compared to countries in the second and third cycles. Countries in this cycle have substantial populations which were and are still displaced by conflict living in other countries. For returnees, a question such as: "are we back for good?" is likely to rank highly. For those still stuck in neighbouring states and other destinations of refuge, questions such as: "should I pack my bags and go back to my beloved country?," "will I be safe?" will arguably rank highly.

The second cycle is very far and seemingly unreachable for states in this cycle unless one major thing happens i.e., consistent efforts have to be made for people to find amicable ways of putting an end to conflict. Can this not be done by the people of the concerned nation itself? It is not easy either. For states in this cycle to dissipate conflict or bring it to manageable levels it takes concerted efforts by fellow brothers and sisters in the continent to reach out. If, however, fellow brothers turn a blind eye, the continent will not move at the desired pace. Taking an example further away from the continent, the Greece Debt burden is a worry not only to the country itself, but to entire Europe. The debt which in 2017 stood at a staggering 177.4% of GDP was the highest in Europe, as such the other preoccupation of European countries is to see how Greece can be eased out of the debt crisis through bail outs from member states.

- **First Cycle Countries**

South Sudan: The country according to United Nations (2018) has about 12.8 million people. South Sudan has over 60 ethnic groups, giving it a rich diversity. This is the continent's youngest nation, after gaining its independence from Sudan in 2011 with Mr Salva Kiir assuming power. He assumed power after a civil war which had dragged for over 20 years killing over 1.5 million people and displacing over 4 million.

Two years later a civil war broke out in the country, which went on for two years till 2015. This saw an estimated 2.2 million people being displaced. Disagreements later led on to the president to sack his vice, Mr Reik Machar when he was suspected of plotting a coup so as to topple the ruling government, resulting into further violence and instability. South Sudan fits neatly into this category in that despite at least gaining independence and having a government in place, it is faced with challenges especially how to build trust between government and the forces loyal to Reik Machar. In 2016, Machar fled Juba, the capital city of South Sudan and sneaked into South Africa claiming that they had been attempts on his life. Thus there is still mistrust among key political players. Machar has been under house arrest in South Africa since 2016.

Neighbouring states such as Uganda have also had a fair share of the crisis in South Sudan. Most displaced people fleeing instability in South Sudan have sought refuge in Uganda. Estimated figures show that Uganda has the most number of refugees from South Sudan. This is also caused by the fact that Uganda has a soft stance towards refugees compared to other countries. Refugees have quickly adopted to living in Uganda.

Currently Reik Machar is in self-imposed exile. He was replaced by Mr Tabong as vice president. Is Mr Machar done? No one knows with certainty. It's not known with certainty either what his loyalists will plot to do next. He may be down but not out. In an attempt to bring normalcy to South Sudan the Kenyan opposition leader Mr Odinga has been appointed to be part of a team to meet Mr Machar as well as Mr Ramaphosa so as to help find a lasting solution to instability of South Sudan.

Somalia: Is a country located in East Africa with a population estimated to be around of 15.1 million people (UN, 2018).In 1969, Mohamed Siadd Barre assumed presidency through a coup de 'tat. His stance was to promote socialism in Somalia, as a result most enterprises were nationalised. He was deposed off power in 1991, leading to instability of the country as a civil war broke out. Since 1991, there was no central government in Somalia until 2012. In the same year the first parliament was sworn in.

So does Somalia belong to the first cycle? The government established starting 2012 has given a modicum hope and some stability for the country. However, the country has to occasionally battle with the problem of insurgents from Al Shabab. Due to them, they pose a security problem to the country. Moreover, there is a problem of pirates which make navigating waters near Somalia extremely dangerous an expedition. The conflict has also affected neighbouring states. When the civil war broke up, Ethiopia had to send reinforcements in 2006 to drive militias away. In 2009, an African Union force, Amisom intervened to help stabilise things, Later, Kenya a neighbour also intervened.

Can Somali move to catch up with the bulk of countries in the second cycle? The threat of militias is so real to the fragile government. This qualifies Somalia to be in the first cycle. Dadaab Refugee Camp, Kenya is one of the largest refugee camps with over 200,000 refugees located in Garissa Kenya, the majority of them came from Somalia. Some came from Ethiopia as well as Sudan. The refugee has five camps- Dagahaley, Ifo, Ifo 2, Hagadera and Kambioos. The old camps were established between 1991 and 1992, with new one in 2011. The old ones were established when a civil war broke out in Somalia in 1991 to accommodate massive influx of refugees. The new one established in 2011 was intended to accommodate people fleeing famine and drought largely from Somalia.

In 2011 refugees at the camp were estimated to be over 463,427. By 2017 over 225,000 refugees had been repatriated to their countries mainly on a voluntary basis. The year 2017 saw residents of Garissa protest for the camp to be closed down. The main reasons being that the locals were losing jobs to foreigners. Also they were protesting against the damage which had been inflicted on the environment. Government later on proposed to have the camp to be closed down citing security challenges. They had been allegations also that the camp was now a haven for terrorists. However, the high court judge quashed the proposal, a ruling which was welcomed by most Human Rights groups.

What could have prompted the government to propose the shutdown of the camp perhaps includes recurrence of incidences of terrorist linked attacks in the country. For instance in 2013, 67 people were killed at Westgate Mall Shopping shooting. Two years later in 2015, armed gunmen stormed Garissa University killing over 150 people in the process. So whilst Somalia battles with insecurity in its backyard, Kenya the neighbour has also shouldered the burden.

Libya: This is one of the disappointing countries for the continent which arguably was in the third cycle, lower case but slid back into the first cycle after the toppling of Mr Gadhafi. Since his ouster, the country degenerated into chaos with no central authority to be fully in charge. Khan and Mezran (2016:9) summarise the Libyan situation as follows: "Libya in 2016 is, in many respects, a failed state. Eighteen months of UN-led negotiations aimed at resolving the country's civil strife did not produce the results hoped for by most, namely a clear agreement to form a national unity government and reunification of the country under a single leadership."

Whilst the above was in reference to Libya in the year 2016, two years on the country has not changed much. Occasionally, there are incidences of conflict among various political and military groups which make Libya one of the unsafest places in the continent. Moreover, in recent times, Libya has acted as a gateway to migrants who make their perilous journey to Europe. This has burdened the already struggling economy as cases of trafficking, terrorism by gangs are increasing due to this chaos, (Khan and Mezran, 2016: 9). Given the preceding background, the current state of Libya fits neatly into the first cycle.

Eritrea. Is a country which is found in East Africa and has neighbours such as Djibouti, Ethiopia and Sudan. The population of Eritrea is around 5 million people. The country is normally vulnerable to droughts due to its overdependence on agriculture. They are two things which make Eritrea qualify to be in this cycle. First is internal, i.e., the state remains one of the poorest countries in the continent. World Bank (2018) notes this:

> Despite recent growth, Eritrea remains one of the least developed countries in the world. Anecdotal evidence indicates that poverty is still widespread in the country where 65% of the population lives in rural areas and 80% depend on subsistence agriculture for their livelihoods, impacting negatively on human development, which is evident in human-development statistics. In 2012, Eritrea's Human Development Index (HDI) at 0.351, was below the average of 0.466 for countries in the Low Human Development group and below the 0.475 average for countries in the Sub-Saharan Africa region.

Second is external, i.e., the long running border conflict with Ethiopia of over three decades. This has not done the country any good in terms of progress. Development and conflict are never allies. Much energy is spent on trying to manage conflict. The 30 year old conflict with Ethiopia is set to come to an end following recent thawing of relations between these two countries.

- **Second Cycle**

This is a semi–progressive phase. There is a thin divide between nations in the first and second cycles. The second cycle is the most interesting of all, it has plenty of "pretenders." A closer look at some of the nations in this cycle will confirm this label. There are nations who pretend to be developing well yet in essence they are not moving much as we shall see. It is a mixed bag of nations. It has some with a semblance to those states in the first cycle, as well as some to those in the third cycle. If these countries are compared to each other, others would appear as if they are doing very well and hence better off than others. However, if they are compared alongside success stories and best practices out of the continent, we realise that the continent still has a lot of work to do for any meaningful development to take place.

The second phase is made up of countries which make up the majority in the continent. Some countries are stuck in this phase despite sitting on vast potential. For a number of countries in this category it is fairly easy to slide back into the first cycle. To these group of countries, the third cycle is so near yet so far. In other words, it is easier to undo the few progress that has been made towards development over the years than to move forward on a sustainable path.

This cycle is a crucial block in that it houses the "critical mass" of the continent, remember there is power in numbers. This group is the cornerstone of the development matrix of the continent. Consider two scenarios. Firstly, if suddenly these countries in their numbers gain traction, transform and migrate into the third cycle (which we shall explain briefly in the next section), Africa will develop. Moving positively further away from the third cycle, the continent will develop sustainably. Africa will catch up with the rest of the world.

On the other hand, if suddenly all these countries in the critical block were to lose the momentum they are having and slide back into the first cycle, there will be pandemonium in the continent. Africa will further sink.

The government is active in the second cycle and has influence on some decisions which shape the path a nation will follow. Whilst the private sector is actively involved in complementing government efforts to develop the economy it often faces hurdles in the process, at times making its role not so strong in some cases.

- **Second Cycle, Lower Case Countries**

Gambia: Is a small country situated in West Africa with a population of around 1.9 million, currently under the leadership of Mr Adama Barrow, after defeating Mr Yahya Jamme who had ruled the state for 22 years with an iron fist. Whilst Mr Barrow's administration is still fairly new in office, what qualifies Gambia into this phase is the period of the authoritarian reign of Mr Yahya Jamme. Due to his heavy handedness, the country enjoyed political stability compared to other West African states, this attribute qualifies them to be in this cycle and not in the first cycle. A mix of bad policies and bad governance during the reign of Mr Jamme justifies South Sudan's inclusion in the first cycle.

In 2007, Mr Jamme announced that he had discovered a cure for Aids, a deadly pandemic which has ravaged the continent using a concoction of herbs he had prepared. These were forcibly administered on over a thousand people. Plenty died due to this, the herbs were disputed by medical professionals the world over. A few months after his exiling, scores of victims of Jamme's medicines have begun legal proceedings against the former Gambian strongman so as to seek justice.

Given the influence of Mr Jamme during his reign this stance on Aids in his country brought more harm than good, hampering any efforts to bring Aids to manageable levels. Gambia remains one the countries with high prevalence of Aids in the continent.

In the year 2013, Mr Jamme introduced a 3 day weekend for civil servants in Gambia so as to allow people to socialise, pray and tend to agriculture. This policy for an already struggling economy heavily reliant on agriculture was very disruptive as most productive hours of time went to waste.

Cameroon: It is a country situated in West Africa with population around 23.5 million became independent in 1960. The country is under the leadership of Mr Paul Biya since 1982. The nation is so diverse with over 200 languages spoken, the Southern part of Cameroon is English speaking whereas the Northern part is French.

Cameroon is stuck in the second cycle, lower case. The nation is heavily polarised such that it is difficult to inculcate peace and stability so as to foster development for the entire nation. For instance the Anglophone region always clamours for greater autonomy of their region, which normally forces government to respond heavily. Existence of over 200 linguistic groups do not foster a spirit of unity in any way. The Northern part of the country due to its proximity to Nigeria has seen the thriving of insurgency spearheaded by groups such as Boko Haram.

Uganda: This country is situated in East Africa and has a population of 35.6 million people, currently with existence of peace, with Mr Yoweri Museveni as the president since 1986 and has enjoyed five terms in charge.

In the present status, despite the stability, Uganda is in the second cycle, lower case of development. As pointed earlier, Uganda by virtue of its location and proximity to countries such as the South Sudan, the country has had contend with influx of refugees fleeing violence. Uganda has had a soft stance towards refugees resulting in huge people choosing to seek refuge there.

Burkina Faso, Mali, Chad, Niger and Mauritania. These states together belong to the G5 Sahel regional organization which was formed in 2014. Its establishment was aimed at strengthening cooperation on development and security in mostly the Sahel region. The states share a lot in common in terms of proximity, vulnerability to insurgency, droughts, weak development despite endowments such as oil and minerals.

What makes us to bunch these states under same category is the prevalence of insurgency, a major stumbling block to stability and hence development of these states. Terror groups such as Boko Haram among others often wreak havoc in these states.

To show that development and security is still a challenge for these states, the current chair of the block, Mohamed Ould Abdel Aziz, during an address in Ethiopia had this to say, "There is no lasting development without security nor enduring security without effective development," Abdel Aziz said at the meeting. "We have agreed to unite our efforts to tackle this double challenge of security and lasting development in the Sahel" (Reuters, 2014).

Chad following its independence is still battling with instability among its northern part which is mostly Muslim and the southern part predominantly Christian. Hence post-independence Chad still has problems such as internal strife, infrastructure gaps etc. Mali faces threats of insurgents mostly in the northern and central parts of the country making the country volatile. For instance in 2012, insurgents captured a sizeable territory of Mali which saw the French government intervening. In 2015, in Bamako, the capital city attacks at Radisson Blu Hotel left scores of people dead. On the other hand, Niger despite its vulnerability too to insurgency, droughts is now facing fresh challenges of migration as it is now acting as a transit route by migrants to Europe. This challenge also increasing insecurity to the already vulnerable state.

- **Second cycle, upper case countries**

Algeria, Sudan and Tunisia: These countries fall into the second cycle, upper case. By now these countries could have developed much more than their present. Interestingly these countries were affected by the Arab Spring which swept through the Arab world from 2011 into 2012. Egypt was also affected but will not be discussed in this book. Morocco also experienced Arab Spring, but better fits into the third cycle than the second cycle. Categorising these countries into this cycle will be centred largely on the Arab Spring phenomena. Although the impact of the protests was not the same, the fundamental causes share a lot in common. For instance in Tunisia and Egypt, regimes which had clung on power were toppled as a direct consequence of the revolts. In Sudan, the protests were dealt with a heavy hand and were easily contained at first. However later on, the masses through protests prevailed which has resulted in Mr. Bashir being overthrown in the year 2019.

Arab Spring in simple terms refers to a series of protests and uprisings predominantly in Arab countries which had origins mainly in Tunisia. In Tunisia, these were caused by the self-immolation of Mohammed Bouazizi in December 2010 in protest over police corruption and ill treatment, (Salih, 2013). Later on these protests spread to other Arab countries in and outside Africa. Our focus is on the major causes of these disturbances. Salih (2013) states that they are ranging views from analysts on the causes of the protests. The main ones being "structural" as well as "spontaneous and direct factors." We shall dwell much on the structural factors, which in essence are the long term factors. Salih (2013: 188) aptly sums up the key long term triggers of the Arab Spring:

> Long-term, embedded structural factors leading to the Arab Spring comprise corruption, state repression, denial of political freedoms, the failure of the traditional powers to accommodate and recognize new youth movements, the development of gaps between the various regions inside one country, the domination of economic resources by the few through the alliance of state authority and the capital of powerful private individuals, and the spread of poverty and unemployment among massive swathes of the population.

From the above, it can be seen that these states just like other African countries would not develop much given, alarming corruption levels, regional inequalities, poverty and unemployment despite exhibiting much potential. In 2017, the countries for instance out of 180 were ranked as follows on Corruption Perception Index Algeria 112, Sudan 175 and Tunisia 74 (Transparency International, 2017). For the same period the Ease of Doing Business Rankings for the countries out of 190 are Sudan 179, Algeria 166 and Tunisia 88 (World Bank, 2017). Tunisia for the period did fairly well.

Causes of the Arab Spring in Tunisia was a convergence of a number of factors pointed by Khan and Mazren (2016: 3) when they note the following:

> Large segments of the population were excluded from political as well as economic participation, and economic disparities were reinforced by development policies that favoured the coastal areas to the detriment of the interior and southern regions. The dismal economic situation coupled with an increasingly brutal police state were among the main causes of the revolts that swept the country in December 2010.

Since the Arab Spring had started in Tunisia before it spread to other countries like Morocco as such its effects were so severe in Tunisia such that the economy went into a recession. In the year 2011, GDP fell by 1.8% whereas unemployment was around 19%, (Khan and Mazren, 2016: 7)

Algeria's economy mainly depends on oil and gas, thus risk of exposure of the economy to external shocks still remains very high. Prices of oil have not been stable lately such that the economy has been affected due to declining oil revenues. The economy is still very vulnerable when compared to its counterparts like Morocco.

Nigeria, Ghana, Ethiopia and Kenya: Inclusion of these countries in the Second Cycle, upper case might come as a surprise package to many readers, but what they have failed to do to date qualifies them to this category. Ghana for instance, is among the pioneers of independence in the continent, she could have done more to show the way to sustainable development to the bulk of the states in the continent. Of these countries, we will discuss only Nigeria at length in Chapter 4.

- **Third Cycle**

The third cycle is the progressive phase. There is significant divide between states in this cycle and those in the first cycle. It is most desirable as countries in this phase show momentum to develop which has the propensity to propel them to be high above with the rest of the progressive world. Also there are plenty of signs and signals to show that there is progression towards meaningful development. There is a marked difference between states in the third and first cycle. Those in the latter if they do not get enough support they risk collapsing, yet those in the third phase if they continue with the current momentum, they can be shining beacons of development for the continent reaching sustainable levels of progress.

Internal structures within states in this phase make them very fragile and vulnerable such that pursuing a sustained development trajectory is often met with hiccups. This means that necessary development traction can be gathered, but cannot be sustained for a long time due to these.

The other disappointing fact concerning this cycle is that countries in it cannot do much to change the continent on their own, because their other "critical friends" are stuck in the second cycle. Moreover, these are just few in their numbers. Ideally, the critical friends would help to add traction to the development momentum of the continent.

Even if countries in this cycle were to escape from the third cycle so as to join the league of countries which have since developed sustainably in the world, still the continent as a whole will not change much. These countries are few in numbers, so their impact will also be less compared to those in the second cycle as discussed above.

Whilst states in this cycle cannot do much about the missing friends stuck in the second phase they have issues also in their own backyards making them unable to match with the rest of the advanced states which are floating high above. These issues are the magnet which continuously pull them down. In essence, these issues act as a mortar which in some way binds them to their allies in the first as well as the second cycles in the continent.

- **Third cycle, lower case countries**

Morocco. Whilst Morocco was also affected by the Arab Spring due to having conditions resembling its neighbouring states discussed in the second cycle, the country fits into the third cycle, lower case as we shall explain. Morocco has an economy which is more diversified with agriculture, mining, tourism being the drivers of its economy. This allows it to be on a better path of development than countries like Algeria over relying on oil and gas and Sudan on oil.

What makes Morocco not in the upper case of the third cycle, is that like most countries in the second cycle, the role of private sector participation in growth and development of the economy is still slow. The government and the king still wield much power in the economy. For instance, the King has a 60% shareholding in the country's largest company, SNI whilst the government owns the OPC the world's largest company which manufactures phosphates, products (Khan and Mazren, 2016: 2). Such interests in a strategic entity will not allow much growth neither will it lay a foundation for sustainable development of an economy.

Botswana. It is a Southern African country with a population estimated to be around 2 million under the leadership of Mr. Mokgwetsi Masisi currently. It is one of the better performing economies buoyed by mining of diamond. Botswana has a stable economy which has experienced much progress over the years compared to most African countries. The country is a destination of choice for investors the world over due to its favourable policy environment. Botswana, is considered clean when it comes to corruption rankings in the continent and being among the third least corrupt.

The country qualifies to be in the third, but lower cycle. This is mainly because the country is currently heavily dependent on diamond as an anchor of its economy. Diamonds currently contribute more than 50% to the country's exports. Thus it becomes difficult to sustain development basing on one major avenue. For instance the advent of synthetic diamonds may disrupt Botswana in future.

Rwanda. Despite the disturbing genocide of 1994, which saw the massacre of over 800 000 people, majority being Tutsis and moderate Hutus, Rwanda has since moved on to becoming one of the shining examples of functioning economies. Rwanda is located in East Africa, with a population of over 11 million people.

The country has seen stability and progress under the leadership of Mr Paul Kagame, scoring healthy indicators in aspects such as World Bank's Ease of Doing Business ranks, with latest score being 41 as at 2018. Government also under Kagame is known for intolerance towards corruption, currently Rwanda is among the least corrupt countries in the continent after Botswana and Seychelles, ranking number 48 as provided by Transparency International. All this has encouraged development.

However, the big question is can Rwanda maintain its momentum? Also beyond Kagame, what awaits Rwanda? This is a big unknown. Moreover, the economy is largely anchored on agriculture with tea and coffee being among key exports. All this makes Rwanda, in the lower case of the third cycle of development.

Mauritius. The country is doing fairly well and managed to transform itself from a sugar dependent economy into a financial services hub. Furthermore, the tourism sector of the country has grown tremendously over the years and has contributed much to the economy. The country has fairly good business climate which has seen it outperforming other big economies in the continent.

- **Third cycle, upper case countries**

South Africa and Egypt. Egypt rightfully belongs to this cycle according to the analysis we carried out, it will however, not be profiled. South Africa is one of the largest economies in the continent with over 50 million people in population. Given its good performing economy buttressed by sectors such as manufacturing, mining, the country has developed well over the years. South Africa is in the third cycle, upper case. This is due to its vibrant infrastructure and robust social security systems when compared to other African countries.

South Africa cannot progress forward and out of the third cycle, due to the following issues i.e. corruption and crime. These militate against efforts to sustainable development. When it comes to crime, South Africa has a lot to do so as to bring issues such as gun violence, rape etc. to manageable levels, this makes the country an unsafe destination. Corruption is still deeply entrenched in South Africa and remains a big problem working against sustainable development efforts. In 2017, the country ranked 71 out 180 and ranks lowly when compared with countries such as Rwanda, Botswana.

Also South Africa cannot move forward given that much of Africa is underdeveloped. She continues to receive thousands of economic refugees from countries such Zimbabwe, Somalia, Nigeria etc. In the process this has put a strain on her economy. She is thus burdened by her other counterparts from the first and second cycles. Migration has also fuelled xenophobic attacks as locals feel threatened by influx of foreigners.

References

Barnett, T. *Sociology and Development*. London: Hutchinson, 2005.

BBC. "Country Profiles." 2018. http://news.bbc.co.uk/2/hi/country_profiles/default.stm

Bond, P., and M. Manyanya. *Zimbabwe's Plunge: Exhausted Nationalism, Neoliberalism and the Search for Social Justice*. Harare: Weaver Press, 2003.

El Bouhali, C., and Grace J. R. "Post-Millennium Development Goals in Sub-Saharan Africa: Reflections on Education and Development for All." In *Rethinking Post-colonial Education in Sub-Saharan Africa in the 21st Century: Post-Millennium Development Goals*. Edited by E. Shizha and N. Makuvaza. Taipei: Sense Publishers, 2017.

Esteva, G. "Development." In *The Development Dictionary: A Guide to Knowledge as Power* 2nd edition. Edited by W. Sachs. London and New York: Zed Books, 2010.

Harrison, D. *The Sociology of Modernization and Development*. London and New York: Routledge, 1988.

Khan, M, and Karim M. "Aftermath of the Arab Spring in North Africa." *Atlantic Council*, October 2016.

Makuvaza, N., and E. Shizha. "Introduction." In *Rethinking Post-colonial Education in Sub-Saharan Africa in the 21st Century: Post-Millennium Development Goals*. Edited by E. Shizha and N. Makuvaza. Taipei: Sense Publishers, 2017.

Mishra, C. *Development and Underdevelopment: A Preliminary Sociological Perspective* [Digital Image]. Occasional Papers in Sociology and Anthropology—Volume 1, 1987. http://www.dspace.cam.ac.uk/handle/1810/229100

Mlambo, A. S. *A History of Zimbabwe*. New York: Cambridge University Press, 2014.

Nkurunziza, E. "An overview of development Studies." *Religion and Development Working Paper* 2. School of Public Policy. University of Birmingham, 2007.

Nyerere, J. *Freedom and Development*. Dar es Salaam: Oxford University Press, 1973.

Rodney, W. *How Europe Underdeveloped Africa*. London: Bogle-L'Ouverture Publications, 1972.

Rostow, W. W. *The Stages of Economic Growth: A Non-Communist manifesto*. Cambridge: Cambridge University Press, 1960.

Sachs, W. "Introduction." In *The Development Dictionary: A Guide to Knowledge as Power* 2nd edition. Edited by W. Sachs. London and New York: Zed Books, 2010.

Salih, K. "The Roots and Causes of the 2011 Arab Uprisings." *Arab Studies Quarterly* 35.2 (2013): 184–206.

Sen, A. *Development as Freedom*. New York: Oxford University Press, 1999.

Todaro, M. *Economic Development*, 5th edition. London and New York: Longman, 1994.

United Nations Millennium Declaration, Resolution Adopted by the General Assembly, A/55/L.2, New York, 2000.

· 3 ·

UNDERDEVELOPMENT OF AFRICA IN THE PRESENT: THE LINKS

Dearth of development of Africa is an economic, social as well as political conundrum. Countries in most continents have made tremendous strides in development. Incomes and economic growth figures have been robust, translating into stable standards of living for their respective citizenry. For most African states, the journey to development is still a bumpy ride, with fruits of development still beyond the reach of the general masses and remain a distant and inconceivable dream.

Extricating the whole of Africa from the jaws of poverty is no easy feat. Factors exacerbating poverty in Africa are intricately interwoven. It is thus a puzzle with many delicate pieces in disarray. These pieces act as crucial links which aid us to fully appreciate why development of Africa is still way behind most continents and will remain like that for some time. Fitting these pieces together is a gargantuan task, for the continent to realign itself towards the rest of the world. We explained the position of Africa relative to the rest of the world in Chapter 1.

Africa of yesteryear is slightly different from modern day Africa. Today we talk of a liberated Africa, an Africa which managed to successfully dismantle the colonial yoke. The greatest challenge of colonial Africa was how to break free from the colonial masters, as such most states waged bitter and often protracted armed struggles to gain freedom and control over their respective territories. This dates back to the early 1950s through the early 1990s, which saw countries such as Ghana, Zambia, Zimbabwe, South Africa, Tanzania etc. being born. Faces of struggle of colonial Africa include founding fathers such as Julius Mwalimu Nyerere, Kwame Nkrumah, Samora Machel, Nelson Mandela, Kenneth Kaunda to mention but a few.

Most colonial masters presided over the demise of their colonies by orchestrating plunder of resources from the continent en masse, with most loot destined to colonial master countries. The colonial period was largely a pre-globalized era, as such most of Africa was linked mainly to their respective masters. For example, an African country could act as a source of raw materials, which were siphoned to the colonizers country. Some would then come back as finished or semi processed to be traded in the colony. All this stalled development of the continent.

Inasmuch as contexts of pre and post-colonial Africa are different as we briefly articulated above, there is one outstanding similarity between these episodes. Thus colonial Africa lagged behind most continents development wise. This was explored fully in Chapter 1. Modern day Africa still faces development hurdles although under a different context. The much connected global economy presents with itself, a sea of opportunities for the continent to tap into, to develop sustainably and improve lives of the people. Modern Africa's development aspirations are constantly hitting a snag and remain a mirage.

During the colonial period, Africans then were perceived to be underdeveloped due to their limited access to their resources which the colonial masters had usurped and benefitted from exclusively much to their chagrin. Fast forward into the 21st century, the bulk of Africa now has unlimited access to its plenty resources i.e., the gold, copper, oil, wildlife, forests, land etc., but still cannot shine on. How then do we understand the state of development of modern Africa? This section will explore essential links in contemporary Africa which still hold back the continent. More specifically, we examine how these links have compounded the problems of developing Africa sustainably.

Pioneer Post-Colonial States and the Development Trajectory

Colonialism will forever remain a part of the history of transformation of Africa. The numerous states of the continent were not occupied at the same time. Also liberation was not attained simultaneously across the continent. There are states which gained self-rule earlier than others, whereas others gained it late. 1950s began to see countries such as such as Ghana beginning to experience freedom which was not there during colonial subjugation. Most pioneers of independence for the continent do not have much to show for that early attainment of freedom. They still face similar challenges to those states which gained self-rule later on in the history of decolonization of the continent. The greatest challenge being that of poverty of the masses which in turn scales down chances for sustainable progress.

Attaining self-rule, enables a country to a path of self-determination. To us independence is synonymous to seeing "*light*." The light to allow a country to venture on a chosen path, whether perilous or prosperous that's what matters most. We borrow a verse from the New International Version Bible, Matthew 5:14–16 during a sermon on the mountain when Jesus was addressing multitudes. The verse reads:

> **14** You are the light of the world. A town built on a hill cannot be hidden. **15** Neither do people light a lamp and put it under a bowl. Instead they put it on its stand, and it gives light to everyone in the house. **16** In the same way, let your light shine before others, that they may see your good deeds and glorify your Father in heaven.

The above verse can relate to the development narrative of the continent. The pioneers of independence indeed saw light first. How many then decided to shine to the continent with regards to development? How many led the way to progress? If we examine the numerous challenges plaguing the greater part of the continent, are we far from the truth if we opine that these pioneers hid their lamps under their bowls hence the bulk of the continent still fails to discern proper light? Sustainable development still remains a big issue for the continent, hence volumes and volumes of books can be written on this narrative. It is however encouraging to point out that there are states which discerned light later on which are trying to let others see the same light. Rwanda for instance, they experienced internal conflicts in the 1990s in which many lives were lost. Despite this setback, the country managed to pick up the few remaining pieces and began to rebuild. Although its development model has its own challenges, the small East African country's lamp is shining to the entire continent. Currently, according to our own classification hence we have shown (in Chapter 2) that Rwanda qualifies to be in the first cycle (lowercase) in terms of our cycles of development hypothesis.

South Africa, on the other hand attained self-rule in 1994, after most states had become independent. The country is arguably the most advanced in relation to standards of the continent. Although they are a number of issues still pulling her down as explored briefly in Chapter 2, her lamp is high up there and continuously shines to greater parts of not only Africa, but other countries outside the continent. For quite a number of giants of the continent, although they may be flickers of light here and there, there are not so bright for the rest to see.

Africa is a promising continent. Everything being equal, by now the continent could be boasting of its own internal development partners who are able to prioritise and tailor make specific development programmes to drive the continent's sustainable development agenda. Sadly, however, development plans to jump start real transformation of the continent espoused in blue prints such as Agenda 2063 will remain nothing but distant dreams. There are countries which became independent way back (i.e., they saw the light), by now they should have been torchbearers of hope of the continent. Whether consciously or unconsciously some decided to hide their lamps under their bowls. The few with their lamps still on and on their lamp stands, occasionally switch them off, many at times without choice to the disadvantage of the continent. For example in Chapter 3, we examined how unfolding global events mostly impact negatively on Africa in particular on her quest to sustainable development. The increase in global terror does not make countries such as Egypt, Nigeria, Tunisia etc. better off. Rather, their security challenges are further complicated. On the other hand, the trade protectionism indirectly advocated for by Mr Trump one of the powerful leaders on this planet will only worsen trade positions of African countries, the majority which are anchored on primary exports and their associated problems as shown in Chapter 5. This is not by choice.

In this section we want to explore three countries which are among the pioneers of independence in the continent. Most of them by now are supposed to be stable, prosperous giving not only light to their inhabitants, but the continent in its fullness. Youngest nations of the continent such as South Sudan could actually be learning a lot from them. Sadly however, their progress has not been very impressive.

By virtue of their sizes in their respective locations in the continent, their light could be far reaching. Take for instance further away from the continent, the case of countries such as England. She was instrumental in pioneering industrial revolution. For the greater part, she dictated the rhythm of advancement in Europe. She never looked back. In doing so, she shone to other European countries and beyond. Like a veld fire, the revolution spread across Europe and the continent advanced. Presently she is still a shining beacon perched high up with the same traction in Europe and beyond.

Is it justified to partly blame lack of progress of the continent on other fellow African countries in the continent? Basing our argument on the "biblical light" we explored a few paragraphs earlier, its logical. If you encounter light and raise it high up you shine to everyone. If, however, you hide the light, effectively you are putting everyone in the dark. For example, mature democracies such as the US strive to uphold human rights, a critical component of advancement of human beings. Why is that so? In part, they want everyone else in the world to take a cue, thus shining to the rest. We will thus explore Nigeria, Tanzania and Angola to see the extent to which they hid their lamps. The idea of this section is not to heap all the blame on these member states, but to challenge them and others in their several capacities to shepherd Africa to a sustainable path of progress, thus more was expected of them. Some of these pioneer post-colonial states acted as Front Line states that spearheaded the political independence of neighbouring states by virtue of being liberated earlier. Front Line states provided support to neighbouring states in form of war supplies, training, ideological orientation and military bases upon which wars of liberation were launched. Countries such as Ghana, Tanzania, Zambia and Mozambique were instrumental in the political independence of most states in the continent. Each nation state in its capacity has had its own way of burying its lamp, starving the continent of the much needed light. Thus if you have a lamp, you have a greater responsibility to ensure everyone else sees the light. Should you decide to hide the lamp, everyone else is plunged into darkness.

Seeing the Light and Hiding the Light

This section examines the political economic orientations taken by some African states that were the first to be independent on the continent. Nations such as Ghana, Tanzania, Nigeria and Angola played a central role in defining the political and economic ideological orientations for most African states. By virtue of gaining independence early, these pioneer post-colonial state were at the fore front of assisting other states to gain political independence as well as charting ways of developing the newly independent states, ideally spreading the much coveted light to the continent.

These four states have been selected because they have been independent for long, their first leaders have been African icons and revered statesmen. Major drawbacks to development efforts identified in the analysis of these states include policy somersaulting,ideological zig-zagging, externally oriented economies, excessive state intervention and lack of value addition.

Tanzania: Despite being one of the earliest states to break from the shackles of European imperialism, by 2013 Tanzania was rated as having a fragile economy, increased poverty level and weak institutions (UNDP, 2014). The political economical trajectory that Tanzania followed from 1961 is characterized by policy zig-zagging, inconsistencies and top-down state driven development process. Tanzania initially adopted a market-driven economy in which most of the colonial economic systems remained intact. The first five years of independence were a continuation of the colonial establishment, albeit under an African leadership. There were no significant changes in the lives of Tanzanians, the economy remained primarily in the hands of Asians and Europeans. The market economy failed to improve the fortunes of most Tanzanians as they remained marginalized from control of the economy.

It is worth noting that the market economy lacks human face as the market recognize only those with the money and leaving in the cold those without. Thus, the market was inadequate when it came to resource distribution for most Tanzanians that had been economically excluded and marginalized during the colonial era. Where the market dominates, the state is often relegated to regulatory duties (Ngowi, 2009).

The Tanzanian economy remained unchanged. During the first five years Tanzania continued with the economic model that had been developed during the colonial era. Tanzania economy remained primarily oriented towards supplying raw material in the form of minerals and agricultural produce. Tanzania failed to diversify its industries to realize more from its raw materials. Most of its finished goods were imported from overseas. The economy remained oriented towards feeding European industries and economies. There was, however, growth in the Tanzanian agriculture and manufacturing sectors, while the economy remained oriented towards feeding European economies. Market-economy driven development failed to take-off and left out the majority of Tanzanians (Mandalu, Thakhathi, and Costa, 2018).

The realizations that market oriented development failed to deliver led to a policy shift. Through the Arusha Declaration, Tanzania embraced African Socialism dubbed *Ujamaa*. Tanzania shifted from market-driven economy to socialism which was driven by the state. From 1967 Tanzania aimed to improve the standards of living for its citizens through nationalization and villagization. The state took ownership of major productive sectors of the economy. Private sector and capitalism were shunned and their operation reduced. In rural areas people were coalesced into villages in which they worked and accessed social services communally in established villages. A look at non-economic indicators of development show that *Ujamaa* improved Tanzanian's access to education, health, food and security. Most villages were equipped with facilities that most people required to lead a comfortable life. Looking at economic indicators, *Ujamaa* failed dismally. State -led collectivization failed to achieve the intended goals due to a number of factors. As the state nationalized the productive sector of the economy, it failed to capacitate and train most officials on proper ways of managing state enterprises. Corruption, mismanagement and incompetency were rampant. Furthermore, force was used to settle farmers into established villages. Resistance to state driven collectivization limited Tanzanians' meaningful participation in the development process (Mandalu et al., 2018; Ngowi, 2009).

The failure of *Ujamaa* and the change of national leadership in 1985 paved way for another shift in economic and development trajectory of Tanzania. From 1986 to date Tanzania has been bouncing between neo-liberal policies prescribed by IMF and the World Bank and efforts by the state to reduce poverty. Lesson that can be drawn from the Tanzania case is that policy zig-zagging remains a hindrance on African state's development efforts. The adoption of socialism during the Cold War exposes the dependence and outward orientation that African state develop. Furthermore, the need to de-link is disastrous as nations cannot do it alone. Tanzania use of indigenous language cut-off Tanzanians inclusion in the global economy. African states have fragile economies that are affected by market prices of commodities, droughts and demand from European countries. Economies need more diversification and value-addition as well as entering the global economy as an equal player. Despite being the torchbearer in decolonization process, Tanzania's economy continues to be weak, increased poverty, poor infrastructures and dependence from outsider aid and donors. Its early independence has not adequately transformed Tanzania into a regional economic powerhouse that assist other nation-states that got their political independence later (Mandalu, 2016). It remains to be seen if Mr Magufuli, the current president will be able to bring real transformation of Tanzania. When he assumed office, he has been perceived as a no nonsense president who intends to break away from the past, through shining his light his own way. Will he get enough support to maintain this tempo? Will Tanzanians be better off? Only time will tell.

Angola: Angola got its independence in 1975. The post-independence government inherited an economy that had been ravaged by South Africans, Zairean and Portuguese military during withdrawals. Productive sectors of the economy were destroyed. Furthermore, the Portuguese externalized their funds and transferred movable properties and resources to Europe. The Portuguese never transferred skills and knowledge to locals, this crippled the post-colonial administration. Their withdrawal left a huge void as locals lacked the competency to take-over the residual economy. Angola was adversely affected by the Cold War, Cuban army was stationed in Angola to strengthen its Marxist-Leninist drive. The state took it upon itself to be the major driver of development and distributor of wealth (Bhagavan, 1986). This resonates with the situation that obtained in Tanzania during the implementation of *Ujamaa*.

Angola has never been politically stable. After the 1991 general election, a civil war broke between National Union for Total Independence of Angola (UNITA) and Popular Movement for Liberation of Angola (MPLA). In a year, the civil war was estimated to have caused destruction that shrank Angola's GDP significantly. The civil war ravaged the extractive economy that Angola has always depended on. MPLA financed the war through proceeds from oil. UNITA on the other hand controlled the area that was rich in diamonds. The diamonds funded the war that UNITA was waging against the governing MPLA. It was not until 2002 that the civil war ended and 2008 that MPLA managed to assert its full control over Angola (Goncalves, 2010).

Angolan economy over-relies on oil production and diamond mining making it a vulnerable economy. Post-colonial governments in the continent continue to build their economies on the foundations that were established by colonial administrators. The economies continue to provide raw material to former colonial masters. The inability to fully diversify and promote value additions continue to burden the Angolan economy like other African states as we discussed in Chapter 5. For Angola its oil exports have rose significantly over the years from USD 8 billion in 2002 to USD 40 billion in 2007. Petrol dollars have been channelled to food importation and provision of educational and health facilities.

Lastly, Angola flirted with economic liberalization in late 1980s and 1990s through the Economic and Financial Cleanup (EFC) blueprint. This policy shift led to some degree of liberalization in economic and financial sectors.

Angola adopted EFC as way to get admission into the IMF. Both the above cases show that post-colonial African states economies are shaped by global processes and external actors. From independence Tanzania and Angola attempted to adopted Socialism and aligned them to Marxists-Leninist ideology during the Cold War. This saw massive state driven development process marked by intensive nationalisation of productive sectors and forging of villagization. The end of the Cold War saw most post-colonial state changing ideological stance and fully embracing capitalism in the form of neo-liberalism. IMF and World Bank were at the forefront to pushing for liberalization through Structural Adjustment Programmes. Policy somersaulting and ideological zig-zagging kills the momentum of these states. Policies, both socialism and neo-liberalism, are not pursued to their logical conclusions. The zig zagging and shifts kills momentum and reverse some of the achievements realized previously. Across Africa, neo-liberalism reserved non-economic indicators due to introduction of user fee payment and removal of subsidies on health, education and food items.

Nigeria: Nigeria became independent in 1960. It stands out as one of the not so convincing stories of the continent. Given the diversity of the continent's populous nation and more than half a century of independence, by now it should be among leading development partners in the continent. The light Nigeria saw has not fully shone to benefit the entire continent, let alone the nation itself. Instead problems have been mounting in this state ranging from poor planning to corruption as noted by Onah (2006) cited in Onyenekenwa (2011):

> All development visions and programmes fail in Nigeria because of poor handling by corrupt and poor/hungry politicians/bureaucrats, leading to growing poverty symptoms, including electoral fraud; untrue and inefficient representatives; violence: religious crises, crises in Middle belt and Niger Delta regions, hostage taking and cult; food insecurity; low agricultural production; illiteracy (that also weakens democracy); crime; high mortality and morbidity rates; prostitution and poor health and national image; low GDP and GNP and high unemployment rate.

The above aptly summarises how the continent's biggest country has fared over the years. Discovery of oil, simply transformed the country into a monolithic economy which effectively became a bane for its slow progress. The oil sector simple resulted in overreliance on oil revenues for functioning of the economy. So depending on prices of oil at any given time, Nigeria's economy is very vulnerable to global oil price shocks.

Extraction of oil has had its own challenges for the economy of Nigeria. Disaffected armed groups have often mushroomed in the Niger Delta where they fight for control of oil. For instance, groups such as Movement for the emancipation of the Niger delta (MEND), are driven by the desire to have a share of the oil wealth in their respective regions. This has resulted in vandalism of infrastructure, kidnappings and general chaos in oil fields. Government has made significant gains in dealing with these groups although the groups keep on regrouping and strategizing. Some of the grievances being expressed by these armed groups are very genuine. Every community should benefit from its locally available resources, but this can only come if leadership creates an enabling environment for all this. Sadly for most African countries leadership has feasted on crisis, looting massively at the expense of economies and people they purport to serve.

Manufacturing, agriculture and other potential sectors were left to collapse as soon as oil was discovered. The present day Nigeria is a net importer of most basic items for domestic consumption. Due to poor performance of revenues from oil owing to depressed global prices, the Naira is always weakening further punishing the economy. Goodluck Jonathan, the former president of Nigeria came up with the Transformational Agenda which was to run from 2011 to 2015. One of its key pillars was to also focus on the manufacturing sector of the economy, probably this was upon realization that oil alone will not sustain the economy. Given this brief on Nigeria, most states in the continent cannot get much inspiration to advance as chaos obliterates real progress gained by the country.

Language Diversity—A Lethal Weapon

Traversing the length and breadth of the African continent, one will experience the continent's diversity in terms of culture, religion, ethnicity, language etc. The focus of this book is to look at one aspect of this diversity, i.e., language diversity. Of utmost importance in this book is that we want to examine how language diversity has influenced attaining sustainable development in the continent. Linguistic heterogeneity in Africa is observed by Chumbow (2009: 2):

> From the linguistic perspective, the single most important characteristic of African nations is linguistic diversity. All African countries are, indeed, multilingual and multicultural in varying degrees. This fact establishes the existence of a multiplicity of ethno-linguistic communities within each nation state.

We should note however that language diversity is closely linked to ethnic diversity in most cases, Chumbow 2009 pinpoints this, "Multilingualism in Africa is paralleled by multi-ethnicity in that the multilingual nations are characterised by multi-ethnicity. To attack multilingualism is to attack ethnicity to which members of the ethnic group are emotionally attached." We can understand language diversity of the continent by observing the sporadic distribution of numerous ethnic groups in the continent. In support of linguistic diversity of Africa due to ethnicity; existing is a study by Murdork in 1959 of Africa. The renowned American anthropologist developed thereafter an ethnicity map to show the rich ethnicity diversity of the continent. Regions such a North West Africa, Central, East Africa as well as Southern Africa have much diversity from the study by Murdork.

Part of the thesis of this book, *Africa's Incomplete Cycles of Development* is grounded on examining the centrality of language diversity as contributing to the problems which explain the current state of backwardness of the continent which is often overlooked. Is language a veritable tool for development of a society? Has language diversity done any good to the continent? Has it really complemented the continent's efforts at development? Are we better off as a continent with this diversity?

Importance of Language in Development and Language Diversity

Language is a means by which people communicate in a society. Having language is one thing, but using it effectively to develop a nation is another. Unity in language is the lifeline of any society. A language can make or break a society depending on how it is used. Language has been significant in the destroying or building of civilizations, Rayed cited in Words (2007). The importance of language has been noted. Bamgbose (2015) in a language conference contribution in Cape Town observed that:

> . . .as long as development is about people, the contribution that they are called upon to make by way of participation will require communication, dissemination of information, sharing of knowledge, feedback and acquisition of skills. None of these activities can be achieved without language.

Rayed further posits that language is central in that it is a way of self-expression by humans of their thoughts. As a result of this, it follows that this will give us an idea of the *quality of thoughts* generated by a society. With regards to the *quality of thoughts* in a society at this juncture we borrow a technical term associated with the language of computers, "GIGO" to emphasize a point here. The acronym stands for Garbage in Garbage Out. Thus if a computer is loaded with bad data, the resulting output will be bad as well. Equally if the *quality of thoughts* generated by a society are bad, we can logically posit that the end products can be bad as well. These take the form of bad decisions, consequently leading to unsustainable development. For example, if leadership of any society given its influence is bent on peddling hate language on its subjects we expect dire consequences to the concerned society.

For the development of a nation, language plays a pivotal role. Several blue prints and programs have been tried and tested in the continent. For instance, the Structural Adjustments Programs (SAPs) of the 1990s, NEPAD, MDGs etc. Most have failed dismally. Several explanations have been proffered in explaining why these have failed. However, none of the explanations mentions the issue of language, notes Bamgbose (2015: 100):

> It is significant to observe that in all the reasons advanced for failure to attain development goals, no mention has been made of language as a contributory factor. This is not surprising as the tendency has always been to view development narrowly in socio-economic terms and to the neglect of the human factor.

In the paper the author views the omission of language in the causes of failures of the various developmental programs in Africa as a *missing link*. Whilst, this view point may have its own problems, the role of language in development trajectory of any society should not be underestimated. Underestimation of the significance of language in development of the African continent given by Bamgbose (2015) is also corroborated by Chumbow (2005) cited in Chumbow (2009:3). He notes:

> The relative achievements of African nations since independence in relation to the contrasting evidence of extensive abject mass rural poverty, is best described as growth without development. This sorry state of affairs is due, in part at least, to the fact that the language factor in development has not been fully and comprehensively addressed or has been addressed only haphazardly and half-heartedly.

Language is also fundamental in building a nation in order for it to be able to have a sense of identity and be counted among other nations. In the process language serves also to differentiate among nation states. Gellner (1994) in Caviedes (2003: 250–251) postulates that:

> The survival of a nation and the success of its drive towards nation-state status are predicated upon the existence of a language that its people can speak, and more

importantly, read and write. While it is important to be able to communicate effectively within the modern nation-state, even more crucial to the manifestation of identity is the demarcation and boundary function which language can play.

The above implies that if a nation has no *lingua franca*, effective communication will be rendered ineffective. It's logical to say that without effective communication in a society development will also be difficult to attain.

Language Diversity refers to various languages spoken at a given area, Pool (1972). Pool further argues that language diversity is one aspect of the language problem which is usually given much attention. An extensive study on languages is provided by Dallas based Summer Institute of Linguistics (SIL) International among other results found that of 25 most linguistically diverse countries, 20 are African (Christian Science Monitor, 2015). SIL International is one of the most used databases on data on languages, (Miller, 2016).

Languages in Africa are estimated to be in the range of 3000 by some scholars. Arguably the continent is one of the most diverse in terms of language compared to other continents. Chumbow (2009: 6) with respect to language diversity of the continent also notes that "Africa is the most linguistically diversified continent with more than 2,086 languages of the over 6,600 languages of the world."

In the European Union for instance with its 27 member states has only 58 languages of which 11 are the most recognisable and are in use throughout the EU, i.e., Danish, Dutch, English, Finnish, French, German, Greek, Italian, Portuguese, Spanish, and Swedish. (Dacheaux, 1994 cited in Caviedes, 2003). Looking at Africa, a continent with 54 countries, assuming that all the languages are shared equally among the countries, it gives approximately a staggering 55 languages spoken per country on average! African countries are rich in languages.

For example, in Nigeria approximately 150 to 400 languages are spoken, Bamgbose (1991). According to Centre for Language Studies (2010) a small country like Malawi has approximately 16 languages. Zimbabwe has close to 14 languages with Shona and Ndebele being the most spoken in the country. Whilst language is significant for development as has been shown above in general, language diversity in many instances brings problems. Pool (1972: 1) had this to say about language diversity in relation to development:

Language diversity of one sort or another is held to cause the retardation of development, both political and economic. Language diversity, it is claimed, aggravates political sectionalism; hinders inter-group cooperation, national unity, and regional

> multinational cooperation; impedes political enculturation, political support for the authorities and the regime, and political participation; and holds down governmental effectiveness and political stability.

In line with the above, Chumbow (2009) also observes the limitations of language diversity in the pursuit of development of a nation, in particular the continent as a whole. He opines that, "One of the most daunting challenges to the enterprise of national development is the very fact of linguistic and cultural diversity which makes the cost of multicultural development in a pluralistic ideology relatively high" (p. 5).

For the continent of Africa, much of the problems observed by Pool (1972) above are quite visible and are deeply entrenched in a number of countries, we will look at South Sudan and Cameroon shortly in this regard. It's easier to witness cooperation and cohesion among various groups of the people in the continent towards a common developmental cause difficult to attain. In most instances due to the diversity national unity has also been threatened in a number of states of the continent, in the process creating vicious cycles of conflict and instability at the expense of sustainable development.

At this juncture we want to reiterate however that we are not implying a causal relationship between language diversity and sustainable development. We nevertheless, observed that for the continent of Africa there is a tendency of slow sustainable development in instances where language diversity is profound. The continent itself has over 3000 languages, (Epstein, 1998) and it is struggling to really move forward and catch up with other continents as we showed in Chapter 1.

Language diversity of the continent is not only about the indigenous languages abundant in different countries. The crushing colonial yoke which most of the states shouldered for years undeniably left a legacy of development problems with links to language diversity in some instances. Coordinating and uniting people towards a common shared national vision of development has not been easy. We shall have an appreciation of this when we look at the case of the country Cameroon briefly.

The relationship between language diversity and development has been done extensively by some scholars. Notable studies include one by Fishman cited in Pool (1969). The study by Fishman according to Pool concluded that linguistic diversity often brings more undesirable results in a society than positives. Pool goes on further to say that Fishman postulates that, "linguistically homogenous polities are usually economically more developed, educationally more advanced, politically more modernized, and ideologically-politically more tranquil and stable" (p. 90).

The experience of large parts of Africa with language diversity has not been very pleasant. Most parts of the continent remain heavily underdeveloped, to which language diversity plays a major factor in ensuring that other regions or parts with those who in most cases may have less representation and are often marginalised.

Language diversity engenders divisions among people in a society, which sometimes fuels clashes. Owing to diversity of languages in the continent, the divisions so created have, spilled even into national development programmes, aid etc. Ensuing confrontations due to diversity normally result in instability and development is sacrificed. However, there are critiques to this view. They contend that language diversity does not on its own create divisions, instead it is the attitudes of the speakers and the sentiments and symbolism attached to the language, Caviedes (2003). It's typical in the continent to find those countries where developmental projects, basic infrastructure etc. servicing those regions where those in charge come from. The dominating and vocal stand better chance of "pushing" for development to their respective regions. Thus some areas can have excess, whereas others may have none at all of the basic amenities. Thus the development model in most cases has been skewed in favour of even the focal opposed to the passive.

South Sudan. In South Sudan, conflict is still rearing its ugly head. National unity is still difficult to achieve making the country very fragile. Finding common ground and peace is so far not easy. Given its numerous tribes, there are over 60 languages spoken in that country with tribes such as Dinka, Nuer, Zude having the most speakers (Miller, 2016). Furthermore she says that language diversity of South Sudan is common in the Northern part of the country where 38% of the people are the Dinka. The issue of language, its diversity in particular, has propagated problems of all sorts for South Sudan. Miller (2016:3) observes the following with regards to language policies in South Sudan:

Language policies have been among the factors fuelling the long Sudanese civil wars. The two main peace agreements between the South and the North (Addis Ababa in 1972 and Naivasha in 2005) included important language decrees concerning the status of the different Sudanese languages. The current president of South Sudan is Mr. Salva Kir comes from the Dinka tribe whereas the former vice president Rick Machar is a Noel. Machar still commands a sizeable opposition force. Numerous efforts to bring stability to this nation have failed, with several peace deals being violated. Fighting is still prevalent in South Sudan.

To further show that addressing language diversity is still key in finding a lasting solution to the crisis in South Sudan, a number of conferences have been held in the country since the independence in 2011. The multi stakeholder forums were aimed in trying to bring the different tribe compositions of South Sudan to be able to tolerate one another and have a peaceful coexistence. In March 2012, a "Language in Education Policy Conference" was held in South Sudan. Miller (2016) says that the conference specifically for language for this country underscores the centrality of the issue of language in the context of South Sudan. She also points out that this conference was one of the first major conferences in post-independence South Sudan.

In addition to that language conference, SIL International also organised a 10-day workshop. Miller argues that this follow up conference by SIL was prompted by the realisation that due to instability which had dragged on for years, there was need to strengthen the issue of language by bringing 10 of the largest language groups to participate.

Cameroon. It is a fascinating bilingual country in the continent when looking at official languages spoken. These are French spoken largely in the Southern parts of the country consisting of 83% and English spoken in the north making up the remainder. The actual number of indigenous languages of Cameroon is a subject of debate. SIL International database, Ethnologue estimates the figure to be around 279, a number which some say is too high. The linguistic divide of Cameroon goes as early as the 1960s.

Language diversity with the colonial background we have just mentioned above has not helped much in the progress of Cameroon. Due to this diversity, there are constant protests from Southwest and Northwest inhabitants of the country who are predominantly English speaking. Their main grievances are marginalization and discrimination in mainstream economy and even public institutions such as courtrooms where French language is mostly used for communication. Can a country move progressively with this background? It's not easy.

The Unforgiving Global Economy

The global economy is ever dynamic, always turning and twisting giving birth to fresh challenges to countries, requiring a considerable degree of astuteness amongst them to gingerly navigate the broader global space. Often, many developments emanating from the global economy have had adverse effects by posing a number of challenges to fragile African economies. These developments increase risk and vulnerability of these weak economies.

Of particular interest are adverse developments which normally occur in the context of bigger economies, these in turn directly weaken African countries, now that they are slowly fusing into the global economy. An observation by Global Economic Prospects (2018), illustrates this with respect to slow down of China, a worrying trend, given its strategic importance on the global economy:

> On the downside, an abrupt slowdown in China could generate adverse spill over to the region through lower-than-projected commodity prices, which would exacerbate economic imbalances and complicate adjustment needs in many commodity exporters. Oil producers in CEMAC and metals exporters are particularly vulnerable to this risk.

On the other hand due to some global developments, Africa's existing problems are further exacerbated. So expecting Africa's vulnerable economies to escape unhurt won't it be asking for too much? So will the continent develop?

Many African economies are largely primary commodity driven with many exports ranging from minerals, oil and agriculture. This has hampered even local efforts at regional integration, we will observe this when we turn to Chapter 5. Against this background, African economies growth prospects have been disturbed by recent developments in China. Of late China has been having excess capacities in sectors such as steel, this has slowed its demand, and in the process global demand has been on the downturn dislocating weak economies. This is a tip of the iceberg of how economies of Africa sneeze in the wake of certain key global developments taking place. It suffices at this point to say that the global economy in many instances has been "unforgiving" to Africa, as we briefly look at key events unfolding in the global space in contemporary times.

Global Developments, Sources of Deep Trouble for Africa

Africa is progressing, albeit at a snail's pace. The broader global economy is getting connected by each passing hour, day and year bringing countries together forming a massive global village. In this village only the vigilant players reap maximum rewards at the expense of laggards. Africa with her myriad of challenges is a subset of this global village, it has to compete also with other successful economies around the globe. What has the global economy done to her? Contemporary Africa has been bruised and battered relentlessly by factors constantly emanating from the global space clipping her wings to fully express herself, in some instances reversing the little gains the countries in the continent had achieved. Against the backdrop of these challenges, Africa has to swim to remain afloat or risk drowning.

There are many developments affecting the global economy other than the slowdown of China we looked at earlier on. As they unfold, one problem erupts after another hitting hard on the feeble Africa. The principal focus of this section is to examine only three of these global developments which expose Africa due to her fragility. Current features of most African countries make them very vulnerable to developments which occur in the global economy. Much of these features will be explored in depth in Chapter 5, they include massive infrastructure gaps, primary commodity dependence etc. all these adversely expose African countries to global development. Specifically, this section is inspired by the following developments on the global economy, the phenomena of globalization, the "Trump" quake and the threat of terrorism and insurgency.

Phenomena of Globalization. The globalization train is accelerating at a tremendous speed. Arguably one task that is difficult to achieve is turning back the hands of time so as to halt this phenomena, so countries have to shape up. Many countries are traversing the path to globalization with much gusto and agility, this has facilitated trade among countries globally. Resultantly, those that have made the most out of globalization have thus been able to attain maximum gains through technological advancement, interconnectedness and networking, high gross domestic products (GDP) and general high standards of living for their respective citizenry. To Africa, the narrative is quite different, no one would expect the continent to be languishing in perpetual poverty in the midst of plenty. Africa has not benefited much from globalization as noted by one of the presenters during a Africa Development Forum (ADF) preparatory workshop (2000):

> Yet the share of the poorest or least-developed countries, most of them in Africa, in global trade has declined since 1980. The majority of these low-income developing countries have failed to integrate into the global economy to the same extent as the industrialized countries and the middle-income developing countries.

Thus in as much as Africa has been trying to follow the rest of the world and cooperate in a way of trade and various engagements with other global players, so little has been achieved in the process. The continent is still in the peripheries. At ADF workshop, the presenter went on further to issue a stern warning on Africa's continued lethargic pace of joining the bandwagon of globalization with the rest of the world when he pointed that, "Unless steps are taken to remove the external and internal barriers to integration, Africa faces the prospect of being further marginalized as the inexorable pace of globalizations continues or even accelerates."

In line with the above, Chapter 5 we will explore in detail regional blocs and their contribution to development of the continent. A host of factors currently militate against inter Africa cooperation among nations in these groupings. Moreover, the rate at which globalization is changing the outlook of the global economy makes it even more distressing for African countries. In addition, regional groupings which are sporadically scattered across the length and breadth of the continent have done less to support this integration as shall be pinpointed in Chapter 5 as well, more was expected of them.

More than one and a half decade has passed since ADF forum in 2000, the present state of affairs continues to be deplorable. Internal and external barriers hindering doing business are still very high as will be shown in Chapter 6, these hedge against efforts by the continent to fully integrate in the broader global space. Many African countries will continue to be mercilessly shoved out of the globalization train as long as they remain exhibiting few signs of serious progress towards meaningful transformation whilst finding comfort in mediocrity. The marginalization of the continent will perpetuate unabated.

Given the laboured baby steps Africa is making towards embracing globalization, much gains have been elusive, sadly however, these countries have borne the full brunt of negative costs of this phenomenon due to their failure to express themselves on the global stage. Globalization has increased industrial activity in countries due to the need to produce goods and services to spruce up international trade making hazardous emissions on the environment. The ensuing climate change has hurt poor countries more than the developed countries. Droughts often linked to climate change are slowly becoming a feature of most poor countries of which most of them hail from Africa but emit less on the atmosphere.

It is saddening to note that one of the top emitters US, is now reneging on its climate change commitments. For instance, the US was supposed to contribute US$ 3 billion towards Green Climate Fund following the Paris

Agreement. President Trump on 1 June 2017, announced from the White house of United States intention to withdraw from the Paris Agreement, which was an addition to the United Nations Framework Convention on Climate Change (UNCCC). His main arguments being that if the accord is implemented, it would cost the US, USD $3 trillion in lost GDP and 6.5 million jobs, (BBC, 2017). Controlling climate change has to be shared responsibility and with top emitters supposed to be the main contributors than for them to pull out like the plan of US. African countries will also be greatly affected given how they are struggling to industrialize.

Due to interconnectedness of countries owing to globalization, phenomena such as "offshoring" and "outsourcing" are increasingly becoming preferred models of production in manufacturing industries, where production networks will be spread across countries or even continents. Large corporates normally do this so as to take advantage of costs such as low labour and taxes, flexibility and allow for specialization. This is predominantly in electronics industries (Dedrick, Kraemar, and Linden, 2008). An iPod is assembled in China, one destination where labour is abundant. The production network of iPod spreads across countries such as US, China, Japan and South Korea (Timmer, 2014). However, only those countries which have conducive environments are increasingly benefiting from offshoring of tasks. A country like South Africa, one of a few encouraging stories of the continent is a major beneficiary of major global firms as a destination of choice for investment due to favourable conditions despite a few setbacks.

Globally, incisive countries which are able to attract most offshoring and outsourcing activities are able to swim with others in the globalization tide. However, for the foot-draggers the global economy is unforgiving, opportunities remain elusive. Losses are huge. Jobs find their way to conducive and better locations. Consequently, incomes and standards of living remain at disappointingly low levels to the losers. At the same time, better countries will march on.

The "Trump" quake. The vote of November 2016 in the United States ushered in the new administration of Mr Donald Trump. Many people were puzzled. Here are a few reactions to Trump victory, we take these words from a publication by Wilson Centre Africa Program (2016):

> The election of Donald Trump created surprise and shock across the political spectrum and around the world. While some see opportunity for Africa from this

non-traditional politician, others are concerned about the president-elect's campaign rhetoric and how it might translate into foreign policy come January 20, 2017.

The election of Donald J. Trump as President of the United States on November 8 signalled what may be a major shift in U.S.-Africa relations and policy. The simple answer is that we currently don't know what the Trump Administration's policy toward Africa will be. President-elect Trump's presidential campaign did not shed much light on his foreign policy approach toward Africa.

The first reaction is an excerpt from a letter by the Program Director of the centre Dr. Muyangwa. The second is also an excerpt from Dr. Nedelcovych, in a contribution to the same publication. We can infer from those above few reactions that the result brought with it shock and uncertainty to the world. The world has to brace for more surprises from Mr. Trump, his utterances and policy adjustments more often shake global markets. This justifies why we devote this section to explain how development of Africa partly hinges on this global development.

The world has to brace for more surprises from Mr. Trump, his utterances and policy pronouncements more often shake global markets. This justifies why we devote this section to explain how development of Africa partly hinges on this global development.

Africa is slowly integrating into the global village despite her problems which are seemingly insurmountable. Given Mr Trump's ambiguous and often inconsistent rhetoric during run up to the US elections often capped by the catch phrase "*America first*," why did he emerge the winner? Before we look into some of the reasons, we decided to put the phrase "America first" in italics to emphasize a point. Thus regarding any deal or transaction which is perceived not to promote the interests of Americans it is likely not to be pursued and if possible whatever had been done by his (Trump's) predecessors can easily be reversed as long as it stands in the way of promoting America (according to how he wants his people promoted) no matter what it takes. So if say any deal on trade for instance is perceived hurtful on Americans, then it is better to do away with or it has to be stopped forthwith. Using the same line of thinking we can conjecture that if assisting poor countries to get to their feet is becoming a burden to America, it is better to immediately stop.

Thus Trump was able to convince voters on their losses emanating from global trade. Implicitly we can say that Trump was indirectly advocating for "deglobalization" by emphasizing on how Americans had been disenfranchised by trade, a product of globalization.

Since Mr Trump shepherds one of the largest economies of the world, developments in the US cannot be ignored. We choose to focus on the US in this volume due to its role on the global stage, as such any policy pronouncements she makes have a direct bearing on the world economy. The US plays a leading role in directing global trade system through helping in setting up of rules and institutions for global trade, e.g., the establishment of World Trade Organisation (WTO) in 1995.

Trade is often regarded as an instrument to uplift poor countries from poverty as such the election Mr Donald Trump does matter in the context of development of Africa as well as the rest of the world in general. Tariffs had fallen considerably over the years since the formation of WTO and volume of traded merchandise had increased as well. Evidence from WTO (2015) shows that average tariffs levied by members have gone down from as high as 12% in 1996 to around 9% in 2013. For the same period, global trade in merchandise had grown tremendously to reach $19 trillion, a fourfold increase.

Now that Mr. Trump is in charge, most probably these gains are likely to be reversed. Global trade is likely to be affected both in terms of direction and volume. Mr Trump has already started cracking the whip. Trade wars are being renewed. The major target of US being China which has seen the latter being slapped with 25% tariffs on USD 50 billion worth of goods. China has since responded by also levying tariffs of the same magnitude (Pramuk, 2018). It remains to be seen how this trade war between the two world's largest economies will end, but the first round of tariffs was effected in the month of July 2018. However, if the war escalates small economies will not be spared. Currently, most Asian economies are caught up in the middle of this war due to their link to China via supply chains. What do these economies do? They can only stand aside and watch.

As an African adage goes, "when two elephants fight, it is the grass which suffers." This aptly relates to this. If the trade war persists unabated, it will hurt weak economies. For instance China, arguably the world's largest consumer of raw materials such as iron ore, copper, oil etc. will consume less if tariffs take their toll, this will have a knock on effect on the global economy, most affected commodity economies of which the majority are in Africa—the map on global commodity dependency in Chapter 5 will confirm this.

Mr Trump also took the trade war to Turkey, who have been slapped with tariffs of 50% on steel and 20% on aluminium, (Pramuk, 2018). This move comes as a slap on the face as the Turkish Lira has been on a free fall and has lost over 20% of its value since its troubles begun, further hurting the economy. One of the reasons why Turkey has met this fate is their continued detention of American religious figure Pastor Andrew Brunson, (Pramuk, 2018). Turkey is a key emerging economy as such this move by US is likely to hurt also other emerging economies.

Focusing on Trump's trade wars on Africa, Rwanda has been the first casualty. Just a brief background to this development is necessary at this juncture. In 2000 the US enacted the African Growth and Opportunity Act (AGOA), whereby in order for African countries to qualify for AGOA they were supposed to reduce barriers for American goods, (The Economist, 2018). Under AGOA, African countries would be able to access American markets, 39 countries are currently eligible. Rwanda however instead of reducing the barriers, they actually raised tariffs for American apparel. Whilst, The Economist further argues that this move will not be very hurtful to Rwanda given that its exports under AGOA are valued at approximately USD 2 million, Mr Trump is showing what he is capable of doing to champion his "America First" mantra. This is just the beginning until he hits where it hurts most, like he has just delivered a technical knockout blow to the Turkish economy. This has potential to plunge emerging markets into chaos given the strategic position Turkey has in these groups of economies.

Zimbabwe is also set to experience the tremors of the "Trump quake." On 8 August 2018, President Trump signed into law Zimbabwe Democracy and Economic Recovery Act (ZIDERA) amending the 2001 Act. The renewal of ZIDERA implies that restrictions previously in place will stay. This will further dampen prospects of jump starting the comatose economy which has been battered for over two decades. Fresh lines of credit from major sources such as the US will remain depressed.

Africa still subsists mainly on aid in sectors such as health, education, water and sanitation etc. where significant strides were made. USAID, a US agency has presence in several countries in the continent including countries such as Zimbabwe, Burkina Faso, Uganda, and Kenya among others. Recently USAID cut funding for Non-Governmental Organisations (NGOs) which carry programs in support of abortion, a rule which was put in place by President Trump in 2017 (Reuters, 2018). Reuters further points that an organisation, Marie Stopes Ladies (MSL) which depended on a grant of USD 1.25 million directly from USAID in assisting in sexual health issues and offering contraception in Burkina Faso has been dealt a major blow. Fertility rates average 5.5 per woman in that country, as such withdrawal of funding will create a huge gap difficult to plug by the already struggling economy, further paralyzing the health sector.

This may just be the beginning also, for a continent hugely anchored on aid it's a bitter pill to swallow, more cuts may be on their way. Significant progress on development in sectors such as health, water and sanitation, education, nutrition etc. will be severely affected. A cut on aid to Africa at least for now, is akin to cutting the umbilical code of a developing foetus.

Potential threat of terrorism: The increasingly connected global space has seen the much dreaded terrorism on the surge raising security fears the world over. Global peace and security is constantly being threatened by increasing terrorism. Without stability, development and progress of humanity remains a big challenge, worse still for fragile economies the impact is likely to be massive.

What is terrorism? Karl Deutsch award winning scholar Fortna cited in Albuquerque (2017) defines terrorism as "a systematic campaign of indiscriminate violence against public civilian targets to influence a wider audience. The ultimate aim of this type of violence is to coerce the government to make political concessions, up to and including conceding outright defeat." Pockets of Africa have and are still experiencing violence with features alluded to in this definition. Terrorism is spreading its tentacles across the length and breadth of the globe. Understanding the complexity of terrorism is not easy in this globalized world especially the motives, tactics employed, funding mechanisms, compositions, networks by terror groups etc. In spite of that, Africa has not been spared of this disturbing phenomenon. Africa of the days gone by was deeply engrossed in armed conflict, which was mainly between colonial masters and respective colonies. Many years of armed struggle against colonizers brought independence for most countries in the continent. That was one problem which was resolved allowing the continent to turn a new leaf in its journey of transformation.

Post-colonial Africa in the 21st century now faces a slightly different challenge—the threat of terrorism. Terrorism makes the continent weak and constantly threatens the few gains garnered towards the path to sustainable development. More often, terrorism has fomented instability in many parts of the continent, forcing economies to shift attention from development as an immediate goal.

Terrorism might not be fully pronounced in the continent, however its potential to undo the few development milestones attained over the years cannot be ignored. Terrorism threat for Africa is real due to its immense problems which often see the few development gains eluding in particular the young who are the bulk of the population.

Reports over the last two years show that Africa is "becoming the new frontier for terrorism," Albuquerque (2017). An annual report on terrorism by the Bureau of Counterterrorism (2017:15) of the US gives a hint of how terrorism is gaining traction in East Africa, in Somalia to be specific:

Africa experienced significant levels of terrorist activity in 2016. In East Africa, the Somalia-based terrorist group al-Shabaab remained the most potent threat to regional stability, having regained territory in parts of southern and central Somalia. As the African Union Mission in Somalia (AMISOM) limited offensive operation to proactively counter al-Shabaab in southern Somalia, the terrorist group gained the time and space needed to regroup and recruit new fighters.

The world over, terrorism is spreading, its impact is however not the same across continents. A study by Albuquerque (2017) on terrorism seeking to map terrorism specifically for Africa overtime found that in the continent it is linked to a number of groups, these groups will be engaged in conflict. The conflict is mostly armed by nature. Notable groups according to Albuquerque (2017) include Boko Haram, Al Shabab, and Tripoli Province of the Islamic State etc. Global Terrorism Data cited by Albuquerque (2017) shows that Boko Haram and Al Shabab account for most terror attacks in the continent.

The distribution of terror across the regions of the continent is not even. Regions such as West Africa, East Africa and Central Africa frequently experience attacks, with Southern Africa has the fewest attacks (Albuquerque 2017). Examples of terrorism related incidences and their respective years in the continent include Garissa University in Kenya in 2015 which armed gunmen stormed the campus opening gunfire. Scores of students were killed. In the same year a gunmen attacked people at a hotel in Tunisia, several tourists died. The tourism industry is having difficulties to fully recover ever since. Mali, often experiences terror linked attacks. In 2015, several scores of people, mostly tourists were left dead following attacks at a hotel in Bamako.

For Africa the impact is likely to be severe as local conditions in the continent still make the continent very vulnerable to it. We briefly shift our focus on ballooning population of the continent with special emphasis on how it has potential to facilitate propagation of terrorism in the continent.

Population explosion without corresponding advancement in standards of living of general populace has had an effect of straining social and economic amenities in the continent. Exponential population growth is largely attributable to high birth rates in most parts of the continent. This has led to proliferation of informal settlements further worsening already existing infrastructure gaps. Due to massive infrastructure gaps, Africa lags behind other continents on urbanisation and industrialization as shown in Chapter 1.

High birth rates are indeed a cause for concern for the continent. These have fuelled massive population growth as noted by Feldman (2009:2), consequently contributing to high possibility of propagating ills like crime, terrorism etc.:

> No problem represents as great a threat to stability in Africa as the continent's extremely high birth rate. The shanty towns that continue to grow, filled with massive numbers of unemployed, poorly educated individuals, are breeding grounds for crime, and an opportunity for extremists to recruit people to their sundry causes, people who are desperate to improve their lot in life.

Almost similar to the above, Bureau of Counterterrorism postulates that incidences of radicalization by ISIS a terror linked organization were rife if people are subjected to social ills like corruption and repression. The report points out that, "In parts of Africa, ISIS's ideology resonated among those with direct experience of official corruption and abusive security-service tactics" (p. 12). Most of Africa's poor surviving in squalid conditions mostly face corruption every day and are subjected to impoverishment, this makes the population much more vulnerable to ideologies such as those promoting terrorism. The most widely cited example we can think of and relates to this is that of the people living in the Niger Delta of Nigeria. Undoubtedly, corruption is one of the biggest challenges of Nigeria, just like most parts of the continent, we will look in detail at how terror associated activities have been easy in the Niger Delta.

To further compound the problem is that controlling birth rates and hence reducing poverty is likely going to be a problem for Africa. This is so due to the overreliance of the continent on donor assisted birth control programs. For instance, the US through USAID has sponsored a number of programs in countries like Burkina Faso, significant gains had been made, however these will be reversed now that Mr Trump steers the US ship as we discussed in detail in the previous section. These high birth rates will continue to create a young, economically active population for the continent. One treasure the continent currently boasts of, is the young population as we highlighted in Chapter 1. It is a source of labour, cheap labour to be specific. We deliberately call this population the "critical mass" due to its strategic importance for the continent. What has been and will continue to be dangerous is the persistent marginalization from the mainstream economy of this group. Due to marginalization, widespread poverty across the continent is still difficult to contain.

Owing to high birth rates, Africa has cheap and abundant labour which however has not been fully exploited. Most companies in developed countries are constantly shifting production due to slicing of global value chains and focusing on those countries where labour is cheap and has some skills or is easily trainable, more so in a business friendly regions. China has become a destination of choice in this respect, it has cheap and abundant labour. Business environment in China is by and large better than that obtaining in most African countries. Most business environments currently obtaining in Africa are *anti-business* and predominantly toxic. The environments are anti-business in the sense that most policies make it difficult for businesses to thrive, capital flight is very common in the continent. We will have a detailed analysis of these business environments in Chapter 6.

At this juncture, we explain briefly what happens with the "critical mass" we introduced in Chapter 2 in the second cycle of development. We focus our attention on two factors i.e., poverty and discrimination stalking the youthful segment of the population of the continent. The bulk of the critical mass currently subsists in alarming levels of poverty and deprivation. What is dangerous for contemporary Africa is the persistent marginalization from the mainstream economy of this group. Due to marginalization, widespread poverty across the continent is still difficult to contain. Mostly there are several options for this population in the midst of grinding poverty. If they feel hard done, they may resort to migration in droves, the global economy is currently experiencing massive migration. However, others may choose to fight from within, of which terrorism and insurgency can be considered an option if it can bring food on the table. Niger Delta in Nigeria frequently experiences disturbances of a terroristic nature.

Who are the people of the Niger Delta propagating the disturbances? It is mostly the young who are yearning for attention to actively participate in the broader economy and feel currently marginalised. Following a visit to Africa, Barack Obama, the former US president at an address once remarked "We need only look to the Middle East and North Africa to see that large numbers of young people with no jobs and stifled voices can fuel instability and disorder," (BBC, 2015).

The Niger delta is now infested with armed gangs which feel disenfranchised e.g. the Movement for the emancipation of the Niger delta (MEND) is driven by the desire to have a share of the oil wealth in their respective regions. The result has been vandalism of oil infrastructure, kidnappings and general chaos in the Niger Delta. Government has made significant gains in dealing with these groups although they keep on regrouping and restrategizing posing serious threats to oil production for Nigeria. As long as grievances of these gangs are not met and they continuously feel alienated from the mainstream economy, pandemonium will rule the roost.

References

Africa Development Forum Preparatory Workshop 2000 https://www.uneca.org/

Albuquerque, Lins de A. "Terrorism in Africa A Quantitative Analysis." 2017. http://webbrapp.ptn.foi.se-pdf-ab7952a8-3bd5-4593-8342-acdbd2ba3b69.pdf

Bhagavan, M. R. *Angola's Political Economy 1975–1985*. Uppsala: The Scandinavian Institute of African Studies, 1986.

Bamgbose, Ayo. *The Language Factor in Development Goals: The Cape Town Language and Development Conference: Looking Beyond 2015*. Edited by Hamish McIlwraith, 2015.

BBC. "Obama Warns on Africa Leaders Refusing to Step Down." 28 July 2015. Accessed 07 September 2018 https://www.bbc.com/news/world-africa-33684721

BBC. "Paris Climate Deal: Trump Pulls US out of 2015 Accord." 1 June 2017. Accessed 11 August 2018 https://www.bbc.com/news/world-us-canada-40127326

Bureau of Counterterrorism. Country Reports on Terrorism 2016, 2017. https://www.state.gov/j/ct/rls/crt/2016/ Caviedes, A. The Role of Language in Nation-Building within the European Union. *Dialectical Anthropology* 27.3–4 (2003): 249–268. https://doi.org/10.1023/B:DIAL.0000006105.16609.f5

Chumbow, B. S. Linguistic Diversity, Pluralism and National Development in Africa. *Africa Development* XXXIV. 2 (2009): 21–45.

Cocks, T. "From Burkina to Zimbabwe, U.S. Aid Cuts Squeeze Family Planning Services." *Reuters.com*, 22 May 2018. https://www.reuters.com/article/us-trump-impact-birthcontrol/from-burkina-to-zimbabwe-us-aid-cuts-squeeze-family-planning-services-idUSKCN1IN0OV

Dedrick, J., Kenneth L. Kraemer, and G. Linden. "Who Profits from Innovation in Global Value Chains? A Study of the iPod and Notebook PCs." Annual Conference May 1–2, 2008, Boston, 2008.

Felter, Claire. "Why Africa Does Has So Many Languages." *Christian Science Monitor*, 21 April 2015. https://www.csmonitor.com/Science/Science-Notebook/2015/0421/Why-does-Africa-have-so-many-languages

Goncalves, J. "The Economy of Angola: From Independence to the 2008 Worldwide Crisis." *The Perspective of the World Review* 2.3 (2010): 73−84.

Linguisticator. "Why Does Africa have so many Languages than Any Other Continent?" 2018. https://linguisticator.com/africa-many-languages-continent/

Mandalu, M. P. "Tanzania's Development Agenda and Poverty Reduction: A Case of Mkukuta." PhD Thesis University of Fort Hare, 2016.

Mandalu, M., D. R. Thakhathi, and H. Costa. "Investigation on Tanzania's Economic History since Independence: The Search for a Development Model." *World Journal of Social Sciences and Humanities* 4.1 (2018): 61–68.

Miller, C. "Language and Ethnic Statistics in 20th Century Sudanese Censuses and Surveys," 2016. https://halshs.archives-ouvertes.fr/halshs-01544597/document

"New International Version Bible." Accessed 12/12/2018 https://www.biblegateway.com/passage/?search=Matthew+5&version=NIV

Ngowi, H. P. Economic Development and Change in Tanzania Since Independence: The Political Leadership Factor. *African Journal of Political Science and International Relations* 3.4 (2009): 259–267.

Onyenekenwa Cyprian Eneh. Failed Development Vision, Political Leadership and Nigeria's Underdevelopment: A Critique. *Asian Journal of Rural Development* 1 (2011): 63–69. DOI: 10.3923/ajrd.2011.63.69

Pool, J. "National Development and Language Diversity." 1972. http://citeseerx.ist.psu.edu/viewdoc/download? doi=10.1.1.169.938&rep=rep1&type=

Pramuk, J. "Trump to Slap 25% Tariffs on up to $50 Billion of Chinese Goods: China Retaliates." *CNBC*. 15 June 2018. Accessed 14 August 2018 https://www.cnbc.com/2018/06/15/trump-administration-to-slap-a-25-percent-tariff-on-50-billion-of-chinese-goods-threatens-more.html

The Economist. "Donald Trump's Other Trade War—with Rwanda—Over Used Clothes." https://www.economist.com/middle-east-and-africa/2018/04/05/donald-trumps-other-trade-war-with-rwanda-over-used-clothes

Timmer, M. 2014. Slicing Up Global Value Chains. Presentation held at Leeuwenborch, Wageningen.

Wilson Center Africa Program. *Africa: Year in Review*. 2016

Words. "The Role of Language in National Progress." 8 June 2007. https://echoingmemories.wordpress.com/2007/06/08/the-role-of-language-in-national-progress/

World Trade Organization. "Trade and Tariffs: Trade Grows as Tariffs Decline." 2015. https://www.wto.org/english/thewto_e/20y_e/wto_20_brochure_e.pdf

UNDP Human Development Report. 2014. *Human Progress: Reducing Vulnerability and Building Resilience*. New York: United Nations Development Program.

· 4 ·

AFROCENTRIC BARRIERS IN CONTEMPORARY TIMES

This chapter explores a number of challenges that militate against Africa's development processes. The challenges outlined in this chapter are a result of historical, cultural and global processes. These challenges are not peculiar to Africa only, they are present in other continents. In this chapter we seek to explain ways in which they play out in Africa and the bearing they have on the continent's development trajectories and processes. The colonial legacy, religion, corruption, electioneering and China's recent involvement in Africa will be interrogated with the aim of bringing to the fore ways these phenomena and process have related to development efforts that African state are pursuing.

The Colonialism Legacy

History of underdevelopment of Africa is partly rooted in colonialism which saw resources being plundered out of the continent. The inhabitants of the continent were excluded from main stream economic activities by the colonisers. Oppression and marginalisation meant that Africans would find it difficult to develop themselves, let alone their own socio-economic and political spaces. Means of production were beyond the reach of natives. The colonizers were the masters.

The focus of the colonizers was to create perfect environments for exploitation of the people as well as the resources by putting in place all forms of oppressive apparatus that fomented inequalities and exclusion of Africans. Numerous pieces of legislations were put in place in several countries to make life for natives difficult to flourish. Most of these disempowered local people. In this book, we will not dwell much on specific case studies and numerous legislations around the continent and where these occurred but we simply want to support scholarly views that trace development narrative of the continent from this episode of history. Moreover, this pre-independence background is essential for this book in that it forms the first cycle of Africa's incomplete cycles of development. What did colonialism leave behind which complicated and continues to make it hard for progress of the continent? We want to focus on the residual economies which were left behind by the colonial masters, these opened a floodgate of problems as we will encounter.

The oppressive infrastructure created by the colonizers acted as great barriers inhibiting development at the same time perpetuating poverty of masses. The Africa of the colonial times with its massive resources ranging from untapped flora and fauna, minerals, virgin lands, oil, natural gas etc. nourished the colonizers at the expense of not only the native people, but also their economies. Virtually all means of production were controlled by foreigners, so the heartbeat of most economies rested firmly in the hands of the colonizers who then repatriated the gains to their motherlands to be savoured by their kith and kin. Thus it suffices to say that the pulses of most pre independent African states economies were engineered and mastered by colonizers.

Political Independence, Without Economic Independence

When the independence era began to dawn on the continent, the euphoria of self-rule and sovereignty swept across the continent. However, without requisite knowledge to operate economies, political independence did not bring with it economic independence. Most economies nearly collapsed since their heartbeats had been controlled by foreigners. Some industries shrunk. Technocrats left in a huff, creating massive skills gap. Most colonizers literally left with their economies, leaving Africans subsisting on leftovers. The daunting task of Africans in most contexts then was how to manage the residual economies left behind, starting with almost zero knowledge base.

Was the political independence going to automatically translate to economic independence?

Just to divert slightly our discussion so as to illustrate an important point here, consider "*leftovers*" in the case of a meal. There are interesting points we can derive from them. Firstly, they can make you desire for a bigger portion, a full meal. Secondly, leftovers in most cases can hardly fill your belly, they cannot be equated to a full portion. Thirdly, if leftovers are not properly managed, you run the risk of starving early—you will not last the distance. Finally, you are not better off with leftovers compared to someone with a full portion. From this analogy, there are important parallels we can draw with respect to African economies which were inherited from the colonizers.

The residual economies left by the colonizers, are akin to "leftovers" in the case of a meal. Most states in Africa just after independence were performing better in terms of economic indicators like exports, balance of payments, quality of education, robust exchange rates, employment etc. At the same time, the population of the continent was still fairly low such that the leftovers in terms of infrastructure among other amenities would sustain people. Moreover, most of these were still relatively new in terms quality, their carrying capacities then would sustain available populations of the time. As time went on, populations in most countries began to increase gradually fuelled by improvement in health care. However the supply side in terms of amenities, industries, associated facilities and infrastructure to improve welfare of people was slow to respond.

In most contexts little was done in place to also look and act beyond the leftovers. There was little realization that the leftovers would soon vanish-as alluded earlier, leftovers cannot be taken for a full portion. To make matters worse some residuals were not properly managed such that they were quick to disappear—they did not last the distance. The little glory and lustre that had been enjoyed just after independence quickly faded away.

As population of the continent continued to grow, the leftovers were no longer enough for sustenance. Demand for essential things like power, housing infrastructure, sewer systems, jobs etc. grew also in line with population growth. Most major cities in the continent found it difficult to cope with growing urban populations resulting in mushrooming of slums as people tried to find alternative shelter. Coupled with poor planning, most slums have common problems such as lack of proper amenities, overcrowding etc. giving constant headaches to city fathers in most cities around the continent. Medieval diseases such as cholera are still a major problem due to health hazard risks posed by poor infrastructure in most urban set ups. Moreover, the leftover infrastructure in some countries is still to be upgraded such that it cannot cope with ballooning populations.

The colonial days therefore saw minimal development of the continent relative to the potential exhibited. The foreigners were largely the ones in control of levers of most economies. The development they did was mostly to facilitate extraction of resources to their mother countries. There was no big incentive to bring real development to transform lives in the colonies. When Africans from most parts of the continent took over at independence, real development is still an illusion.

Leftovers are almost gone. Inhabitants of the continent have to put up with the present realities of inequality, exclusion, poverty, poor local health facilities (yet most powerful Africans especially politicians have a penchant for seeking medical treatment abroad shunning local facilities), promises and more false promises of better days ahead by shrewd politicians, poor infrastructure, epileptic power supplies, overcrowding, constantly bursting sewer pipes with some streets overflowing with raw sewage in most urban settlements, unemployment, congestion in cities, pollution, homelessness, among other challenges. In all this, development is the greatest casualty. Progress is still slow.

Problems continue to accumulate in the continent, hence it was befitting for us to ask in Chapter 1, the question, "*Will Africa ever catch up with the rest of the world?*" given all this. If it doesn't catch up now, then when? We traced the journey of development of Africa partially from colonialism so as to highlight an important thing at this juncture. During colonial times, development and real progress of the people was minimal, creating an incomplete cycle of development. Just after independence, it was a transition period when Africans were largely feeding on residual economies left by colonial masters. Most of the leftovers were not managed properly, unbeknown to most countries was that leftovers will not last the distance. Development thus slowed creating another incomplete cycle. Post-colonial Africa is however not free from troubles. Sustainable development is a moving and elusive target hard to achieve, yet poverty is accelerating when we compare the continent to most continents, creating another cycle of incomplete development. Present day Africa thus has fresh hurdles it has to overcome so as develop sustainably.

Each phase we tried to trace in the journey has its own barriers. For instance, the transition phase marking a break away from colonialism to freedom largely meant inheriting residual economies, but how to move sustainably with the residuals was the biggest issue. Gloating over the residuals and getting entrapped in them without creating more became a big barrier at this stage in Africa's development history. Hence most economies shrank against their potential.

Contemporary Africa is mainly free from wars and instability such that in most parts a modicum of peace prevails. In this section we focus our attention into this independent Africa. Why is she not developing at the same pace as other continents? This phase the continent is now in is still plagued by a plethora of challenges creating an incomplete cycle of development which is however most important than the other two, mainly because it is more complex.

For instance, the phase of colonial times could easily be gotten over by getting your independence either through wedging an armed struggle against your oppressors or settling for a peaceful transition. On the other hand, the period of leftovers was often chaotic and difficult to manage. Economies were quickly run down through mismanagement or people would fight over control of resources. This saw a number of coups being the order of the day in the continent, as aptly observed by Wangome (1985):

> The period between 1960 and 1970 and slightly beyond has generally been called the decade of coups' in Africa. Once coups started in Africa they became like a wild African bushfire. They swept through the entire continent at an alarmingly high speed. They leapt through national borders as if those boundaries did not exist anymore.

A number of problems emanated during the era of leftovers which mainly featured military governments being in charge, as summarised by Wangome (1985):

> In retrospect, the results of military rule in this vast continent have been very disappointing indeed. Besides being unable to solve the problems they set out to solve in the first place, military regimes in some cases have created situations that did not exist with civilian governments. Military rule has not necessarily been free of incompetence, corruption and maladministration that their civilian predecessors were alleged to have encouraged. Soldiers have been known to be more of wealth-seekers, property grabbers and bribe-takers. They have openly engaged themselves in self-enrichment activities through the barrel of the gun and through intimidation. They have become better embezzlers than their forerunners. They have made better smugglers and tax evaders.

From the above, it showed that most "leftovers" were not properly managed. As we hinted earlier on, they quickly dry up-they indeed dried up in some parts of the continent. An example of leftovers not properly managed is given by Decalo (1976:231) cited in Wangome (1985). He gives an account of how mismanagement of the newly inherited Ugandan economy took place under the stewardship of Mr. Idi Amin who had usurped power:

> In Uganda, General Idi Amin expelled the entire Asian community without any compensation. All the Asian-owned businesses, premises, dwelling houses and plantations were literally dished out to fellow soldiers, friends and any other Ugandan who caught the General's fancy. Within about two years most of those businesses had closed down or gone bankrupt owing to mismanagement and neglect.

Leftovers indeed vanished in Uganda, the residual economy collapsed. So one of the greatest errors of Africa just after independence was mistaking the leftovers for full portions. As such during the so called decades of coups, energies were expended on fighting over crumbs, a relic of colonial legacy as opposed to creating new economic models that would address post independent Africa challenges. The main motive for fighting over the leftovers most probably was to simply control the residuals economies as opposed to growing them for the betterment of the rest of the people. It is thus not surprising that the continent is still grappling with the early industrialization stages when other continents have shifted focus to the fourth industrialization. Immediately after independence, primary focus was supposed to be on how to industrialise and modernize the continent through upgrading infrastructures, equipping and capacitating people so as to be able to be much more useful to their respective economies in the continent as opposed to migrating to other continents.

However, the current phase has changed. How the continent was treated 40 years ago is different from how it expects to be treated presently. Africa can no longer be treated with kid gloves and continue to be cajoled. Leadership across the globe has changed, patience with the continent is slowly waning. In Chapter 3 under global developments we highlighted how the coming in of Mr. Trump, one of the powerful leaders in the world has so far changed things in a difficult way for the continent.

Africa has to sweat for her meals-decent meals (full portions) and not crumbs (leftovers). The decent meals have to be honestly worked for, not the grab and take which characterised the era of leftovers. The period of leftovers is over! She has to prove her mettle to the rest of the world. Africa needs to compete in all sectors if she is to develop. Taps of Aid are slowly closing as the world spins around several challenges. Donor fatigue is also gradually setting in. For Africa to stand her ground and be counted among the rest, there are other several hurdles she has to manoeuvre.

Electioneering Mode

During our early days in college at the University of Zimbabwe studying for our first degrees, observing student politics was fascinating. Participating was even an intriguing experience. Students normally jostling for posts in the numerous student bodies especially the Student Representative Council (SRC) were always a marvel to observe and listen to when they "sell" their manifestos to the "electorate" trying to outshine their rivalries. Occupying these positions was often accompanied with some benefits, for instance guarantee of residency on campus and other direct personal benefits. Getting residency on campus normally meant that you had no hustle of commuting early so as catch up with lectures and you would enjoy all the comfy of being a resident –often an envy of many.

Competing candidates often had nothing material to offer to the electorate so as to "buy their votes" except for a few *gifts*, ranging from t-shirts, caps and occasionally cheap beer, but this was strictly for the few and well connected, privileged followers of running candidates. Most competing candidates often had one common indispensable tool− the powerful and choreographed speeches. These were a powerful paraphernalia to shred your rival into pieces. With the speeches you would outwit the other candidates and take the majority of votes with you. Pomposity and verbosity were often the hallmarks of the campaign speeches. Normally this was a season for us to come across vocabulary we often termed "jawbreakers" from the candidates. The speeches were largely laced with big words which we could not readily trace to any known dictionaries. This is what made the campaigns so "interesting." The most verbose candidates normally would garner much votes, simply because they would be so appealing and "entertaining."

The student representatives once elected and are guaranteed of the personal benefits, most of the "beautiful promises" which will have earned the candidates the tickets to the respective offices will never be delivered to the electorate. Most of the times after the elections, electorates seldom made any follow ups to the election promises.

Years now after graduation, recollecting the early college experiences, we find them to be very relevant in analysing the current development space of the continent. The student politics are a microcosm of the macrocosm of the electioneering mode obtaining in most countries in the African continent in current times. There are several parallels we can derive from this college experience. As simple as it appears, it is nevertheless a powerful analogy which relates with broader politicking in the continent and how it has impacted on development.

In the student politics analogy, the elections are an emblem of democracy–most states in the continent are holding elections, despite them having their own challenges, we will look at election *issues* briefly. In the example, *gifts* dished out to the electorate stand for the freebies normally handed out to the masses so as to entice them to vote. They range from free beer, fly by night self-help projects, election regalia, meals etc. The various student candidates vying for posts basically stand for the numerous political candidates running for different political offices, whereas the rest of the voting students stand for the masses. Then comes the powerful speeches, they stand for the "colourful" campaign manifestos which are often sold to the masses at each election season. Those students who finally make it to the numerous bodies such as the SRC stand for the numerous political electives who manage to make it to different political offices such as local authorities, legislature etc.

The main dichotomy between the electorate in the student example and that of ordinary voting masses is that the former tends to be a better informed electorate by virtue of associating as a community of intellectuals, whereas the bulk of the later has a tendency to lack information. This lack of information has challenges of their own and has allowed shrewd politicians to feast on their electorate and enrich themselves without much development of the continent. Collier (2014: xii) in his book, *The Bottom Billion* notes this and says, "Without an informed electorate, politicians will continue to use the bottom billion merely for photo opportunities, rather than promoting real transformation." The bottom billion in the book meant those countries still struggling to attain meaningful development, a sizeable chunk of these are in Africa.

Election Issues in Africa

Increasing elections amongst nations in the continent is an insignia of transformation to democracy, although maturity stages of democracies hugely vary. International Peace Institute (2011:1) has a positive observation with respect to increase in elections and democracy in the continent:

> The post-Cold War period witnessed several positive changes with respect to democratization in Africa. Participatory politics grew in the 1990s and 2010s, as the percentage of African countries holding democratic elections increased from 7% to 40% and in 2010, Freedom House classified eighteen countries on the continent as electoral democracies. During the past two decades, the general trend has been toward greater accountability of political leaders, whose domestic legitimacy is largely linked to the means through which they attain and maintain power. Yet progress has been uneven.

Elections have allowed power to change hands, sometimes smoothly and in other instances violently. Sadly however, since the dawn of independence across the continent, the political landscape has often been marred by a lot problems as notes International Peace Institute (2011:1)

From the 1950s through to the 1970s, decolonization swept across Africa. While freedom was greeted with euphoria in many places, it could not mask the deep political instability that often accompanied independence. Violence and coercion became a common means of changing power. Coups, counter-coups, and aborted coups littered the political landscape on the continent.

Empirical evidence suggests that clean elections actually improve economic policy which nurtures conditions for economic growth and sustainable development. On the other hand frequent and unfair elections often make things worse, (Collier and Chauvet, 2009). Collier and Chauvet (2009) further opine that elections have two effects. First, they have a structural effect, i.e., they increase accountability. Second, they argue that elections have a disruptive effect by causing frictions which may affect politicians' need for reform.

Elections in the context of Africa, are often littered with many problems ranging from vote rigging, deception, violence, intimidation etc. disfiguring in most instances their credibility. Thus credibility, is a major talking point of most elections in the continent. In addition, African elections are often held with much vigour and gusto. "Sugar coated" manifestos often dominate campaigns which however translate mostly into nothing in as far as development is concerned. The gullible electorate normally falls into the same trap of being told lies almost every election season. Development however, is not built solely on manifestos, practical action is called for which goes beyond mere sloganeering.

On electioneering mode we focus on essential issues related to elections, specifically the processes and outcomes. We will pay special attention to election messages normally peddled to the electorate, issues of constitutions etc.

The net effect of most of these issues has been to affect how the continent progresses or simply to drive it to a path of unsustainable development. For instance we shall have an appreciation of why election messages are often used as a subterfuge to hoodwink the electorate yet in actual fact most election promises are not delivered. The thrust of this section is to highlight two interesting but important issues which are normally associated with elections of the continent which we have observed to date. These issues are important in the sense that they shape the development discourse of the continent. More often they weigh down efforts at development by the majority of countries in the continent as we shall highlight.

African Transactional Electioneering and Politicking. Elections in the context of Africa have literally become like a tradeable commodity, I give you my *things* you give me your votes. In this context, *things* are similar to the gifts we covered in the student politics example we explored earlier on. We cannot have sustainable development if we continue on this path as a continent. What we will mostly have is development linked to election seasons. Once the election cycle is over, then elected officials can afford to simply sit back, relax and "save" their "things" waiting for another election season. In Zimbabwe, roadworks often characterised by simple patching of potholes in urban areas and grading of gravel roads in rural areas is a common spectacle during run up to elections as politicians try to "market " themselves with much gusto. Thus we will simply expect to see signs of meaningful development only around elections. In the process we create cunning politicians who are solely driven by elections as opposed to creating statesmen and stateswomen who are development oriented. Once they win, they vanish.

What if I give you my things and you do not deliver on your votes? The remedy is simple. Simply take your things back. Nothing for nothing. Something for something. A recent example of a Ugandan prospective legislator, Mr Patrick Okumu Ringa supports this observation. Mr Ringa's bid to get elected for a parliamentary seat hit a snag when he lost the elections. Despite having provided water through drilling 10 boreholes to the Nebbi Municipal community, he did not take his lose lightly. Mr Ringa confirmed to the local paper, New Vision that he had removed the boreholes, he was quoted as saying "Our people are not appreciative. All I wanted from them was votes. I have educated so many children, but all they tell me is I have done nothing," So to show gratitude for the "*things*" he had done to the people, he wanted their votes, yet they chose to be disloyal to him. Thus if you fake your support and allegiance to me, hence I take what belongs to me. After all it is not illegal for me to take what is mine.

What if we give you our votes and you do not deliver on your electoral promises? It does not matter. We wait for another election season, after all it was just politics. Moreover, I know you are too poor, you cannot afford to ignore me. Give me another chance. It is not uncommon in Africa to see non-performing and often absentee leaders/representatives frequently seeking re-election be it local authorities, house of assembly etc.

This practice is mostly common in very poor areas where it is easy to manipulate voters as opposed to urban areas where voters are much more informed. The powerful are able to force the poor to account for their lack of loyalty with votes, but the poor cannot force the powerful to account for their failure to deliver development goods. In instances they try, they obtain little success. So can we expect very poor and backward communities of the continent to be transformed for real given situations like this? It is not easy.

Jobism. One interesting feature especially in most election campaign messages almost wherever you go is the promise of jobs and more jobs by politicians. Even Mr Trump during his election campaign his promises included the desire to safeguard American jobs in sectors such as coal mining, steel etc. Is the promise about jobs bad? No. Almost everyone needs a job. Coming back to Africa, the promises about jobs has become an anthem, an overplayed song which politicians have well mastered and continues to be a central message in most campaign manifestos. Interestingly, it seems to the gullible masses, the "jobs music" is the melody they love to hear the most. Mostly, the quality of the "promised jobs" to be created does not necessarily matter.

Jobism is defined by Richard McKenzie cited in an article by Sedze (2018) as "the modern public policy philosophy that *mistakenly* focuses on the number of jobs as being the key feature of a country's measure of a country's economic success or failure." Italicising the word "mistakenly" is deliberate by the authors. This part of the definition is key to contextualising the concept of jobism to Africa. The main difference between jobism in the context of mature democracies and continents like Africa is that for the former, politicians try to walk the talk. Jobs, better quality jobs are often created so as to benefit people. For the later however, the job promise is seldom delivered, they remain a pie in the sky. For the few which are delivered, the quality leaves a lot to be desired. Meaningful jobs should bolster competitiveness of the continent to the rest of the world through increasing efficiency and productivity (Sedze,

2018). Thus the dominant strategy of job promises is "mistaken" somehow in that the promises revolve around the physical number of jobs created as opposed to their quality. The quality is measured in terms of efficiency and productivity we stated earlier. As a result most of the lucky jobs created, if any can hardly be banked upon so as to support sustainable development for the continent. We briefly look into some of the reasons jobism is a popular strategy in the context of elections in Africa.

Why not promise jobs in Africa when many people are wallowing in poverty due to massive unemployment? The jobs message is a sweet melody to the electorate. Most youths are out of work in the continent, they are excluded from mainstream economic activities. The promise of eking out a living through getting a job is then most welcome. Jobism strategy therefore is still very relevant in African context since growing number of unemployed is not scaling down.

Earlier on in this section we discussed about how residual economies were not properly managed in some contexts in the continent. The consequence of poor management of these inherited economies and ensuing chaos destroyed some viable industries creating huge vacuums in terms of required industries to cater for fresh challenges and growing expectations from masses brought about by the independence euphoria. The question then was how to fill up this vacuum. With little practical skills to create new economies needed, few industries are being created. However, the politicians have to be seen to be in charge, the other way to justify stay in office is to promise jobs a target which has mostly remained elusive. Industries gap is then filled with promises, resulting in jobism taking centre stage in election messages. Walking the talk on creating and even replacing the destroyed industries is no easy task hence the jobs messages features prominently in most election manifestos.

Jobs is a low hanging fruit especially when coming up with election messages. A sad reality is that there is often a mismatch between jobs pledged and actual jobs which are eventually delivered to the electorate. It's easier to promise than to deliver.

Constitutional "Coups," For Whose Benefit? A disorder which is gradually becoming a disturbing trend in several African countries is amending of national constitutions and electoral laws which is going on and shows little signs of coming to a halt. It is now a cancer which is slowly getting entrenched into the political systems of the continent. Camara (2016) writing for The Washington Post calls these amendments "constitutional coups." Since the

1990s, nearly 30 presidents in African, particularly the Sub Saharan region nations have sought power extensions through playing around national constitutions, (Camara, 2016). In reference to these endless constitutional amendments which have become fashionable in the continent, Mr. Barack Obama, the former US president at an African Union address in 2015 once remarked:

> "When a leader tries to change the rules in the middle of the game just to stay in office, it risks instability and strife, as we've seen in Burundi," Mr. Obama said. "And this is often just a first step down a perilous path. And sometimes you'll hear leaders say, 'Well, I'm the only person who can hold the nation together.' If that's true, then that leader has failed to truly build their nation." (Benen, 2015)

Undoubtedly this comment by the former US president may have been inspired by what is currently happening in several parts of the continent. With the constitutional amendments, the culture of over staying in power has been cultivated and is gradually becoming a custom of several regimes in the continent. Here is a look at evidence from Burundi and Uganda to collaborate this.

In July 2018, the Constitutional Court of Uganda delivered a ruling that would see the scraping off of the presidential age limit of 75 years. Whilst the country will go for polls in a few years to come, the time of the amendment may mean that Mr Museveni will run again. He has been in power for more than 30 years now. In 2005 an amendment was made again which scrapped the limit of terms of office for the presidency from two terms. This allowed him to extend his stay in office (Africa News, 2018).

In May 2018, 76% of Burundians voted in a referendum for a constitutional amendment which would allow the president, Mr Pierre Nkurunzinza who has ruled since 2005 to stay in power till 2034, (Sunday Times, 2018). His party itself according to the Times paper even gave him the title "Supreme Eternal Guide" implying that he is above the law.

So the element of constitutional amendments is spreading across Africa. It is not only the two cases highlighted above, but examples are plenty around the continent. For instance the DRC under leadership of Mr Joseph Kabila has seen moments of when the president would want to change electoral laws to allow him to go beyond stipulated limits sparking protests in the country. In 2014, Burkina Faso, a small West African country was plunged into chaos when Mr Blaise Compaore wanted to extend his 27 year rule via amending the constitution (The Guardian, 2014). On the other hand, Cameroon abolished term limits in 2008. This move allowed Mr. Paul Biya to stand for re-election in 2011, (BBC, 2018). At this juncture then we ask, for whose benefit are these "constitutional coups" being made? Do they promote a path to sustainable development by the continent? Is this not another cycle of incomplete development gradually unfolding across the continent when we thought elections have helped propagate democracy in the continent?

Mostly, the amendments are meant to preserve the status quo and benefit a certain clique, for example to ensure that a sitting head of state extends his term of office at whatever costs. Power is indeed sweet! Through observation about on goings in several places in the continent, these constitutional coups have allowed leaders to cling to power. The result has been to see the same leaders ruling over long periods of time but with development of their respective countries shrinking. Most heads of state in Africa who have had an average of fifteen or more years in power, there has been a tendency to have less and less in terms of progress and betterment of livelihoods of people. Others assumed power when economies were performing fairly well (mostly the residual economies) which they then presided over their demise or grew very little at the same time enriching themselves. The clinging presidents have been stewards of winning political parties (in most cases with landslide margins) which however has given birth to systems which do not promote sustainable development, of their countries as observed by Feldman (2017:11):

> An important offshoot of the problem of winning parties appointing all of the government positions, is that it is difficult for a professional, competent, impartial bureaucracy to arise in such a situation. Cronyism and nepotism are used to fill slots instead of merit and, as a result, governments are incapable of implementing fair taxing schemes, creating schools, providing adequate security, delivering healthcare and so forth.

Following successful constitutional coups in the continent, some leaders have been able to romp to numerous electoral victories, earning themselves fresh mandates to rule people. Whatever mechanism and machinery they have used to win fresh mandates besides the constitutional coups is beyond the scope of this book. Clinging and overstaying in power has come with a price in the continent.

Here is a brief look at leaders who have clung to power for more than two decades, Idris Deby of Chad now has more than 25 years. Mr Teodoro Obiang Nguema of Equatorial Guinea now has more than 37 years since 1979, he is the longest serving in the continent. Mr Museveni of Uganda now has more than 30 years in charge. Development has not been able to move. Corruption, incompetence, deteriorating standards of living of the ordinary populace, failing economies have often been the common outcomes. Some leaders even despite advanced ages and failing health have clung on, burdening the very electorate they purport to serve. Mr Biya of Cameroon often known for his hands-off approach by being mostly absent in the country (BBC, 2018), has earned himself another new term of ruling the country aged 85. This will see him finishing his term at the ripe age of 92 despite having ruled for 35 years. The economy has not been doing much with 60% of Cameroon population under the age of 25 still yearning for better livelihoods and jobs, (BBC, 2018). In the early month of December 2018, an interesting development of a constitutional coup is unfolding in Sudan. Lawmakers signed a petition which seeks to extend presidential term limits. This will allow Mr. Bashir whose has ruled since 1989 to throw his hat in the ring again come 2020 (Africa News, 2018).

Briefly we discuss one other problem of holding on to power and its associated problems using a simple analogy of a common domestic animal in Africa, known as a "goat." Out of the goat we derive the phrase "*goat mentality*." The behaviour of this domestic animal helps us to emphasize what we have observed regards to overstaying in power in several parts of the continent.

- **Goat Mentality**

Growing up as small boys we used to herd livestock. Goats, we found them to be the most fascinating domestic animals. They were the most mischievous. Goats were the last animals to go for grazing, normally late afternoon. We would never make a mistake of releasing them out of their pens at the same time as the rest of the livestock. In most cases, if this was done, goats would never graze at one place. They would take the lead, running everywhere, outpacing the other animals. This meant that, we would be always on our feet the whole day, with little rest as other animals would also follow the goats' crusade.

Before we let them join the rest of the livestock, the remedy would be simply to tie them to small bushes outside their holding pens. Interestingly, they would start grazing around the area within their reach. By the moment they join the rest of the livestock, their bellies would be almost full and they would not give us much problems. We studied this rather interesting behaviour of goats for our entire childhood of tending to livestock. In our imagination we deduced that, these goats thought that they would never get the chance to join the rest of the livestock. So they would rather graze whatever was within their reach to the maximum. During those days as small boys we thought that tying the goats to small bushes out of their pens would be akin to punishing them for their misdemeanours. We often derived pleasure out of this, unbeknown to us was the fact that these goats actually fed themselves to what was within their reach.

Another interesting fact about goats, is that they can thrive under the harshest of conditions. Even desert like. They can graze as well as browse, making them resilient to difficult conditions. In Africa for many countries, even when economies are well below reasonable levels of performance, some leaders have been able to survive financing extravagant lifestyles with whatever little available resources they could put hands on. Like the goat, they have been able to graze as well as browse, showing less signs of distress despite their economies sinking to their knees.

African leaders who often overstay in power fail the human rights test. Gross violations are usually the order of the day. To sustain themselves they trample on any dissenting voices with impunity. In response, the international community sometimes responds with slapping the respective administration with sanctions and restrictions. Just like the noose which tied our goats to the bushes, so are the sanctions to the clinging leaders. The intention being to make them reform after feeling the pinch of sanctions. However, some have survived these tough conditions by being able to run down their economies at the expense of their people, constraining sustainable development in the process. Like the goat in desert like conditions, they have survived through tough sanctions imposed on them. Ordinary masses have paid the price. Sanctions and restrictions imposed by the international community have had the effect of hurting the ordinary people more than the initial intended targets.

One last behaviour trait of goats is their stubbornness emanating perhaps out of their persistence. Sneaking away from the rest of the flock in the grazing fields, they would occasionally invade village gardens so as to have a bite of fresh and succulent vegetables. In response we would drive them away. In no time however, they would come back in the same gardens. The only solution was for us to look for grazing land far away from the gardens and keep a watchful eye on them from there.

The same goat mentality can easily be related to the clinging leadership and how it has been an albatross to progress of the continent. The "village gardens" are the national economies across various nations in the continent. Most of these leaders have been driven away by the general masses through elections. Why? Because of most of their misdemeanours in the economies ranging from corruption, incompetence and general mismanagement subjecting people to poverty and stalling sustainable development. The votes through elections have driven them away, however like the goats we would earlier drive away, they would subvert the will of the people and bounce back with much gusto. In the process they continue with their transgressions.

A recent case in point of "goat mentality" in practice is that of Mr Yahya Jammeh, the former president of Gambia. In 2016 he was defeated in polls by Mr Adama Barrow. The defeat signalled outright rejection by the people-like the goats being driven away out of the gardens, so were the people's votes to Mr Jammeh. People had had enough of his incompetence, abuses, maladministration, failing economy among other transgressions. Jammeh initially conceded defeat, he even made a phone call to his rival and delivered a congratulatory message. Later on he changed his mind and wanted to subvert the will of the people. He was later persuaded to leave the country. Had it not been the threat of force issued to him as a warning, he was prepared like the stubborn goat to invade the garden again. To do what? To continue with running down the tiny West African nation despite having led for over 22 years and having failed to grow the economy.

Religion and Development in Africa

The African continent has been undergoing religious resurgence in the past decades. The Pew Report notes (2011) that the number of Christians in the Global South, Africa included, has risen significantly in the past century. It is worth noting that in Africa, Pentecostalism is arguably the fastest growing strand of Christianity. There has been a rise in studies that aim to understand the relationship that exist between Pentecostal strand of Christianity and development. Put in another way, scholars have been grappling with questions of whether this new strand of Pentecostalism can deliver or initiate development processes.

Modestly, there are attempts to understand if Pentecostalism is a conducive vehicle for improving peoples' lives. There are two lines of thought that have emerged in literature on African Pentecostalism and development. One line of thought, represented by the Centre for Development and Enterprise, argues that Pentecostal movements in South Africa have spearheaded social and infrastructural development in their communities.

The other school of thought dismisses Pentecostalism as lacking pragmatism and spiritualizing and enchanting everything to an extent that it offers no meaning and practical solutions to the challenges that post-colonial African states face. The latter line of thought is found in Gifford's (2002, 2004) work and the Comaroff (2001, a&b). Below we consider this line of thoughts in detail and tease out opportunities and drawbacks that Pentecostalism presents to the development processes and practice.

Literature from southern Africa is starting to appreciate and highlight the role of Pentecostalism in the development processes (Bompani, 2010, 2015; Freeman, 2015; Schlemmer, 2008). Pentecostalism promotes "development from below" in Bompani's words. The argument is framed around Weber's (1930) concept of "the Protestant Ethic" which Weber showed to be "this worldly" as it orients believers to focus on "the here and now." For the Calvinists, the Protestant Ethic encouraged systematic saving and methodical approach to worldly duties. This resulted in a work ethic that contributed greatly to the emergence of capitalism in Europe. Schlemmer (2008) identified some elements of the Protestant Ethic in contemporary Pentecostalism across the globe. Some Pentecostal movements in Africa are encouraging methodical approach to saving, investment and wealth accumulation. A number of Pentecostal churches in Africa promote entrepreneurship among their members.

Writing about Zimbabwe Assembly of God Africa (ZAOGA), David Maxwell (2005) argues that members are taught to start small businesses. Most ZAOGA members vended food and other wares to both members and non-members. ZAOGA and other Pentecostal movements in Africa are breeding a generational of entrepreneurs through initiatives that promote what Maxwell (1998) calls "penny capitalism." Entrepreneurial activities have a direct bearing on household incomes and livelihood (Gukurume, 2018). In such cases, Pentecostalism in building development from below through capacitating members and encouraging avenues for income generation.

Apart from promoting entrepreneurship, Pentecostal movements are building capacity among members. This is achieved in a number of ways. Most Pentecostals movements arrange for business seminars and financial literacy coaching for members (James, 2015). Members are equipped with up-to-date information and skills on investments, budgeting and cost-effective expenditures (Gukurume, 2018). There is visible shift towards pragmatism. The focus on increasing avenues for income generating leads to financially stable families and households. Pentecostalism in Africa focuses on the people, improving their livelihoods and bolstering income generating projects. Development projects from below are direct impact on the lives of the people.

Furthermore, Pentecostal theologies limits unnecessary expenditure on alcohol, extra-marital affairs and traditional rituals that divert funds from being used by families (Maxwell, 2006).

Miller and Yamamori (2007) have shown that contemporary Pentecostal movements across the world have strong social engagement that directly improve the lives of people in communities. Through charity activities such as kitchen-soups, school rehabilitation, support for Orphans and Vulnerable Children (OVCs) and People Living with HIV and AIDS (PLWHA) and funding education for the marginalized children, Pentecostal movements are directly impacting the lives of the marginalized categories in societies. Pentecostal movements are improving the lives and reducing deprivations that characterise societies. Pentecostal movements have large memberships which allow them to pool large amounts of resources that can channelled towards assisting the less fortunate (Miller and Yamamori, 2007). Furthermore, they have a huge coverage and direct access to the less marginalized that are often neglected by state welfare system, NGOs and other actors in development processes.

This far, we have outlined an edge that religious movements have in development processes. They have direct access to marginalized categories in society. Furthermore they tie the concept of development to theology. This inspires members to pursue ways that improve their lives as religious duty. While these strengths can be noted, there are studies that show that some strands of Pentecostalism are detrimental to development processes. Gifford (2002) notes that some strands of African Pentecostalism fail to address real problems that affect people because they tend to spiritualize everything. Structural problems are left unaddressed as Pentecostals seek solutions in prayers and rituals. For Gifford, Pentecostals do not proffer meaningful solutions to everyday development challenges face. Emphasis on spiritual warfare divert some churches from making meaningful contributions to society.

On the same note, Comaroff and Comaroff (2001) blame Pentecostal movements in South Africa for encouraging conspicuous consumption at the expense of production. Pentecostals seek consuming global commodities without the means of supporting such lifestyles. Pentecostalism in this case is detrimental to development as it pushes members in debt and poverty. Comaroff and Comaroff (2001) further argue that Pentecostal movements encourage occult economies in which at time members seek to amass wealth through supernatural means.

Hair raising miracles are often paraded, whether to cow followers into submission or mere show boating, they have become the order of the day for most movements. This discourages working and honesty means of wealth accumulation. Pentecostals, especially the youth lack work ethic and do not plan beyond riches that come supernaturally. To further compound the problem is that, most Pentecostal movements have literally captured youth in most parts of the continent, with promises of instant riches and often miracles have often been used so as to allure followers. Can those "quick fixes" really be relied upon so as to shepherd the continent out of this curse of poverty and regression? These authors however, do not underestimate heavenly powers, but we believe in a culture of hard work. The problems of the continent are complex. The millennials of the continent should toil just like those in other continents, honest hard work driven by traceable formulae will actually promote a youth who can bequeath massive wealth for generations to come in the continent.

Our other challenge with Pentecostalism in relation to progress of the continent is that development attached to religion is piecemeal and mainly focussed on members. Non-members are at times are neglected, alienated and left in the cold as people associate on the basis of religious affiliations. On the same note, religious movements operation are shrouded in mysteries. Development agenda of the economy needs to be built on honestness and hard work. Good and accountable people in the continent will come out of these key virtues. There is therefore a need to monitor religious movements by respective governments in the continent as they now come in as arguments in the development matrix of the continent. This can no longer be ignored.

Chinese Deals with Africa in the 21st Century: Investments or Exploitations?

The past two decades have seen a significant influx of Chinese people migrating to Africa to pursuit of economic opportunities that Africa offers (Park, 2009). Though Chinese engagement with African countries is not new, the current engagement is purely economic unlike the earlier engagements that were ideological (Stahl, 2016: 2). The involvement of the Chinese has been met with mixed reactions and feeling across the continent. This section explores dynamic associated with the Chinese investment in Africa bringing to the fore both opportunities that Chinese bring to the continent and challenges that these investment bring to the continent. China's focus on African countries has witnessed increase in Foreign Direct Investments, infrastructural developments and trade. In the year 2011 Africa received a total of US $ 629 billion in overseas direct investment. Of this total, China's contribution was 3.2% (Dollar, 2016: 22). While its contribution seems small, China's ODI and FDI have been increasing. Furthermore, China has put more money in Africa than in other continents.

The Chinese model of developing Africa is complex and opaque. The Chinese government has encouraged African governments to provide raw material for the Chinese manufacturing industry in exchange for construction of transport, shopping malls, telecommunication, hydro-power and gas and aviation infrastructure. In Zimbabwe the Chinese have moved to procure tobacco, in which they are slowly replacing European buyers, while Ghana provides cocoa, Ethiopians are providing sesame while a number of countries such as Democratic Republic of Congo, Congo Brazzaville and Nigeria have attracted Chinese developmental programmes by virtue of their oil and petroleum (Brautigam, 2011). In Zambia the Chinese deals have developed railway system, while in Democratic Republic of Congo there has been interest in growing iron mining. In Angola the Chinese have shown interest in oil and gas resources.

In this respect, the Chinese have brought with them a model that differs from those of European model of helping Africa. The Chinese are reluctant to interfere with internal affairs and politics. The west has often blamed the Chinese for propping up authoritarian regimes in African by giving them a life-line through mega-deals that they sign. Furthermore, the Chinese model has promoted aid that is linked business simultaneously. Concomitantly, the Chinese model has proved to create more jobs for the locals, develop the infrastructure in African states. Investment is a prerequisite for development and not aid which has been labelled lethal and dead (see Dambisa Moyo, 2009). Furthermore, Chinese approach of underwriting deals might be better than loans. Reasons are utilized to meet current needs and to offset the Chinese investments. This deal enjoys reduced interests, though it jeopardize future generations' utilization of the same resources.

The result of Chinese aid and investment is clear to most Africans. Some get services and products from Chinese linked development projects while others have been employed in various sectors that results from Chinese deals and investment efforts. Creation of jobs is at the heart of all these deals. Africans have rated highly Chinese investors as compared to investor from other parts of the world (Drake, 2015).

Chinese investments in Africa come in a number of ways. There are state-to-state bilateral agreements, Chinese firms moving into African countries to establish businesses and there are also individual Chinese migrants who are venturing into retailing and other small scale businesses. The Chinese are creating employment for locals as well as allowing the locals to be part of the global consumption circuits. Chinese businesses bring with them technology that is lacking in Africa. with these technologies, new skills and expertise is imparted on Africans.

Chinese investment in Africa has been condemned for a number of reasons. There are scholars that have brought to the fore the toxic nature of Chinese investments in the continent. The primary issues raised against Chinese deals and investments is that of neo-imperialism. Chinese firms and the state are in Africa for the appropriation of resources that will later on provide raw materials for Chinese factories and industries. This motive to acquire resources is similar to that of erstwhile colonizers—European imperial powers.

The Chinese are growing their industries through cheap raw materials that are expropriated from African nations. For instance the Chinese acquire iron from Democratic Republic of Congo, tobacco and gold from Zimbabwe and sesame from Ghana. The Chinese are not developing local industries in their investments. They build rudimentary industries that facilitate movements of raw materials and resources out of Africa. The Chinese model stifles value-addition and diversification of industries on the continent. The Chinese process the raw material into finished commodities that they sell for a premium to African governments. Apart from stifling the growth of Africa's industrialisation, the Chinese have made themselves the biggest creditor to most African governments. China extends huge amounts of funds to African nations, which often are not repaid, trapping African nations in a vicious circle of debt. The Chinese push for deals that are attractive but have the potential to ensnare African government when they fail to repay.

The Chinese deals have presented challenges for most African governments. Infrastructural development by Chinese for instance has associated problems in the continent. Despite this seemingly noble initiative, the Chinese have failed to impart skills and capacity to locals. Sino-Africa deals, for example, are spearheaded by Chinese personnel and the bulk of materials are acquired from China. Africa has been reduced to a market for Chinese businesses. For China, Africa is a land where its huge population can be made productive and an avenue for expanding Chinese market globally. The model of investment and engagement that Chinese state and its investor promote in African is regressive. Unlike European and American aid and investments that come with conditionalities when it comes to good governance, democracy and rule of law, Chinese aid and investment are not premised on these. The Chinese have propped up authoritarian regimes that have no respect of rule of law and good governance. The Chinese have opened a life-line for oppressive and authoritarian regimes. The Chinese promote economic prosperity at the expense of democracy. For Sen (1999) development is synonymous with freedom and liberty. The model that the Chinese promote do not place a premium on citizen's freedom and liberties. If development is about freedom, democracy and rule of law, then the type of development the Chinese are promoting in Africa falls short.

In a country such as Zimbabwe, the Chinese have dominated sectors such as retailing and mining where they often pay meagre salaries to the locals owing to lax labour laws internally, evade tax payments and have often being accused of externalizing funds. This reduces revenue to the hamstrung government, negatively impacting its operations and activities. Furthermore, Chinese entrepreneurs are favoured by most African governments as model minorities that are used as a buffer zone against local entrepreneurs. Chinese migrants are promoted at the expense of local entrepreneurs because most entrepreneurs of Chinese origin are not citizens who participate in local politics. Locals are side-lined as they have the ability to fund and contest for political leadership. The Chinese entrepreneurs provide the means through which African governments deny citizen's their rights and deliberately not promote local enterprises.

It is pragmatic therefore that, African states need to be in a position to assess the nature of mega-deals that the Chinese offer and select those that are beneficial to both the current generation as well as to posterity. The Chinese engagement with the African state must recognize African state as equal partners with the ability to choose what development aid and deals they need. African state must move away from opaque deals that are not ratified by citizens. There is need for the Chinese to promote holistic approach to development by promoting rule of law and democracies in which Africans can flourish and thrive. Limitation of freedoms stifled development with a human face.

In conclusion, this chapter and Chapter 3 largely explored challenges that are militating most of African state's progress and development efforts. The colonial legacy heavily dragged African states down as colonialism left most economies oriented towards feeding European industries. There is need to rethink and re-orient African economies to meet the needs of the ever increasing and expectant population. Post-colonial African states also have their own issues such as corruption, nepotism, politicking, electioneering, ethnic and religious diversities that present challenges for Africa nation-state. These issues need to be addressed to clear the way for African states to make progress and improve the lives of citizens. The proliferation of Chinese further complicates the develop terrain that most African states must navigate.

References

Africa News. "Uganda Court Upholds Age Limit Removal, Dissenting Justice Kakuru is Declared Hero Online." Accessed 29/10/2018 http://www.africanews.com/2018/07/27/uganda-court-upholds-age-limit-removal-dissenting-justice-kakuru-is-declared//

Benen, S. "Obama says he 'could win' a theoretical third term." Accessed 13/07/2016http://www.msnbc.com/rachel-maddow-show/obama-says-he-could-win-theoretical-third-term

BBC. "Paul Biya: Cameroon's 'Absentee President.'" Accessed 30/10/2018 https://www.bbc.com/news/world-africa-43469758

Bompani, B. "Religion and Development from Below: Independent Christianity in South Africa." *Journal of Religion in Africa* 40.3 (2010): 307–330.

Bompani, B. "Religion and Development in Sub-Saharan Africa: An Overview." In *The Routledge Handbook of Religion and Global Development*. Edited by E. Tomalin. London: Routledge, 2015.

Brautigam, D. *China in Africa: What Can Western Donor Learn*. Oslo: Norfund, 2011.

Camara, K. "Here's How African Leaders Stage "Constitutional Coups": They Tweak the Constitution to Stay in Power." Accessed 29/10/2018 https://www.washingtonpost.com/news/monkey-cage/wp/2016/09/16/heres-how-african-leaders-stage-constitutional-coups-they-tweak-the-constitution-to-stay-in-power/?utm_term=.e6f71b7f44aa

Collier, Paul, and Chauvet, Lisa. "Elections in Developing Countries: Do They Improve Economic Policy?" *VOX CEPR Policy Portal*, 2009. https://voxeu.org/article/do-elections-developing-countries-improve-economic-policy

Comaroff, J., and J. L. Comaroff. *Millennial Capitalism and the Culture of Neoliberalism*. Durham: Duke University Press, 2001a.

Comaroff, J., and J. L. Comaroff. *Millennial Capitalism: First Thought on a Second Coming*. London: Duke University Press, 2001b.

Dollar, D. *China's Engagement with Africa: From Natural Resources to Human Resources*. Washington, DC: The John L Thornton China Centre, 2016.

Drake, B. *PEW Global Attitude Survey on How the World Views the U.S and China*. Washington, DC: Pew Research Centre, 2015.

Feldman, S. *Authoritarianism, Threat, and Intolerance*. In E. Borgida, C., Federico, C., & J. Miller (eds.), At the forefront of political psychology: Essays in honor of John L. Sullivan. New York: Routledge. In press, 2017.

Fick, M. "Burundi Approves New Constitution Extending Presidential Term Limit." *Times*, May 21, 2018. https://www.timeslive.co.za/news/africa/2018-05-21-burundi-approves-new-constitution-extending-presidential-term-limit/

Freeman, D. Pentecostalism and Economic Development in Sub-Saharan Africa. In *The Routledge Handbook of Religion and Global Development*. Edited by E. Tomalin. Abingdon, Oxon: Routledge, 2015.

Gifford, P. *Christianity and Politics in Doe's Liberia*, Vol. 2. Cambridge: Cambridge University Press, 2002.

Gifford, P. *Ghana's New Christianity: Pentecostalism in a Globalizing African Economy*. Bloomington and Indianapolis: Indiana University Press, 2004.

Gifford, P. *Christianity, Politics and Public Life in Kenya*. London: Hurst & Company, 2009.

Gukurume, S. "Youth Empowerment and African Initiated Churches in Urban Zimbabwe." Religion and Development Policy Brief 02/2018. Series of the Research Programme on Religious Communities and Sustainable Development. Humboldt University, 2018.

International Peace Institute. "Elections in Africa: Challenges and Opportunities." Accessed 08 September, 2018. https://www.ipinst.org/wp-content/uploads/publications/ipi_e_pub_elections_in_africa__2_.pdf

James, D. *Money from Nothing: Indebtedness and Aspiration in South Africa*. Stanford, CA: Stanford University Press, 2015.

Maxwell, D. "The Durawall of Faith: Pentecostal Spirituality in Neo-Liberal Zimbabwe." *Journal of Religion in Africa* 35.1 (2005): 4–32.

Maxwell, D. *African Gifts of the Spirit: Pentecostalism and the Rise of Zimbabwean Transnational Religious Movement*. Harare: Weaver Press, 2006.

Maxwell, D. "Delivered from the Spirit of Poverty? Pentecostalism, Prosperity and Modernity in Zimbabwe." *Journal of Religion in Africa* 28.3 (1998): 350–371.

Miller, D. E., & T. Yamamori. *Global Pentecostalism: The New face of Christian Social Engagement*. Berkeley: University of California Press, 2007.

Moyo, D. *Dead Aid: Why Aid Is Not Working and How There Is a Better Way for Africa*. New York: Farrar, Straus and Giroux, 2009.

Park, Y. "Chinese Migration in Africa. South Africa Institute of International Affairs (SAIIA)." Occasional Paper 24, 2009.

PEW. *Global Christianity: A Report on the Size and Distribution of World's Christian Population*. Washington, DC: PEW Research Centre, 2011.

Schlemmer, L. *Dormant Capital: Pentecostalism in South Africa and Its Potential Social and Economic Role*. Johannesburg: Centre for development and Enterprise, 2008.

Schlemmer, L. *Under the Radar: Pentecostalism in South Africa and Its Potential Social and Economic Role*. Johannesburg: Centre for development and Enterprise, 2008.

Sedze, B. Job Creation is a Mirage. *The Standard*. Accessed 16/12/2018 https://www.thestandard.co.zw/2018/04/29/job-creation-mirage/

Sen, Amartya. *Development as Freedom*. Oxford: Oxford University Press, 1999.

Stahl, A. K. "China's Relations with Sub-Saharan Africa." IAI Working Paper 16:22, 2016.

The Guardian. Burkina Faso: Violent Clashes over Plans to Extend President's Rule. Accessed 29/10/2018 https://www.theguardian.com/world/2014/oct/30/protesters-storm-burkina-faso-parliament-constitution-vote-president-blaise-compaore

Wangome, J. "Military Coups in Africa—The African "Neo-Colonialism" That Is Self-Inflicted." *Globalsecurity.org*, 1985. Accessed on 25/10/18 https://www.globalsecurity.org/military/library/report/1985/WJ.htm

Weber, M. 1930. *The Protestant Ethic and the Spirit of Capitalism*. London: Allen and Unwin.

· 5 ·

REGIONALISM AND DEVELOPMENT IN AFRICA

The African continent is home to 14.8% of the global population; it accounts for less than three per cent of the global GDP and receives only three per cent of foreign direct investment (UNCTAD, 2018). Go it alone in economic development does not work for any forward looking state. Various economic theories push for regional groupings. Barriers to trade need to be minimized. As noted by El-Maghur (2011), states are becoming increasingly more interdependent on one another, the prospects of development are better achieved when states pursue goals as a block than when they pursue goals as unitary entities. The world has been created in a way that each piece of land is characterized by its own endowments, making it harder for states to go alone. It is never possible for any nation to isolate itself because of insufficient endowments in its own backyard. Moreover, for developmental issues, the theory of comparative advantage requires partnership for effective and successful growth. Mansfield and Milner (1999:589) note that the ultimate goal of regional integration is mainly to merge some or all aspects of the economies concerned.

Regionalism, apart from economic issues also considers; socio-cultural, institutional and geographical-centered issues. Mansfield and Milner (1999) argues that regionalization refers to the growth of societal integration within a region and to the often undirected processes of social and economic interaction. Regional integration in Africa represents one of the potential responses to critical challenges and thus solutions to the socio-economic difficulties in the continent and its regions, such as unemployment, poverty, bad governance, and social unrest. The first experiment with integration was within Southern African states, the Southern African Customs Union (SACU) established in 1910, and is arguably the first sub-regional attempt on integration. In 1949 the Southern Rhodesia Customs Union emerged between South Africa and present day Zimbabwe.

Regionalism has various definitions in place, ranging from geographic proximity of countries, economic path—level of income, trading blocks, homogeneity in policies, institutions, languages, religion, common political path, legal systems, labour market systems, among other definitions. Rugman and Verbeke (2004), indicate that the most common approach for grouping countries into categories has focused on economic dimensions. Successful integration requires that, states engage in activities that are purely oriented to promote economic prosperity (El-Maghur, 2011). As noted by Kipruto (2010) effective regional integration requires the mobilization of vast resources, both within and outside the region. Regional integration is viewed by many as a mechanism for developing the industrial sector of a member country; the infant industries which are allowed to operate in the newly protected markets in the regional economic blocs will operate safely by producing and "exporting" within the protected market until they become mature and eventually become sufficiently efficient to face world competition without further assistance (Abdi and Seid, 2013). Regional integration as hinted by Sobhee and Bhowon (2007) can also have negative economic and social impacts, notably when the domestic regulatory framework is inadequate or not implemented effectively.

Regional integration has been seen in Africa as a means of encouraging trade and securing economies of scale (Khandelwal, 2004). In the formation of free trade agreements, the dynamic and static gains associated with regional trade agreements are significant (Simiyu and Mugano, 2017: 4417). The common regional groups in Africa are defined geographically. Africa as a continent is divided into Eastern Africa, Middle Africa, Northern Africa, Southern Africa, and Western Africa. Regional integration in Africa went through several stages and took many forms according to the different objectives and fields (Taha, 2016). According to El-Maghur (2011) geographical boundaries upon which Regional Economic Communities (RECs) are established were determined by colonial occupation. The need for economic integration in Africa has long been noticed. Development-oriented regionalism can contribute on guiding Africa's achievement of development goals, building resilience to external financial and economic crises, and fostering inclusive growth (UNCTAD, 2018).

The Organization for African Unity (OAU) was established in 1963, as a prerequisite for economic development for the continent Africa, which has been lagging behind other continents in terms of development. Since then, Africa has many Regional Economic Communities (RECs) which group together individual countries in sub regions for the purposes of achieving greater economic integration. The RECs are the 'building blocks' of the African Union (AU). The RECs have been crucial to the strategy for the implementation of the New Partnership for Africa's Development (NEPAD) formulated in 2001.

Key Regional Groupings in Africa

Currently, there are eight RECs recognized by the AU, each established under a separate regional treaty. They are:

- Arab Maghreb Union (AMA)
- Common Market for Eastern and Southern Africa (COMESA)
- Community of Sahel-Saharan States (CEN-SAD)
- East African Community (EAC)
- Economic Community of Central African States (ECCAS)
- Economic Community of West African States (ECOWAS)
- Intergovernmental Authority on Development (IGAD)
- Southern African Development Community (SADC)

According to UNCTAD (2018), thirty-nine countries out of fifty-four countries are members of more than one of the eight RECs. There is overlapping of regional groups, and this has posed challenges to effective implementations of different treaties in each bloc. Burundi, Democratic Republic of Congo, Djibouti, Eritrea, Libya, Uganda, and Sudan are each members of three RECs, while Kenya is the only country in the region holding four RECs memberships: CEN-SAD, COMESA, IGAD and EAC (IMF, 2014). Five countries—Algeria, Côte d'Ivoire, Egypt, Nigeria, and South Africa—are responsible for 67% of all intra-African traded volumes in 2015 (IMF,

2016). They represent five out of the eight RECs: ECOWAS, UMA, SADC, COMESA, and CEN-SAD.

Moreover, there are additional regional economic cooperation bodies not officially recognized by the African Union as RECs, including:

- Economic and Monetary Community of Central Africa (CEMAC)
- West African Economic and Monetary Union (UEMOA/WAEMU)
- Economic Community of the Great Lakes Countries (CEPGL)
- Indian Ocean Commission (IOC)
- Mano River Union (MRU)
- Southern African Customs Union (SACU)

The African Union recognizes eight regional blocs as formal. Since inception of each regional bloc, there has been a development path that has been registered, with various changes in the welfare of each nation, either positively or negatively. Formation of a bloc has not been easy in the history of Africa. Cooperation levels have been differing among member states. Some blocs have registered great benefits, while some have witnessed different growth patterns with time passing. Political changes, economic upswings, civil wars among others in various regions have contributed to blocs not attaining their intended purposes within the stipulated time frames.

Overview of Regional Blocs in the Continent: Milestones and Inadequacies

AMU. The Arab Maghreb Union's (AMU), is a regional group in Africa, founded on February 17, 1989, in Marrakesh, Morocco. The group since its inception comprises of five nations; Algeria, Libya, Mauritania, Morocco, and Tunisia. The group is one of the unstable in the world, with the tension caused by the commonly called Sahara conflict. On the day of founding the member states agreed to coordinate, harmonize and rationalize their policies and strategies to achieve sustainable development in all sectors of human activities. The region has for a long time been characterized by distrust among its nations, for instance Algeria and Morocco have highest level of tension. This has undermined development of the region. It has since been the aim of the group to struggle for success by trying to eliminate parliamentarians who do not push for democracy for the common good of the region and its citizens. A 2006 survey indicated that the tension between Morocco and Algeria has not been caused by differences of the people, but the tension between rulers. The state leaders in most Arab Maghreb member states have been in power for decades, thus running the states akin too personal property (El-Maghur, 2011).

A series of negotiations have been done especially in the 1990s, to ensure that the regional group starts to achieve economic and social benefits. By 2006, the regional group has already managed to accomplish common projects, such as the national sections of the North African motorway, the optic fibre extension of the telecom networks, the fight against desertification and cooperation in health matters, among others. Regional integration of the Maghreb has not materialized as it has yet to move beyond the project phase. When AMU was founded, member states agreed on an implementation time table, time table set out tasks that were to be accomplished within specific times, this was done in accordance to standards of integration and against the background of the needs of states in member states (El-Maghur, 2011).

The AMU is seen as an organization disconnected from current global political trends. The founding treaty set to establish a Maghreb bank and a free trade area, but to date, none of these institutions have been established and operationalized. There exist inadequate state cooperation, as well as institutional cooperation. Maghreb countries are reluctant to adhere to integration programs such as eliminating tariffs. Mauritania has particularly not been active in social economic affairs of the Maghreb Union.

EAC. The East African Community (EAC) is a regional inter-governmental organization established under Article 2 of the Treaty for the Establishment of the East African Community that entered into force in July 2000. The member states comprises Burundi, Kenya, Rwanda, Uganda and Tanzania. The ultimate goal as stated in Article 5(2) of the treaty is for member states to have a customs union, a common market, subsequently a monetary union and ultimately a political federation in order to strengthen and regulate the industrial, commercial, infrastructural, cultural, social, political and other relations.

The community has made significant progress during the last 10 years of integration; the Customs Union in particular catalyzed remarkable trade expansion, with intra-EAC trade growing by 40% between 2005 and 2009. Mergers & acquisitions and cross-border investments have become key drivers and contributors to investment growth in the EAC region. East African Legislative Assembly (EALA) and East African Court of Justice (EACJ) establishments are great models in Africa in terms of regional legislative oversight and jurisprudence.

The greatest impediments to EAC democratic consolidation are the recurrent conflicts within the horn of Africa and the Great Lakes region, terrorism and piracy that have led to proliferation of small arms and influx of refugees into the region. Satisfactory strides have been made by the EAC community in forging strong cooperation in political issues especially in areas of defense, peace and security that are critical prerequisites for regional integration process. The EAC has gained recognition as a fully-fledged regional economic community. The EAC bloc has maintained strong ties of collaboration with COMESA, SADC under the Tripartite arrangements and IGAD sub-regions in an effort to establish a broader regional market to support fast industrialization, trade expansion and fast-tracked development of linking infrastructure between the member countries.

Despite the challenges in the implementation of the EAC regional integration process, the community ranks globally as the fastest integration economic bloc (Kipruto, 2010). EAC is, so far, the only REC that has the objective to attain a Political Federation, in an incremental progression through the stages of a Customs Union, a Common Market, and a Monetary Union (EAC, 2013). This progress is mainly rooted in consensus as the EAC's central approach to decision making; and maintaining this rate of progress demands avoiding issues around which consensus eludes states during negotiations in order to avoid fractures within the Community (Rwengabo, 2016). The EAC was rattled in 2013/2014 by the emergence of a "Coalition of the Willing", comprising of Kenya, Rwanda, and Uganda, sidelining Tanzania and Burundi., hence creating a 'community' within the community.

ECCAS. The Economic Community of Central African States (ECCAS) was established in 1983 in accordance with the Lagos Action Plan, as one of the pillars of the African Economic Community. ECCAS aims to achieve collective autonomy, raise standard of living of its populations and maintain economic stability through harmonius cooperation. The initial goal of ECCAS was to promote exchange and collaboration among the members and give an institutional and legal framework to their cooperation. ECCAS GDP is unevenly distributed among its ten states members: Angola (36.9%), Burundi (1.6%), Cameroon (19.8%), Congo (7.24%), Gabon (9.09%), Equatorial Guinea (8.07%), Central African Rep. (1.4%), DR Congo (10.18%), Sao Tome and Principe and Chad (4.7%). The community was planning to become a customs union in 1997 after the creation of a Free Trade Area (FTA) in 1993, but financial difficulties, due to the non-payment of membership fees by member states, and conflicts in the Great Lakes area did not allow the achievement of these goals (Fotso, 2014).

IGAD. The Inter-Governmental Authority on Development (IGAD) is one of the regional integration arrangements in Eastern Africa which came in to existence in 1996 replacing the Intergovernmental Authority on Drought and Development (IGADD) which was founded in 1986 with the aim of establishing a regional cooperation arrangement and enhancing the economic and social development of the region (Abdi and Seid, 2013). IGAD comprises of seven nations, Djibouti, Ethiopia, Eretria, Kenya, Somalia, Sudan and South Sudan. South Sudan and Eritrea are the youngest to join the group, being admitted in 2011. However, Eritrea admitted in 1993, withdraw in 2007, and readmitted in 2011.

Dersso (2014) indicated that IGAD is the only region of Africa where colonially drawn borders have been redrawn; the region is also known for being very prone to violent conflicts and various forms of transnational security threats. IGAD addressed not only drought and disaster prevention, but also political and economic issues. Food security and environmental protection, conflict prevention, management and resolution, and economic cooperation and integration has been further emphasized by re-engineering of IGAD. Over the years, IGAD entered into strategic partnerships and alliances with stakeholders to advance its development objectives.

The European Commission (EC), Germany, Netherlands, Denmark, USAID, Norway, Finland, Spain, Sweden, Italy, Ireland and Canada are among the partners who have been supporting IGAD for a long time (IGAD, 2007). The IGAD region is also characterized structural weaknesses, and include differences in governance and national development policies, major imbalances among the economies of the region, and the similarity of the countries' major export items (Dersso, 2014).

To strengthen IGAD capacity to deliver on its mandate of peace, prosperity and regional integration, there was introduced IGAD Institutional Strengthening Action Plan (ISAP), with three phases, 2009, 2012 and 2016-2020. ISAP III was formulated on the basis of achievements of the first two phases. IGAD mobilizes resources to implement ISAP III activities through a Joint Financing Arrangement (JFA) and other bilateral agreements/ arrangements (IGAD, 2017).

CEN-SAD. The Community of Sahelo-Saharan States (CEN-SAD) was established on 4 February 1998 by a conference held in Tripoli, Libyan Arab Jamahiriya, of the leaders and heads of State of Burkina Faso, Chad, the Libyan Arab Jamahiriya, Mali, the Niger and the Sudan. The CEN-SAD was designed to establish between the African countries members a knowledge-based economic union, to face drought and aridity, two global threats whose ecological, socio-economic and political consequences are felt in all circum-Saharan space.

The principal originality of the CEN-SAD lies in the fact that it gathers the majority of the countries which are exposed to drought and aridity and their ecological and socio-economic consequences such as desertification, degradation of the grounds, impoverishment, the migration, the sedentarisation. CEN-SAD is a young REC and it copes with the largest plagues which strikes Africa. CEN-SAD community contributed to change the frozen and tense relations between the Sahel-Saharan States turning them into relations that are characterized by mutual co-operation in economic and political fields (Taha, 2016). The regional group failed to attain political and cultural exchange, hence has no economic weight compared to other RECs that are more active in Africa.

ECOWAS. The Economic Community of West African States (ECOWAS) was established in 1975 with the formal aim of promoting economic co-operation between 15 countries with different historic trajectories (colonisation, language, and administrative cultures) yet sharing similar socio-economic conditions (Bossuyt, 2016). The inspiration for the creation of ECOWAS came from the United Nations Economic Commission for Africa (UNECA), which had divided Africa earlier in the1960s into regions for purposes of economic development (Komla, 2007). ECOWAS comprises of Benin, Burkina Faso, Cape Verde, Côte d'Ivoire, Gambia, Ghana, Guinea, Guinea-Bissau, Liberia, Mali, Niger, Nigeria, Senegal, Sierra Leon and Togo.

The member countries of ECOWAS have small economies that are highly susceptible to external economic and political influences and this situation affects their socio-economic and political development (Komla, 2007). ECOWAS adopted the new trade theory (NTT) which emphasizes the impact of increasing returns to scale on the pattern as well as on the mutual benefits from international trade (Alao et al., 2012). All member nations of ECOWAS concentrate on the production of goods which a nation has comparative advantage over others.

ECOWAS since its inception has managed to achieve increased levels of awareness on integration, free movement protocol of humans, goods and capital, enhancement of transnational transport system, trade liberalization, peacemaking, and financial integration among other achievements. The pace of economic development was affected in the 1980s due to political crises including civil wars and military coups. Insecurity due to civil strife and unstable governments easily spreads to neighboring states (Komla, 2007). This, however forced ECOWAS to fully embrace the security agenda as a core business, and regional diplomacy and military intervention has been used to address the political crises.

ECOWAS bloc has managed to contain conflicts, successfully dealing with rigged elections, peace restoration, infrastructure development (including trans-coastal and trans-Sahelian roads) and free movement of people. Events in Gambia is a recent case of how ECOWAS intervened in Gambia in 2016 to avert a potential deterioration of security situation. Following the elections held in 2016, the then president Jammeh initially conceded defeat to Barrow. Later on he changed his mind citing several irregularities. However, ECOWAS's mission ECOMIG intervened. The legal basis being, "…Article 4(j) of the AU's Constitutive Act (2000); Articles 3(h), 10(c) and 25 of the ECOWAS Protocol Relating to the Mechanism for Conflict Prevention, Management, Resolution, Peacekeeping and Security (1999); Article 7(m) of the Protocol Relating to the Establishment of the Peace and Security Council of the African Union (2002); as well as Articles 24 and 25(7) of the African Charter on Democracy, Elections and Governance (2007)." Williams (2017). This has been a big positive not only for West Africa but the entire continent.

Although there has been progress, there is broad recognition that the core business has not been fully achieved due to various obstacles. The Sahel is being increasingly destabilized by cross-border crime, drug trafficking, the Tuareg conflict, terrorism and the spread of Al Qaeda in the Islamic Maghreb (Bossuyt, 2016). There exist numerous check points, arbitrary and discriminatory treatment of citizens of other countries and tight migration laws; making it difficult to fully attain free movement protocol as expected. Obstacles to residence permits still persist. Despite the existence of own resources, levels of aid dependency are high, particularly for regional programmes. The bloc managed to set up financial institutions namely ECOWAS Bank for Investment and Development, ECOWAS Regional Investment Bank and ECOWAS Regional Development Fund.

SADC. Southern African Development Community (SADC), formerly known as the Southern African Development Coordination Conference (SADCC) was established in 1980. SADC replaced SADCC in August 1992 (Mugano, Brookes, and Le Roux, 2013:998). SADC has 15 members: Angola, Botswana, Democratic Republic of the Congo, Lesotho, Madagascar, Malawi, Mauritius, Mozambique, Namibia, Seychelles, South Africa, Swaziland, Tanzania, Zambia and Zimbabwe. South Africa accounts for over 60% of all intra-SADC trade, as well as 70% of the total SADC gross domestic product (Bell, 2017). The aim of SADC is to strengthen socio-economic cooperation and integration as well as political and security cooperation of southern African states. Through regional integration, SADC objectives include; achieving development and economic growth, alleviating poverty, promoting employment, enhancing the standard and quality of life, and supporting the socially disadvantaged. Economic convergence lies at the heart of the SADC and constitutes a major catalyst for deepening regional integration (Sobhee and Bhowon, 2007). Trade between the member countries is relatively high compared to other regions in Africa and is disproportionately high in processed and more sophisticated products (Mashayekhi, Peters, and Vanzetti, 2012). Bell (2017), noted that a major achievement of the SADC is its regional Free Trade Agreement, which was inaugurated in 2012. Across member countries of the SADC, there are large discrepancies in economic well-being and stage of development.

The effects of regional integration has seen some members eliminating or reducing their tariff barriers between the member countries as early as 2000. SADC trade integration also faces challenges derived from overlapping memberships of several member states. One of the major challenges impacting negatively on the implementation and completion of SADC's projects are the capacity, skills and expertise to drive key business processes (Magakwe, 2013). The bloc is also bedeviled by civil wars and there exist tension among its states; xenophobia attacks in South Africa have shaken the relationships of member states.

SADC has poor human rights records and the potential for instability exist, derailing the benefits of integration objectives. Illicit trafficking is among the most challenging forms of crime in the region. The bloc is known for setting up ambiguous targets, and this has led to various issues being postponed to future dates, as they cannot be attained with set dates. The formation of the customs union and the common market has been pushed to future dates, and may not be attained in few years to come. The establishment of a monetary union and single currency have also both been delayed, due to the complications caused by the postponement of the common market (Bell, 2017).

COMESA. The Common Market for Eastern and Southern Africa (COMESA) is the successor organization to the regional Preferential Trading Area (PTA), and came into force on December 8, 1994. Member states for COMESA are Burundi, Comoros, Democratic Republic of Congo, Djibouti, Egypt, Eritrea, Ethiopia, Kenya, Libya, Madagascar, Malawi, Mauritius, Rwanda, Seychelles, Sudan, Swaziland, Uganda, Zambia, and Zimbabwe. COMESA main goals are to eliminate the structural and institutional weaknesses of member states and to promote political stability and sustained economic development.

The 19 COMESA Member States represent over 440 million people, $32 billion/year in imports, and $82 billion/year in exports. The GDP average growth rate was 6.6% in 2013 (COMESA, 2014). In 2014, the annual import bill was USD 170 billion while the export bill was US$112 billion (COMESA, 2014). The COMESA design aimed to eliminate the structural and institutional weaknesses in the Member States by firming up collective action chiefly in pooling of resources to sustain development efforts. In the quest to develop, India has been one of the cooperating partners of COMESA, and India's relationship with Africa was given a new structure during the First India-Africa Forum Summit (IAFS-I) held in New Delhi in April 2008, (COMESA, 2012).

As alluded to earlier in the section there are other blocs domiciled in the continent. Whilst they are not recognized by the African Union, they nevertheless serve different purposes to enhance welfare of their respective member states. In this section we will have a brief look at these blocs, their achievements to date as well as contemporary challenges.

SACU. The Southern Africa Customs Union (SACU) is a customs union established in 1910. It comprises of five countries namely Botswana, Lesotho, Namibia, South Africa and Swaziland. The headquarters is in Windhoek, Namibia. SACU is the oldest existing customs union in the world (WTO, 2003). In 1994, SA initiated re-negotiation; negotiations concluded in 2002 and new SACU Agreement entered into force in 2004 (Mlumbi-Peter, 2015). SACU objectives include maintaining free interchange of goods between member countries. There exist a common external tariff and excise tariff. Customs and excise collected in the area paid into South Africa's National Revenue Fund; and a revenue sharing formula exist for the member states. SACU revenues also represent an important source of foreign inflows and contribute to the stock of international reserves (Honda et al., 2017). SACU negotiates deals with other regional groups for the benefits of its member states. In 2008, SACU and United States signed a trade, investment, and development cooperative agreement (TIDCA). South Africa is by far the most industrialized economy in the bloc.

MRU. The Mano River Union (MRU) comprises of Sierra Leone, Liberia, Guinea and Côte d'Ivoire. MRU was established October 1973 by the Malema declaration. Guinea joined 1980 and Côte d'Ivoire joined the union 2008. The Mano River basin countries are closely linked not only by their common borders and ethnic groups but also by their history and conflicts (Poole and Mohammed, 2013:4). MRU aims to strengthen the capacity of members to integrate their economies and coordinate development programs in the areas of peace building, as a prerequisite to any development, trade promotion, development of industry, energy, agriculture, natural resources, transport and telecommunications, monetary and financial affairs in short, all aspects of economic and social life.

One achievement of the MRU is the setting up of Mano River Youth Parliament, which is supported by budget allocation, and helps in linking the activities of the Liberian youths and other youths from member countries. The Mano River basin has experienced violent conflict since the late 1980s, and conflicts have caused an estimated 300,000 deaths in Liberia and Sierra Leone, brought massive social dislocation, devastated the countries' infrastructure, eroded the social fabric and led to crippling economic hardship for the majority of the population (Poole and Mohammed, 2013: 7). Dialogue between communities in the border regions and their governments was necessitated, since 2007, and contributed to improved governance, accountability and transparency in the border areas. Unemployment among the youths is very high in the region, and many your women are engaged in informal border trading. In the border villages and communities there are a range of people with different ancestral origins and tribes (Poole and Mohammed, 2013:17), and this has been the source of conflict within the borders. The region has been heavily affected by outbreak of Ebola, causing great deaths and decline in productivity. Sub-regional Post Ebola Recovery Plan was developed with great levels of political commitment.

IOC. The Indian Ocean Commission (IOC) is a regional organization established in 1984. IOC member states are Comoros, Madagascar, Mauritius and

Seychelles. The bloc comprises of one member outside the African continent, France/Reunion Island. The IOC member states have heterogeneous economies, geographies, populations, and social indicators (ADB Group Report, 2013:11). The member countries also vary widely in size. Madagascar has a population of almost 20 million, which represents 87 per cent of the total population of the IOC region and is more than 200 times the population of Seychelles (ADB Group, 2013: 11). The economies are islands which are vulnerable to natural disasters like cyclones, tsunamis, drought and floods, hence are of special interest from a sustainable development and environmental point of view (IOC, 2012: 1).

IOC has for long concentrating on issues of climate change adaptation, natural disaster prevention and management, agro-ecology, sustainable land management, and marine conservation and terrestrial biodiversity. According to IOC (2004: 18), objectives and missions established by the founders of the IOC were primarily to strengthen links between the peoples of its member states and improve their standard of living, promoting cooperation in a number of areas: diplomacy, economy, trade, agriculture, fishing, the conservation of resources and ecosystems, culture, science and education. The bloc is characterized by high food production cost. The vulnerability of IOC stems from fluctuations in global food commodity markets highlights the demand for enhanced regional market integration (Nimarkoh, Koroma, and Sablah, 2017: 1). IOC countries also belong to COMESA; however, Mauritius and Madagascar are also members to the COMESA-FTA, and thus these two countries benefit from reduced trade tariff.

CEPGL. The Economic Community of the Great Lakes (CEPGL) was founded on the 20th September 1976 in Gisenyi, Rwanda, and has Democratic Republic of Congo, Rwanda and Burundi as its members. The main aims of CEPGL are to foster economic integration and promote cross-border cooperation. Achievements of the bloc include; International Great Lakes Energy Company (SINELAC) which produces electricity, Development Bank of Great Lakes Countries (BDGL) which finance community projects, Institute of Agriculture and Livestock Research (IRAZ) which does research in areas of agronomy and zootechnics, CEPGL identity card for free movement of people, and Energy Organization of the Great Lake Countries (EGL) for increased cooperation in the energy sector.

There was low pace in integration growth in the mid-90s (1994), due to conflict among member states, until 2007 when there was decided to re-launch the CEPGL activities. Although deterioration of the security situation in the GLR manifested itself throughout both the colonial and post-colonial periods, the 1994 Rwandan genocide has become the defining moment for GLR security (Nzaramba, 2010:2). Lack of the political will of regional leaders contributed to the slow growth of the bloc. Belgium and the EU have provided budget for CEPGL's first year of renewed work (NCA, 2007: 1).

UEMOA/ WAEMU. The West African Economic and Monetary Union (UEMOA/WAEMU) is an economic, integrating and cooperation organization which was found in 1994. The member states of WAEMU are Benin, Burkina Faso, Côte D'Ivoire, Guinea-Bissau, Mali, Niger, Senegal, and Togo. Two economies Senegal and Côte d'Ivoire are more industrialized as compared to other nations in the bloc. The bloc works towards greater regional integration with unified external tariffs. The member states share the same money, West African francs (CFA francs), monetary policies, and French as an official language (Koma, 2012:1). The Custom Union became effective since January 2000.

WAEMU has experienced distinct phases of peaks and troughs in economic growth and growth turning points have been abrupt (Balima, 2018:5). The formal financial system of WAEMU is underdeveloped and the banking system is concentrated in two or three commercial banks in many of the countries. Health wise, WAEMU adopted a Community Action Plan on promoting essential generic drugs and improved traditional medicines, the local manufacture of essential medicines and quality control, to improve accessibility to populations of the Union to care quality (Amari et al., 2014: 21). Various successes have been noted for the bloc.

As supported by Seck (2013: 19), WAEMU has recorded some undeniable successes, particularly in its currency management, its exchange policy and in the organization of its stock market; and has managed to preserve the solidity and reliability of its institutions and its members' adhesion to the community project. However, there has been a problem for WAEMU to address new issues affecting the community that are not covered in its scope, but with hampering effect on the progress of the bloc.

CEMAC. The Central African Economic and Monetary Community (CEMAC) is one regional bloc found in Africa. CEMAC region comprises of six different countries: Cameroon, Central African Republic (CAR), Chad, the Republic of Congo, Equatorial Guinea and Gabon. As an achievement, within CEMAC, the Central African Monetary Union (UMAC) is the institution responsible for monetary policy; it has specialized bodies, including BEAC which issues the currency of the Union and guarantees its stability (ADB, 2005: 7). The region has a diverse climate and land availability, and hence pastoral activities are undertaken. The region has also minerals which include oil deposits, natural gas, diamonds, gold, manganese and uranium. There has been little or no extraction of most minerals (except oil and timber) in the region due to lack of private investment. According to IMF (2014:2), the region's most pressing challenge is to implement structural reforms to promote sustainable and inclusive growth while adopting macro policies to preserve financial stability, ensure an efficient use of oil revenues and increase resilience to shocks.

Regionalism Synthesis

There is no doubt that regionalism has brought some positives in the history of Africa. Regionalism has also shaped many economies in the world hence determining the future prospects of nations involved. Improvements have been made in areas including trade, communications, macroeconomic policies, and transportation (AU, 2006). Regionalism in Africa, however, cannot be matched with other continents in the world over. It is defined in its own kind, related to history and path of economic development including the political path that African economies have gone through. Regionalism in Africa is yet to benefit its citizens to the maximum the concept can provide, as resembled in more economically developed nations.

Major Issues Militating Against Integration in Africa

This section looks at the major issues that explain the slow success of regional blocs to achieve the overarching goal of sustainably developing the continent. It is a summary of the issues raised in the previous section when we discussed individual regional blocs. These major issues in essence cause slow integration, let alone development of the continent.

Institutional Settings. This is among the key issues is the complex institutional setting under which regional integration schemes have been operating (AU, 2006). While regional integration came as a wave, of which every nation has no chance to turn it away, most nations lack high levels of commitment to attain the stipulated objectives. Each African nation has various tribes and cultures which for long has remained difficult to brand. Colonization history of Africa has also shaped the regions in Africa. Some economies has been testing regional blocs for their suitability, hence pulling out from one group and joining another. Political leaders have also determined the regional blocs effectiveness, where there is no political friendship, the regional group has failed to implement the set objectives in time and in full. The willingness to implement what has been agreed has been a challenge over the years. In one regional bloc, some member states are working towards set objectives seriously while others just lag behind. For example, SADC has postponed its objectives several times, indicating that it is a serious challenge to have those objectives fulfilled.

Political Instability. Political instability has contributed to poor implementation of regional blocs targets. Moving forward on Africa's integration agenda will require sustained effort from the continent's leadership (AU, 2006). Africa is full of various conflicts, both internal and external. Peace and security has become one major aim of each regional group. The common Sahara conflict has for decades continued to affect the efficiency of countries involved. Xenophobia attacks in South Africa has impacted on relations of South Africa and other nations. Political tension of the Hutu and Tutsi. Political leaders of some nations rigging elections in an effort to maintain power, leading to various challenges and dragging back the pace of regional integration. Some nations failing to honor their roles in the regional group, hence low levels of cooperation.

Over-reliance on Primary Commodities. Currently inter-Africa trade is weak hampering success of the regional blocs. One such factor causing weak internal trade in the continent is the over reliance of most of the member states in primary commodities.

Commodity dependency in Africa is largely in primary sectors such as oil, natural gas, agriculture and mining. Countries such Angola, Libya, Nigeria are well known oil economies. Zambia, Botswana, Zimbabwe are noted for mining activities. The severity of commodity dependency is shown by those regions which are heavily shaded. For Africa, dependency is in the region of 80%–100% relative to other continents. The major implication of commodity dependency is noted from observations by Czinkota et al (2011). They argue that the major difference between developing and industrialised nations is that the former rely on export of primary products and raw materials.

Conversely, industrialised nations export manufactured goods. Further they assert that this background of reliance on primary commodities has several important implications:

- The level of price competition is higher among primary goods exporters since they are largely many sellers and offering the same product
- Export earnings for primary products are very volatile and are likely to be affected by e.g., weather vagaries such as droughts, famine etc. or some other shocks on the global market.

To corroborate the observation by Czinkota et al. (2011), Feenestra and Taylor (2014) opine that dependence on primary commodities by an economy brings us to a study carried out by two economists Prebisch and Singer. They argue that prices of primary commodities tend to decline overtime. The studies became to be known as the Prebisch–Singer hypothesis. This was empirically observed for commodities such as wool, aluminium, tin etc. Most African states are likely to be caught in this trap if predictions of the Prebisch–Singer hypothesis are anything to go by.

Infrastructure Deficits. Infrastructure is in various forms, and plays a crucial role in the growth and development pattern of any nation including Africa. Tafirenyika (2014: 6), indicated that lack of progress in implementing agreements along with the absence of reliable transport, energy and information and technology infrastructure make the journey towards regional integration long and arduous. The link between economic infrastructure and growth is widely recognised (United Nations, 2013: 8). Saghir (2017: 1) also indicated that infrastructure development and financing are an indispensable component of growth for any economy. Main four types of infrastructure include; transport infrastructure, power generation, information and communications (ICT) highway and irrigation. Considering such definitions of infrastructure, Africa remains underdeveloped in the setting up of infrastructure, and this has slowed down the development process for many years.

Saghir (2017: 1) noted the existence of infrastructure gaps in Africa, indicating that SSA countries lack adequate and sustainable infrastructure to support increased economic growth. Despite the clear link between growth, development and infrastructure and the consequently high payoffs to investment in infrastructure, a variety of studies have identified a significant infrastructural deficit in Africa (United Nations, 2013: 8), and deficit refers to social and economic infrastructure.

Africa's infrastructure stocks inherited from the colonial powers supported reasonably strong economic growth from the early 1960s until the 1970s oil shocks (Brunel, 2004), and later on deterioration and improper adjustments took place. Infrastructure quality in Africa is also a challenge (Estache, 2006: 18), and this remains the case despite reforms made in various countries through innovations adopted. There is greater need to first prioritise infrastructure development for easy networking within states and with the outside world, hence on e of the key aspirations of Agenda 2063 of AU is to lay out infrastructure grand plan for the continent. Good infrastructure prevents trade delays and reduce costs of communication and transacting hence bring forth efficiency in development path. According to the Africa Construction Trends Report (2016: 12), investment in infrastructure also tends to increase business confidence and at the same time lowers transaction costs by making it easier for businesses to move people, goods and services. Currently, it is costly in Africa to transport goods whether by road, ship, rail, or sea as compared to other non-African states. Communication is also more expensive in Africa, thereby making it more costly to transact.

Overlapping membership. This has also contributed to poor levels of regional integration. Many countries belong to more than one regional blocs in the continent. AU (2006) indicated with concern that overlapping mandates and objectives, duplicated integration policies, and the multiple memberships by African countries appear to be slowing integration, reducing the regional economic communities' effectiveness, and stretching thin limited financial resources. The performance of countries with multiple regional groups is less effective and hence pose as a challenge to attainment of one group objectives. Duplication of programs by regional economic communities is another inefficiency of Africa's regional integration efforts (AU, 2006). The AU has tried to have some regional blocs to have ties to lessen the negative effects of one country being part of other regional blocs. Multiple membership is very costly given the level of resources African states have.

Size of member states. This is also militating against the efficacy of efforts towards contributes to integration. Africa comprises of many countries with different sizes, both in geographical size and population. In COMESA, the most populous country is 993 times larger than the least populous country (Mo Ibrahim Foundation, 2014). Contribution towards infrastructure development has always been a challenge, given the different sizes of nations within regional blocs. Some countries are poorer than others, while some depend on donor aid.

Sovereignty and protectionism. Issues of sovereignty play a critical role to determine the pace of implementation of regional blocs objectives. According to Mo Ibrahim Foundation (2014), only 5 out of the 54 African countries (Comoros, Rwanda, Seychelles, Mozambique, and Madagascar) offer visa-free access or visas on arrival to other African citizens. African citizens, on average require visas to visit 60% of African countries. Hence the free movement of people, goods and capital objective is far from being attained in the regions. Some economies have refused to lower their tariffs of commodities in the region; hence trade objectives have yet to be made. Some nations still do not allow foreign business launches in some sectors of their economies, therefore Free Trade Zone, is just a blue print whose contents is yet to be implemented. COMESA-EAC-SADC Tripartite was established in 2005 to strengthen and deepen economic integration of Southern and East Africa by harmonizing policies and programs in areas of trade, customs and infrastructure development (Mo Ibrahim Foundation, 2014). COMESA-EAC-SADC Free Trade Area (FTA) was initiated in 2011 with implementation starting 2016.

As noted by Nnanna (2006:2), and the fact is still the same to current date, African sub-regions are pursuing economic and monetary cooperation at different speeds. Development partnership requires equal efforts to be applied by each member for full benefits to be received. The fact that members within each bloc apply different efforts to the agreed treaties, has on its own affected the success of many regional blocs in Africa. Various deadlines have not been met due to lack of seriousness of some members states. Committed nations have reciprocated such bad behavior, leading to poor integration results. Further divisions have also risen within blocs, as a result of lack of accountability of other nations within the bloc. Lesson from European Union are instructive. EU has forged regional integration in most aspects synchronizing laws, currency, policies, parliament and migration. The integration allows member states to benefit from other members comparative advantage.

Sluggish Private Sector Buy In. Private sector participation is minimal in all major integration efforts, yet it is the goose that should lay the golden egg in an economy. Nnanna (2006: 3) indicated that during the 1980s and early 1990s, most African countries adopted economic policies that entrenched the state in all aspects of economic activities, thus relegating the private sector as marginal player in the development effort. Lack of private sector participation is a serious factor, that has impacted on the integration effectiveness in Africa. In Europe private sector participation is well supported, hence regional integration has come with best results. There is a lot of inefficiencies for programs run by the state without private sector involvement.

Technology. It has impacted Africa regionalism. Africa for years has been characterized by poor pace of technology uptake. This has hampered many programs of regional integration, due to poor communication within member states, among other challenges brought about lack of effective communication channels and high technology use. Development of communication networks is very essential for regional integration to reap significant benefits.

International Cooperation: Africa and the World

Apart from forming regional groupings in Africa, African nations have gone further to form partnerships with the outside world. There is a cooperation known as the South-South cooperation that has gained mileage as far as partnerships is concerned for development purposes. South–South cooperation (SSC) is not a new phenomenon in the region, since the late 1950s, Africa has had relations with Southern countries focusing mostly on political issues (United Nations, 2010: 2). As of date, the focus has shifted from political to economic issues, hence development. SSC concept and its characteristics have evolved in many different international, regional and bilateral forums, as well as within each country (Cabana, 2014: 9). South-South Cooperation is about partnerships among equal partners who both learn from each other (Dimitra Newsletter, 2014: 1). Uneze (2015: 3), indicated that SSC refers to various forms of co-operation ranging from technical, to political, economic and educational co-operation among developing countries in order to foster their common development objectives.

The SSC has been recognized by various world organization, FAO has been supporting SSC for more than 17 years, and so many projects since 1997 have been implemented in support to special and national programs for food security. According to Dimitra Newsletter (2014:9), through FAO's SSC initiative, China has deployed nearly 1000 aid workers in more than 25 countries, including Ethiopia, Namibia, Nigeria, Uganda and Senegal. The SSC has aided African nations to work towards the achievement of Millenium

Development Goals (MDGs). Uneze (2015: 5) highlighted that most countries in sub-Saharan Africa (SSA) are on track on a few MDGs, but are making slow and 'painful' progress in most of them.

Various agreements have been undertaken and are operative with different achievements being noticed. The agreements include; Forum on China–Africa Cooperation (2000), Republic of Korea-Africa Forum (2006), India-Africa Forum (2008), Turkey-Africa Cooperation (2008), Africa-South America Strategic Partnership (2006), New Asian-African Strategic Partnership (2005), and Afro-Arab Cooperation (1977), among other ongoing engagements. Africa's exports have been on the rise to developed nations, however important to note is that exports are primary in nature, and the trend if not strongly monitored may lead to poor development of the manufacturing sector for processing products. Sustainable development in Africa, requires that the Southern partners should pay more attention to the environmental consequences of their activities in Africa (United Nations, 2010: 9).

China-Africa Relations. China, in history has been a major provider of development assistance to African countries with a socialist orientation during the Cold War (Uneze, 2015:20). With SSC there is lack of policy conditionality, which has both negative and positive implications. Zimbabwe, has been ignored by its traditional donors due to weak governance and politics, but has benefited a lot from SSC. As noted by Uneze (2015: 28), SSC main strength lies in the predictability of financing, promotion of domestic ownership and use of technologies across the Global South.

The African Growth and Opportunity Act (AGOA) has also come with its notable offers to Africa. AGOA is a nonreciprocal trade preference program that provides duty-free treatment to U.S. imports of certain products from eligible sub-Saharan African (SSA) countries (Williams, 2015:2). AGOA defines cooperation of African countries with USA. AGOA has since been amended multiple times. The set-up of AGOA in 2000 was to encourage export-led growth as well as economic development of SSA economies and improve economic relations of U.S. with the region. Apart from apparel and energy products, South Africa accounts for the bulk of U.S. imports under AGOA. Lesotho registered a 36% increase in employment, just two years after AGOA execution (Páez et al., 2010), as new manufacturing firms were established in textile, apparel and footwear industries. Zimbabwe and Kenya also recorded significant rise in employment as a result of AGOA, while Swaziland and Malawi textiles industry registered growth. AGOA has supported a growing African middle class, reduced dependence on development assistance, and further opened African markets to American companies (Mpela-Thompson and Jack, 2013:5). The most cited weaknesses of AGOA is that, it is a one-sided agreement, it its preparation there was little African involvement, participating African countries are not obliged to oppose US foreign policy, and AGOA is dominated by oil and raw materials.

There is a continuous evaluation criteria for country eligibility under AGOA, hence conditions attached. Some countries have failed in some years to match the eligibility criteria, hence booted out. The agreement lacks certainty, despite the benefits in improved trade for exports. Gresser (2014: 1) argues that, the greatest challenge to Africa's ability to take full advantage of global market opportunities such as AGOA is a remaining weakness in infrastructure and trade logistics.

Korean Economic Development Cooperation Fund (EDCF). There has been growth in Korea's investment outflow into Africa in the last decade, rising from $157m in 2000 to $372m in 2011 (United Nations, 2013:74). Kim (2012) argues that the increase in Korea's investment in Africa was because of the search of natural resources like energy, ores and minerals. Tanzania benefited most from the EDCF, as the loans were limited to few African nations. Korea's aid has mainly been provided through bilateral channels, and Korea has a relatively high rate of participation in social infrastructure (United Nations, 2013: 75).

Other Inter-continental agreements. Apart from the discussed international cooperations, there exist many other between African states and the outside world. Such agreements have yielded some positives in both trade and social aspects of African states.

In conclusion, Africa comprises of various regional blocs, some that are formally recognized by the African Union, while others exist but have no African Union endorsement. African states also belong to development partnerships across continents, like the South-South cooperation, and many others. The wave for integration has managed to shape Africa to become what it is today. However, greater analysis shows that, if there were no internal and external challenges to integration, more should by now could have been achieved from integration. The ultimate goal of regional integration is to create a common economic space among the participating countries; monetary and economic integration may evolve from trade links, as well as, historical and cultural ties (Nnanna, 2006: 2). The chapter has narrated the various regional blocks in Africa, their motives and progress since their founding dates and various challenges hampering their intended objectives.

The chief noticeable characteristic of regional integration in Africa is multiple and overlapping membership. Many countries in Africa belong to several groupings and sub-groupings that in some cases conflict, compete, or overlap amongst themselves rather than complementing. Overlapping and multiple memberships cause regional integration to be costly, inefficient and ineffective. This adds to the burden of harmonization and coordination, and is wasteful duplication in view of constrained resources. Nations seek deliberate membership to numerous groupings with the hope of integration benefit maximization and spreading risks to minimize losses. However, membership to more than one REC will arguably divert loyalty of states.

Common in Africa are the internal challenges. Nguena (2011: 1) noted that, poverty, civil war, human rights violations, lack of democracy and bad governance are common issues in Africa. Such aspects have for many years contributed to the delaying of benefits of integration. Some blocs have later included such aspects as part of the regional agenda so that full benefits of integration be met. Civil wars have dominated many states in Africa. Political willingness to implement regional programs has been missing.

More is expected for regionalism to be effective in Africa. Capacity building interventions that support macroeconomic and sectoral policy reforms at the national and regional levels are vital for the emergence of a responsive domestic and regional policy environment.

References

Africa Construction Trends Report 2016. "Africa's Changing Infrastructure Landscape." *Deloitte*. https://www2.deloitte.com/content/dam/Deloitte/za/Documents/manufacturing/Deloitte Africa_Construction_Trends_2016_Nov2016.pdf

Abdi, A. I., and E. H. Seid. "Assessment of Economic Integration in IGAD." *The Horn Economic and Social Policy Institute (HESPI)*, Policy Papers No. 13/2, pp. 1–31, 2013.

African Development Bank. "Economic Community of Central African States (ECCAS): Regional Integration Assistance Strategy Paper (RIASP) For Central Africa 2005–2009." *Country Operations Department*, West Region, 2005.

African Development Bank Group. "Indian Ocean Commission Countries A Flagship Study on Regional Integration, Summary Final Report." *African Development Bank Group*, Tunis Belvédère, Tunisia, 2013.

African Union. "Assessing Regional Integration in Africa II; Rationalizing Regional Economic Communities." *Joint Publication of Economic Commission for Africa and African Union*, Ethiopia, 2006.

Alao, D. O., C. O. Atere, O. Ayomola, E. Adewumi, and B. A. Irewumi. "An Analysis of the Achievement of Economic Community of West Africa Since Inception." *Singaporean Journal of Business Economics and Management Studies* 1.3 (2012): 76–85.

Amari, A. S. G., A. N'Guessan, J. G. Sackou, A. C. Amonkou, P. M. Alloukou, and R. Duncan. "Medicines Harmonization in West African Economic and Monetary Union (WAEMU) Countries." *International Journal of Drug Regulatory Affairs* 2.1 (2014): 18-28.

Balima, H. W. "Growth Acceleration in the West African Economic and Monetary Union." *IMF Country Report No. 18/107*. African Department, International Monetary Fund, 2018.

Bell Wilson. "The Southern African Development Community: Solid Achievements and Future Challenges." Strategic Analysis Paper, Future Directions International, pp. 01–07, 2017.

Bossuyt, Jean. "Political Economy of Regional Integration in Africa." *The Economic Community of West African States (ECOWAS) Report*, 2016.

Brunel, S. *L'Afrique: Un continent en réserve de développement*. Rosny-sous Bois: Editions Bréal, 2004.

Cabana, Lopez S. "Chronology and History of South-South Cooperation." *Working Document Number* 5, Ibero–American Programme, 2014. https://www.segib.org/wp-content/uploads/Chrono-South-South2014.pdf

COMESA. "Brief on COMESA." *Common Market for Eastern and Southern Africa*, 2012.

COMESA. "Brief on COMESA." *Common Market for Eastern and Southern Africa*, 2014.

Czinkota M. R., Ilkka Ronkaines, and Michale Moffett. "International Business." Danver, MA: John Wiley & Sons Publishers, 2011

Dersso, Solomon. "East Africa and the Intergovernmental Authority on Development. Mapping Multilateralism in Transition NO. 4." *International Peace Institute*, 2014.

El-Maghur, Mohamed Ahmed. "Evolution, Challenges and Prospects of the Arab Maghreb Union, 1951-2010." *Masters Thesis*. Institute of Diplomacy and International Studies, University of Nairobi, 2011.

Estache, Antonio. "Africa's Infrastructure: Challenges and Opportunities." *IMF Institute and the Joint Africa Institute*, Tunis, Tunisia, 2006.

Feenstra, C. Robert, and Taylor M. Alan. *International Trade 3rd Edition*. New York: Worth Publishers, 2014.

Fotso, A. D. "The Potential Effects of the ECCAS Free Trade Area on Trade Flows." *MPRA Paper No*. 59863, pp. 1–31, 2014.

Gresser, Edward. "AGOA At 14: Successes, Failures, and Next Steps." *Progressive Economy*, 2014.

Honda, J., M. Nose, C. S. Padilla, J. L. Torres, M. Morgan, F. G. Im, and N. A. Koliadina. "Fiscal Rules: Coping with Revenue Volatility in Lesotho and Swaziland." *International Monetary Fund*, 2017.

ICTSD. "African Integration: Facing up to Emerging Challenges." *International Centre for Trade and Sustainable Development (ICTSD)*. Geneva, Switzerland, 2016.

IGAD. "Annual Report." *Inter Governmental Authority on Development*, 2007.

IGAD. "Mid-Term Review of IGAD Institutional Strengthening Action Plan (ISAPIII) 2016 2020." *Inter Governmental Authority on Development*, 2017.

IMF. "Central African Economic and Monetary Community (CEMAC): Staff Report On Common Policies of Member Countries." *IMF Country Report* No. 14/252, 2014.

Indian Ocean Commission. "The Indian Ocean Commission: regional solidarity in the face of globalization." *Indian Ocean Commission*, 2004.

Indian Ocean Commission. "Advocacy of the Indian Ocean Commission to the United Nations Conference on Sustainable Development." *Indian Ocean Commission*, Government of Seychelles, 2012.

Khandelwal Padamja. "COMESA and SADC: Prospects and Challenges for Regional Trade Integration." *IMF Working Paper*, WP/04/227, pp. 1–43, 2004.

Kim, D. "Korea's Investment in Africa." 2012. http://www.eurasiane.eu/?page=eMAP&id=112&id_dossier=12

Kipruto, Kipkoech Joseph. "Challenges and Prospects of East African Community Regional Integration Process (2001–2009)." MA *Thesis*, Institute of Diplomacy and International Studies, University of Nairobi, 2010.

Koma, Olgie. "The West African Economic and Monetary Union WAEMU (UEMOA)." *Housing Finance Africa*, 2012.

Komla, G. I. "Economic Community of West African States Regional Integration Process: A Study of the New Regionalism Phenomenon in Africa." MSc *Thesis*, Department of Management and Engineering, Linkopings University, Sweden, 2007.

Magakwe, Jack. "The Activities of the Southern African Development Community in Relation to its Purpose Statement." *Masters Thesis*, University of South Africa, 2013.

Mansfield, E., and Helen Milner. "The New Wave of Regionalism." *International Organization* 53. 3 (1999): 589-627.

Mashayekhi, M., R. Peters, and D. Vanzetti. "Chapter 13: Regional Integration and Employment Effects in SADC." *Policy Priorities for International Trade and Jobs*. Ed. Douglas Lippoldt. OECD, 2012. 387-414.

Mlumbi-Peter, Xolelwa. "South Africa and the Southern African Customs Union." Department of Trade and Industry, South Africa, 2015. https://www.thedti.gov.za/parliament/2015/SACU.pdf

Mo Ibrahim Foundation. "Facts & Figures: Regional Integration: Uniting to Compete." *Mo Ibrahim Foundation*, 2014.

Mpela-Thompson, Dineo, and Jack, Kel Ibifuro. "Strengthening the African Growth and Opportunity Act: Delivering on Africa's Promise through NEPAD and the African Diaspora to Reinvigorate the Commercial Relationship Between the United States and Sub-Saharan African Countries." *New York City Bar Association Committee on African Affairs*, 2013.

Mugano, G., M. Brookes, and P. Le Roux. "The Impact of SADC Customs Union on Zimbabwe." *Southern Africa Institute for Management Scientists*, 2013.

Nguena, C. B. "The Role of the Economic Community of Central African States in the Maintenance of Peace and Security in Central Africa." *LLM Thesis*, The Faculty of Law, Addis Ababa University, 2011.

Nimarkoh, J., S. Koroma, and M. Sablah. "Linking Trade and Food and Nutrition Security in Indian Ocean Commission Member States." *Food and Agriculture Organization of the United Nations*, Accra, 2017.

Nnanna, O. J. "Economic and Monetary Integration in Africa." *G24 Secretariat September presentation*, Singapore, 2006. https://www.g24.org/wp-content/uploads/2016/01/ECONOMIC-AND-MONETARY-INTEGRATION-IN.pdf

Norwegian Church Aid. "Country Programme Plan: Great Lakes." *Norwegian Church Aid*, 2007.

Nzaramba, Pascal. "The Effective Integration of the ICGLR Towards Sustainable Securityand Economic Development in the GLR of Africa." *MSc Thesis*, LLM, University of Sussex, Brighton, United Kingdom, 2010.

Páez, Laura, Stephen Karingi, Mwangi Kimenyi, and Mekalia Paulos. "A Decade (2000-2010) of African-U.S. Trade Under the African Growth Opportunities Act (AGOA): Challenges, Opportunities and a Framework for Post AGOA Engagement 24." *African Development Bank Group* Sept. 15, 2010.

Poole, Maureen, and Janet A. Mohammed. "Border Community Security: Mano River Union Region." *Conciliation Resources*, 2013. https://www.c-r.org/downloads/MRU_bordercommunitysecurity_ConciliationResources.pdf

Rugman, A. M., & A. Verbeke. "A Perspective on Regional and Global Strategies of Multinational Enterprises." *Journal of International Business Studies* 35 (2004): 3-18.

Rwengabo, Sabastiano. "Consensus and the Future of the East African Community." *ACODE Policy Brief*, EAC - Series 36, 2016.

Saghir, Jamal. "Sustainable Infrastructure Development in Sub-Saharan Africa." *Center for Strategic and International Studies*, 2017.

Seck, Diery. "Fifteen Years of WAEMU: Results and Strategies for the Future." *International Development Research Centre*, 2013.

Simiyu, E. J., and G. Mugano. "The Influence of World Trade Organisation Free Trade Agreement Tariff Rates on Kenya." *International Journal of Social Science and Economic Research* 2.9 (2017): 4414–4433.

Sobhee, S. K., and V. Bhowon. . "Deepening Integration in SADC: Mauritius Achievement and Coming Challenges." *Regional Integration in Southern Africa* 8 (2007): 1–227.

Tafirenyika, M. "Intra-Africa Trade: Going Beyond Political Commitments. Africa and Europe search for an elusive agreement." *Africa Renewal* 28.2 (2014).

Taha, Saeed Ali Ahmed. "Efforts of Integration in the African Regional Groupings (The Community of Sahel-Saharan)." *African Perspectives* 13.44 (2016): 17–29.

Uneze, Ebere. "Impact of South-South Co-operation in achieving the Millennium Development Goals (MDGs) in Low-Income Countries." *European Report on Development, Europe Aid*, 2015.

United Nations. "Economic development in Africa: South–South cooperation: Africa and the new forms of development partnerships." United Nations Conference on Trade and Development, 2010.

United Nations. "Infrastructure Development within the Context of Africa's Cooperation with New and Emerging Development Partners." Office of Special Adviser on Africa, United Nations, 2013.

Williams, Brock R. "African Growth and Opportunity Act (AGOA): Background and Reauthorization." *Congressional Research Service*, 2015.
Williams, Paul D. "A New African Model of Coercion? Assessing the ECOWAS Mission in The Gambia." *IPI Global Observatory*. March 16, 2017. https://theglobalobservatory.org/2017/03/ecowas-gambia-barrow-jammeh-african-union/
WTO. "WTO—Trade Policy Review—Southern African Customs Union." *World Trade Organization*, 2003.

· 6 ·

IS AFRICA READY FOR BUSINESS?

The success of Africa in achieving sustainable development rests not only in the local conditions of the individual countries, but on how these states interface with the rest of the world. In Chapter 5 we traced the numerous blocs dotted across the length and breadth of the continent. The diversity of the blocs, has had a bearing on the development path the continent finds itself in today. In their great numbers, can they push the development agenda of the continent, in particular the African Union's Agenda 2063? The African Union adopted Agenda 2063 in 2015 in Ethiopia at the 24th Ordinary Assembly to steer development agenda of the continent. The all encompassing goal of the framework is to transform the fortunes of the continent for the next 50 years to ensure sustainable development for the continent.

Agenda 2063 aims to build on the momentum set by previous as well as current initiatives to develop the continent. Notably, the Abuja Treaty (1991), the New Partnership for Africa's Development (NEPAD) (2001), Comprehensive Africa Agricultural Development Programme (CAADP) (2003), Malabo Declaration (2014), the Programme for Infrastructural Development in Africa (PIDA) (2017), among other programs aim to develop the continent. These programs also fit into numerous action plans adopted by different member states at national as well as regional levels. In terms of successes, some have but others have had more challenges as has been highlighted in Chapter 5. In the previous chapter, the significance of regional groupings with their diversity was shown.

In the global village, there is massive power in numbers, especially where countries have the economic muscle. As shown in Chapter 5, some of the economies in Africa are too small when it comes to economic muscle. As such their impact is small as well. In this chapter we want to show how ease of doing business in Africa still poses a challenge to some development initiatives for the continent. The idea of this chapter is to combine a sizeable number of countries in the continent and empirically examine them using data available from the respective countries. As such we choose member states of the Africa Free Trade Zone which still face development challenges. This is not to say that those left out are not facing them, instead it gives us a picture of how then the bloc is likely to perform.

The second guiding thought is to prove that some of the developmental agendas of the continent fail even at infancy stages mainly because the individual countries themselves are not ready to do business within the continent with each other as shall be shown by the empirical results. This on its own will militate against any noble development initiatives the continent can think of. For example a country without good and sound infrastructure cannot really expect to benefit from integrating production networks. Transport and logistics networks thrive where there is vibrant infrastructure, a country without is left in the cold, furthermore doing business with such a country becomes a nightmare.

Finally, in the chapter we discuss the "ease of doing business" concept with respect to the continent, mainly because globalization has brought unprecedented cooperation and closeness among nations in the global space. Openness to trade are the wheels which drive 21st economies. Countries with too much obstacles to the outsiders will be as good as closed. For example, as of November 2017, a country like Zimbabwe is currently preaching the gospel of, "Zimbabwe is open for business." after realising that decades of international isolation will not help her in her endeavours to develop. What remains then is, will she walk the talk? Zimbabwe is not the only country which for so long had challenges regarding doing business with. Several countries in the continent still have plenty of challenges making doing business with them not an easy task. The main issues making doing business difficult is the primary focus of the next and subsequent sections.

An Overview of Africa Free Trade Zone (AFTZ) Member States

The year 2015 witnessed a historic event on the African continent which saw the creation of Africa's largest trading bloc, the Africa Free Trade Zone (AFTZ). It consists of the following regional trading blocs in the continent: SADC, COMESA and EAC. Total membership is 26 states with a combined GDP of USD1.2 trillion and 620 million inhabitants, IPS (2016). AFTZ covers the bulk of Southern and Central Africa and partially stretches to North Eastern.

The region encompasses a mixed bag of countries with diverse dynamics in terms of economics, politics etc. For instance, in the zone you find some of the most corrupt, poorly managed states relative to some transparent and better managed states. Sadly, all these states have to find common ground for this initiative to work the desired magic through the continent. The puzzle then is, mixing the good and the bad member states, targeting to achieve the best possible regional grouping.

AFTZ member states have unique economic and political systems. Member states in the respective trading blocs, have internal challenges which even makes regional integration not so easy a task. So is this newly created bloc the panacea to Africa's economic growth, economic integration challenges etc.? Will this bloc unlock the roadmap to attaining the continent's broader agenda 2063 highlighted above? Will the bloc leverage sustainable development initiatives for the continent?

It is worthwhile at this particular juncture to briefly look into some of these member states, in particular those which have a lot of issues to do on their respective business environments and those that have fared fairly well in their environments. Also how some of these countries have been rated in as far as corruption is concerned shall be highlighted.

In Southern Africa, Botswana and South Africa, are countries which have progressed impressively in business environments relative to their other counterparts. For instance, on Doing Business as at 2016, the countries are ranked 71 and 74 respectively. Botswana is doing well buoyed by performance of its diamond mining sector. The corruption perception index (CRPI, hereafter) score for Botswana as at 2015 results is 63, which implies good accountability.

South Africa on the other hand, is a powerhouse of the continent which has strengths in key industries such as mining, manufacturing and processing.

Whilst it is a powerhouse of the continent its CRPI score has been 44. As at May 2016, Moody's, a rating agency assigned South Africa a credit rating of Baa2 although with a negative outlook. According to the report, corruption among other factors were the sources of risks which this country faces. Between March and April 2017 after the infamous cabinet reshuffle in South Africa, in particular the sacking of the finance ministry team among other factors led to downgrading of South Africa to "junk" status by S & P as well as Fitch- these are also reputable rating agencies. The ratings indicate that the business environment of South Africa has plenty of challenges. All this increases costs of doing business.

As at 2016, Zimbabwe and Tanzania were ranked a disappointing 161 and 132 respectively, with CRPI scores of 21 and 30. Angola, the other potential giant for the continent was ranked at 182 and a low CRPI score of 15, signifying heavy corruption and a toxic doing business environment.

Egypt despite being a potential economic powerhouse for the continent, for the same period it was ranked 122 and had a score of 36, implying substantial corruption. Kenya, is the powerhouse in particular for the East African Community (EAC) regional bloc, despite a ranking of 92, a CRPI score of 25, points to huge corruption. Recently USA suspended aid to Kenya, one of the reasons cited was presence of corruption. Rwanda is a success story for the EAC bloc, which has made significant progress, with an impressive ranking of 54 and a score of 56 for CRPI for the same period.

The preceding brief discourse on conditions of member states of AFTZ, affirms that the countries are so diverse and worlds apart. Harmonising and marrying this diversity together will be the mortar which will bind this regional arrangement into one piece with a shared vision. Besides the discussed factors, other countries for instance Burundi, Somalia, DRC etc. occasionally have incidences of instability. Owing to fragility of states doing business becomes difficult. For instance, countries in the horn of Africa, Somalia, and Eritrea etc. often experience conflict and instability. This obviously makes ease of doing business difficult and investments in other potential sectors complex. All this adds, to hurdles regards to doing business. The disturbing corruption scores shown by most countries, implies that it is a cancer which is embedded in the structures of these economies. Thus it is reasonable for us to opine that the success of AFTZ will also hinge partially on how problems like corruption are decisively dealt with, besides attending to the conventional doing business indicators.

Ease of Doing Business Concept

The concept refers to "an index published by the World Bank. It is an aggregate figure that includes different parameters which define the ease of doing business in a country." Economic Times (2018). 10 key parameters are considered when doing business in a particular country is measured. These areas are:

- Starting a business
- Dealing with construction permits
- Getting electricity
- Registering a property
- Getting credit
- Promoting minority investors
- Paying Taxes
- Trading across borders
- Reinforcing contracts
- Resolving insolvency (World Bank, 2017)

Ease of doing measures have been in use since 2005. According to World Bank there are two aggregate measures for assessing doing business of a country i.e. the ease of doing business ranking and the distance to frontier scores. The later shows the performance of an economy on 41 indicators for 10 doing business categories relative to the benchmark. For instance, if a country has a score of 50, on a category it means it is 50 percentage points away from the frontier as reflected in the performance of other countries in a given period.

On the other hand, the ease of doing business ranking aims at assigning a rank for a country from 1–190, on how it will have performed on the indicators relative to other countries. The best rank being 1 and the worst a country can be ranked relative to others being 190. Problematic areas of Doing Business according to the World Economic Report Forum 2014–2015 include corruption, government bureaucracy and poor infrastructure among other areas. So does Ease of Doing Business matter to states in Africa when looking at sustainable development of the continent as a whole? Several factors attest to this.

Globalization, here to stay. The globalization train is unstoppable and world has much to offer in terms of opportunities especially to those nations which are much more adaptable to the negatives and positives which have been brought by globalization. Globalization arguably increases integration of countries into Global Value Chains (GVCs), so Africa still needs to catch up. For instance, capital flies out of very volatile business environments and lands where it is most welcome. If it takes unnecessarily too long to get permits for starting a business, an investor will not have the patience to wait.

Low Private Sector Participation. Whilst investment flows keep on trickling to the continent, however, facts show that flows directly from private sector players such as Transnational Corporations (TNCs) remain very low globally. According to World Investment Report (2000) investment flows by TNCs into the continent is still around 1.2% of total global FDI flows. Further the reports says that Africa only has 5% of flows from TNCs when compared to what other developing countries are receiving. This is a worrying trend given the role of TNCs in the continent, in terms of employment, foreign currency generation given huge endowments of the continent in sectors such as oil, mineral resources. Low private sector participation is arguably due to hurdles partly reflected in the doing business parameters such as Paying Taxes, Getting Electricity, Getting Credit etc.

Overregulated Business Environments. Most business environments are faced with too many hurdles, in most cases they often scare away investors. For most developed continents, government role is minimal and interventions are done when necessary. For instance provision of public goods, law and order are mainly done by government. However, it is not uncommon in Africa to find the government interfering regularly with normal flow of business, in the process scaring away private players.

Foreign Direct Investment Deficits. Africa is still experiencing low FDI inflows as pointed above. Furthermore, the little that the continent is getting is not evenly shared. It means there are other countries in the continent which are getting more than others. For instance for the FDI flows received by the continent in 1999, 70% of it was just in five countries, i.e., Angola, Egypt, Nigeria, South Africa and Morocco, UNCTAD (1999). It may imply that other countries receive very little of the flows.

Weak Inter Africa Trade. Currently, trade amongst African countries remains low. Several factors explain this sad state of affairs. For instance, as we shall see in the coming sections, empirically Trade Across Borders (a parameter of ease of doing business) within member states of the continent is still low. Barriers such as visa requirements, across states makes mobility of factors of production such as labour, a challenge.

Falling of barriers to trade globally. One of the phenomena the global economy has been witnessing over time has been increasing openness to business among states until recently when U.S president, Donald Trump started to crack the whip on Chinese imports destined to the US. Falling trade barriers globally has increased world trade and cooperation among nations. Sadly Africa remains one destination where barriers still remain high enough so as to prohibit trade. The high barriers owe much to the vulnerable nature of most economies of this continent hence the need to protect most industries of the continent.

Empirical Analysis of Ease of Doing Business for AFTZ Member States

Since the inception of doing business indicators by the World Bank, there is now a vast body of literature of studies trying to explain, this concept. In particular, a number of studies on how economic growth or Foreign Direct Investment (FDI) for a country or region is affected by the ease of doing business in a particular country or region. Overtime, the World Bank is always refining these indicators, in terms of, for example, methodology of how some of these indicators are determined and expanding on how some of them are captured.

To assess performance of several countries in the AFTZ we had to ground our analysis on previous studies on the similar subject. Most of the studies examined focused on the major indicators given by World Bank as the key explanatory variables. A brief look at some of the studies on the subject will suffice at this juncture.

Ani (2015) carried out a study on selected Asian countries so as to see how ease of doing business parameters impacted on economic growth within the countries under study. Dealing with construction permits and getting credit had a negative effect. On the other hand, registering a property and trade across borders were found to have a positive effect. Other variables were found not to be significant.

A study by Kasongo (2013) on 40 sub Saharan Africa has important results on link between doing business and FDI inflows. Using seven panel data sets for the countries and FDI as the regressand, doing business indicators were used as explanatory variables. Factors such as starting a business, cost of registering a property were found to be significant in determining FDI inflows in the region. The researcher also found that cost of starting a business, time to register a property, time to export were not significant.

So as to explain how doing business indicators affect economic growth, Haidar (2012) used a sample of 172 countries using panel data spanning 2006–2010. The major finding of the research was that each additional improvement of business regulations resulted in 0.15 increase in economic growth for the period under study.

Mahuni and Bonga (2017) in their study for the Zimbabwean economy explored how various Doing Business parameters impacted on FDI inflows. The study results showed that the country has a difficult ease of doing business environment in areas such enforcing contracts which stifles FDI inflows.

Messaoud and Tehem (2014) conducted a study to investigate the link between business regulations for 162 countries from 2007 to 2011.The majority of indicators were found to be significant in explaining growth, with the exception of trading across borders and dealing with construction permits.

World Bank's International Financial Corporation (2012) is a report which is based on doing business with respect to countries in the Arab league. Its aim was to find out those factors which inhibit or promote Doing Business in the Arab region. The report shows that the Arab world is still grappling with problems like unemployment, low private sector investment etc. Governance was found to be the major hindrance which if manipulated well will help open up economies in the Arab world. Governance influences how institutions are run. In turn variables like enforcing contracts, corruption, getting credit, getting permits etc. will be affected directly or indirectly by governance.

Marek (2012) writing for the World Bank, sought to analyse the relationship between Doing Business, economic growth and regulatory reform. The goal of the paper was to see the importance of instituting reforms as a means of unlocking private sector investment so as to spur economic growth. The researcher acknowledges that whilst the Doing Business indicators cannot be relied upon entirely, they nevertheless help policy makers have a starting point. The research shows Doing Business aspects focusing on costs, have the greatest impact on explaining growth. The researcher singled out factors such as getting credit and enforcement of contracts.

In examining how countries in Africa are performing in terms of doing business and economic growth we used secondary data for 26 countries collected from World Bank, Transparency International and UNCTAD statistics. Due to data unavailability, the study used 2010–2016 data sets. The AFTZ has 26 countries, however the study dropped Libya due to serious data problems, the study failed to obtain relevant data for the variables for the period under study. We therefore used 25 countries in the analysis.

As shown above, most studies mainly use 10 indicators given by World Bank. However, this study added corruption also as the 11th variable. Corruption Perception Index as given by Transparency International assigns scores ranging from 0–100. A score such 100 implies a clean country, whereas a low score, for example, 10, signifies presence of high level of corruption. Doing business indicators, are taken as distance from frontier scores, a score of 100, is the benchmark and ideal for an economy while 1 is the unfavourable country position. Inclusion of corruption as an extra variable besides the usual 10 indicators given by World Bank is justified given the serious nature of the scourge in the continent. Chapter 3 has shown how corruption has stagnated development efforts by the continent.

The 25 countries have been classified into 3 groups using the average GDP levels for the 2010–2016 period. Group I with higher income has 7 countries, South Africa, Egypt and Angola topping the group. Group II has 8 countries, Uganda, Zambia and Botswana topping the group. Group III has 10 countries, with Madagascar, Rwanda and Malawi on the top, while Comoros, Seychelles and Djibouti on the bottom list.

The study employed the Panel data regression technique to analyse the data for the AFTZ member states. The study assumed the Pooled OLS model for the entire group. However, recognising the panel tests (chow, LM and Haussmann) for a better and efficient model, the study also has to run the Random Effects and the Fixed Effects models. Time effects and country effects models have been done, leading to the further division of the group into 3 using the average GDP as the dividing parameter. Four data sets have been run, the whole group of 25 member states, and the 3 divisions of the member states.

Table 6.1: Summary of regression results.

Dep. Variable: GDP	25 AFTZ MEMBERS			GROUP I [7 Countries]			GROUP II [8 Countries]			GROUP III [10 Countries]		
Variables	**POLS**	**REM**	**FEM**	**POLS**	**REM**	**FEM**	**POLS**	**REM**	**FEM**	**POLS**	**REM**	**FEM**
CRPI	***			***	***				*			
RI			*			***				***	***	
EC				**	**		*	*				
TAB	***									***	***	
PT				*	*	***				**	**	**
PMI		**	*			**						
GC	***						*	*		***	***	*
RP	*			**	**				***	**	**	
GE				**	**	*	***	***		***	***	
DCP	*			**	***	***						
SB	*			*	*	***	***	***	*			

Significant; *10%, **5%, ***1%. **POLS**-Pooled OLS, **REM**-Random Effects Model, **FEM**-Fixed Effects Model.

The table above gives a summary of the data analysis done by the current study. The AFTZ as a region to improve economic growth has to pay immediate attention to 6 key variables affecting the economic growth of the region. These include corruption levels, boarder trading, credit issues, registration of property, construction permits handling and starting business issues. The bloc has to check on the effect of these variables on the economic growth and act to improve accordingly. Corruption levels, boarder trading management and controls, and credit lines are the major significant variables to be dealt with. Not undermining the results of the REM and FEM, the bloc should also address how it resolves issues of insolvency and also improves on investor protection to attract foreign direct investment.

The study results also indicated that, in as much as the bloc might need to address collectively on issues affecting economic growth of the member states, there is greater need to separate the member states into smaller groups and examine further the most impacting variables. Thus, the study came up with 3 groups (I, II and III). Each nation within the AFTZ bloc, should also check on what group it falls and check on which variables it should address strongly for the attainment of high levels of growth.

Group I countries, being the high income nations, have resolving insolvency, payment of taxes, dealing with construction permits, starting business, investor protection and getting electricity as significant variables confirming economic growth levels of the member states. The results are drawn from the FEM, which is the best model as per panel tests. Countries in this group should also address issues of corruption, contracts enforcements, and property registration as reported from the POLS and REM regressions, whose results should not be neglected. Worth to note for this group is that, country differences are significant as reported by country effects test, implying that there are differences that prevail for individual nations, which has to be investigated separately. Time effects are insignificant.

Group II countries, rated as middle income for this study among AFTZ bloc, have registration of property, starting a business and corruption as the significant variables affecting economic growth of member states as reported by the FEM (the best model from panel tests). The group should also have a concern on factors, namely, enforcement of contracts, getting credit and getting electricity, which have been reported as significant by the POLS and REM. Time effects have been found significant for this group, indicating that economic growth has been changing with the effect of time, implying a transition. Country differences have also been noted for this group, implying that individual analysis is recommended for efficient analysis.

Group III, composed of lower income countries among the AFTZ bloc, have reported crucial results as well. The Haussmann test, failed to meet the asymptotic assumptions and hence could not report. The Chow test favoured the FEM, while the LM test favoured the REM. Therefore, both models will be reported, and worth to note is that the POLS and the REM have results which are in agreement, from coefficients to p-values. Member states in Group III, should pay attention to variables namely, insolvency resolving, trading across borders, payment of taxes, getting of credit, registration of properties, and electricity provision (reported by the REM and POLS, the FEM also supported the results, though it only mentions PT and GC as the only significant variables). Country differences have been reported, implying further separation required for efficient results. Time effects are insignificant for this group of countries.

The methodology adopted in this study, has an efficiency tracing component, and hence recommended for policy use. The initial model for the whole bloc, reported an adjusted r-squared and an overall r-squared of 0.177 and 0.0177 for the POLS and REM respectively; and further division of the bloc to 3 groups have led to the reporting of higher figures of the parameters (0.9196:0.9412, 0.7078:0.7747 and 0.7840:0.8272, for the 3 groups respectively). The FEM reported the same efficiency improvement, though the greatest was for Group I, reporting an overall r-squared of 0.6079. There is greater encouragement for member states to work on improving various doing business indicators, so as for the bloc to improve economic growth.

Discussion of Results

The empirical analysis explored on the study has shown how Ease of Doing Business indicators should be at the heart and soul of AFTZ trading bloc. Attending to the issues explored in the analysis will help a great deal in steering the development cause of the countries concerned as well as the continent in general. Furthermore, resolving the pertinent issues explored will be the mortar, which will bind the member states together by bringing them to some uniform platform.

In the analysis we pinpoint how diversity of the member states on their own largely makes it difficult for cross border transactions to be carried with efficiency. The results on the variable trading across borders corroborates this. Thus the member states should strive to open up their borders so as to increase inter Africa trade by reducing barriers among member states. Previous studies on the similar subject have largely dwelt on only the 10 Doing Business indicators given by the World Bank, however as we pointed earlier, the empirical analysis added corruption as an extra variable, giving a 11 variable model. The results on corruption have been robust, thus success of this trading bloc will depend too on attending to corruption.

It has also been shown that the diversity of the member states also requires individual efforts by the member states in addressing issues around, credit, registration of property, construction permits handling and starting business issues within their respective domains. This is corroborated by country effects carried out during the regressions. This will allow convergence around the bloc to be much easier.

AFTZ Study Outcomes and the Probable Development Discourse of Africa

In this section we want to explore the significance of the study of ease of doing business of the countries which make up the AFTZ member states in the context of leveraging sustainable development for the continent. The empirical analysis helped us to appreciate the major sticking issues dominating business environments of some countries in the continent. Paying taxes, starting a business, getting credit, registering a property are prominent factors making doing business with countries explored difficult.

The model we used encompassed World Bank indicators and an additional variable, i.e., corruption. From the results obtained corruption is and still remains one of the biggest challenges of the continent, corruption has been explored at length in Chapter 3. The current trend of corruption is only sinking the continent to its knees further dampening prospects of development. Nipping it in the bud would help the continent a great deal in sprucing up the image of the continent and send positive signals to the outside world.

The Sticking Issues on Ease of Doing Business

The ease of doing business measures which were significant in the study across the member states, need attention. Without serious address to these and other *sticking issues*, the continent will remain behind, scuttling major efforts at development. The issues are sticking in that they "close" the business environment of Africa not only to the outside world, but to Africans also amongst themselves.

The empirical analysis in as much as it gives insights into how doing business is like in the continent, it has a few limitations. The main problem being that of data availability. Data remains a pricey commodity in most developing countries, mostly its collection and accessibility by various stakeholders. At times key information is missing. For instance as alluded earlier, instead of using data for all the 26 AFTZ member states, the study used data for 25 member states. Moreover, the data span was also narrow. Possibly with availability of more data, the robustness of results can be improved.

The factors covered in the study are mainly expressed in quantitative terms in fitting the model as well as explaining the results. However, opining that only quantitative aspects matter most in aiding us to understand ease of doing business in the continent will only give a misconstrued view of the ease of doing concept. Qualitative factors should also come into the fold in assessing openness to business of a destination. For example issues such as perceptions and attitudes of say, investors about a particular destination are not captured since they are qualitative aspects, but are nevertheless important for any destination. For example in Zimbabwe, following the new administration of November 2017 with its "Zimbabwe is open for business" mantra, there has been a growing increase expression of interest and trickling in of real investment from investors the world over as perceptions are taking on a positive dimension.

What are Africa's development prospects in light of the above analysis? Why are the barriers so high? The empirical analysis showed major issues which constrain doing business in the AFTZ bloc. Dreaming of sustainable development in light of the above hurdles is not easy. Here is a look at two major sticking issues explored above.

Trading Across Borders. At the present mobility across international frontiers in Africa is currently constrained by numerous restrictions and regulations we indicated earlier. For instance mobility of labour and other factors of production across countries even within Africa remains a major challenge. Coordination across various agencies and authorities across national frontiers. In 2016, a World Bank feature story observed the following;

> Restrictions on the legal forms of entry to hospitals in countries such as Tanzania and Uganda or limits on the repatriation of earnings in Kenya and Uganda constrain the establishment of foreign hospitals in the region. Finally, the high cost of visa and work permits in many countries impose stringent restrictions on the movement of health and education professionals to provide services abroad.

This is just an example from the continent on how factors of production, labour and capital in particular cannot be positioned where maximum returns can be realised due to excessive barriers stifling their mobility as implied by the above quote. The barriers are not only in the service sectors, but others as well. A good example of how barriers are doing more harm than good is given by Brenton and Gozde cited in Charalambous (2012) in a report on Global Tax news, of the hurdles a South African firm, Shoprite has to endure in a way of barriers. They note that Shoprite spends USD20, 000 a week on import permits to distribute products to its outlets located in Zambia. Effectively, this increases operational costs for this firm.

Paying Taxes. For the continent, paying taxes remains one of the challenges observed in the analysis. PwC South Africa 2018 on its Tax in Africa survey, notes the following with respect to how taxes are making doing business difficult in Africa:

> The most significant findings confirm that doing business on the African continent is still a fairly large challenge. In particular, areas such as obtaining certainty around the

application of legislation and discussing/negotiating with the tax authorities remain challenging. Another interesting conclusion is that tax is still considered to be one of the primary constraints on doing business in Africa.

For any state, taxes raised from individuals and businesses are a central plinth supporting the provision of services, the maintenance of infrastructure, the employment of civil servants, and the smooth functioning of the state (Isbell, 2017:1). Taxes remains the major source of income for African countries. Despite such a fact, tax systems in Africa have received criticism related to their characteristics. Taxation systems to be regarded as a "good tax system" should be economically efficient, effective and equitable (Fjeldstad, 2011).

Using the standard concept evaluation, tax systems in Africa need to be improved. Ghosh (2016) indicated that tax systems in most African countries—as in other low-income countries—are underdeveloped. For the past decades, there have been various tax reforms to improve tax systems in many African nations. Some tax reforms undertaken in Africa include a shift from sales tax to value added tax. Despite efforts of African countries to match up with global trends by implementing self-assessment, they are left behind in tax compliance measured by tax revenue as a percentage of GDP (Carter and Cebreiro, 2011). The capture of the informal sector is still a great challenge in the continent. Countries in Africa are not good tax collectors.

The most befitting theory for taxation systems in Africa is the "tax handle theory," which states that developing nations concentrate on the easy to tax sectors in their collection. Such system tends to over strain other sectors leading to unfair competition. The system also encourages tax evasion and non-compliance of tax payers. Well-designed tax systems can strengthen the relationship between citizens and government—giving citizens a stronger stake in what their government does and a stronger incentive to demand accountability (Ghosh, 2016).

Generally taxes collection is low in African countries. Various combination of reasons may be cited as the causing factors to low taxation in Africa. Taxation generally not high on the domestic political agenda—politicians do not support complete tax reforms yet they tend to run away from considering tax reform agenda as a policy priority. A tax law voted by parliament can be different from its effective enforcement (Laporte, De Quatrebarbes, and Bouterige, 2017:7). The political and economic elite often not part of the tax base—politicians in Africa rarely pay taxes, if they do they partially pay using their political muscle. Politicians do evade taxes, yet many of their activities requires remission of taxes to the same government. Isbell (2017: 1), supported the fact indicating that, in many African countries, however, tax evasion leaves states with major holes in their budgetary pockets. Extremely narrow tax bases—tax bases are generally low in Africa, the tax system is not efficient to cover all sectors including the informal sector.

Large untaxed informal sectors—due to poor industry development in Africa, small businesses and the informal sector form a greater part of the industry, yet accountability of taxes remains difficult for the sectors. Extensive/increasing tax exemptions—in an effort to promote industry growth and also government purchases tax exemptions occupy a significant portion worth concern. Massive revenues from natural resources are lost—accountability of revenue from natural resources like oil, diamond, gold among other minerals is difficult because of political relations. Illicit capital flows facilitated by tax havens entrench inefficient tax systems.

Tax compliance levels in Africa is very low. Low tax compliance weakens the state's ability to invest and develop (Isbell, 2017:1). Non-compliance or low level of compliance may be caused by the complexity levels of tax systems and/or the enforcement levels of authorities. Self-assessment methods have been developed and promoted in many African countries, yet tax education is still necessary for individuals and businesses. Aiko and Logan (2014) report, majorities of Africans say it is difficult to find out what taxes they're supposed to pay. Non-compliance is also caused by the public not knowing how the taxes are used by the government, and also the knowledge of negative use of collected amounts by the government. Ali, Fjeldstad, and Sjursen (2014) have found that not understanding how taxes are used is negatively correlated with tax compliance. Compliance can be through enforcement by relevant authorities or through voluntary willingness of the taxpayers (Wahl, Kastlunger, and Kirchler, 2010). Enforcement compliance is also a challenge in many African nations. The enforcing authority do face administration and expert challenges in identifying taxable transactions as well as efficient methods to make collections. Processes to collect taxes are defined as too long in Africa leading to individuals and businesses opting for non-compliance. Long verification processes are more visible in borders where traders spent too much time in ques to formalize their transactions. The inefficiency in tax collection is linked to poor ease of doing business indicators for African countries.

Besides complications around areas of taxes legislation and compliance pointed above, tax rates in the continent, still remain on the high side relative to other destinations. According to Tax Foundation (2017) the global average statutory corporate tax rate was 22.96%. A comparison by region for the same period shows Africa topping the list with a higher rate of 28.73%, Europe with the lowest of 18.35%, North America 23.08%, Oceania 23.67% and South America 28.73%. A country such as South Africa for example, although it is in the first cycle of development, as we have shown in Chapter 2, its taxes constrain growth and hence development to sustainable levels. Trading Economics show that the average Corporate Tax Rate of South as at 2018 is around 28%, in the years 2008–2012 it was averaging a whopping 34.5%! Thus given such average corporate taxes which are punitive, business environments simply scare away potential investors, consequently development is stifled.

Another example of how taxes do burden not only people but business too in the continent is the recently introduced Ugandan tax levied on social media platforms such as Facebook, Twitter, Instagram, Linked In among other platforms (Muhumuza, 2018). This tax was effected in July 2018, at the rate of 200 Shillings (about 5 cents). The incidence of the tax will not only hurt especially the poor sections of the Ugandan community who use social media, but will also complicate ease of doing business for those relying on online businesses and even those mulling to venture into such.

Just recently in Uganda, popular opaque beer manufacturer Nile Breweries a subsidiary of South African based SAB Miller has been forced to shut down. According to Otage (2018) of the Daily Monitor the main reason was the Excise Duty of 30% currently levied on the manufacturer. This effectively raises operational costs. Over a 1000 farmers who directly supply maize to Nile Breweries will be the immediate casualties if government fails to reverse this tax. Downstream jobs as well as incomes will be lost.

So in essence Africa, is open for vast opportunities, but is not very ready yet to do business with the rest of the world as our empirical analysis has reflected. The evidence we have shown above shows that much has to be done in improving openness of Africa to the rest of the world. Barriers stifling mobility should be eased through opening up of borders, taxes should converge with global average rates, utilities such as electricity should be affordable, as well as credit should be accessible at fairly reasonable rates. Improvement on these and other areas will lead to real transformation of the continent towards a path of robust development.

References

Aiko, R., and C. Logan. "Africa's Willing Taxpayers Thwarted by Opaque Tax Systems, Corruption." Afrobarometer Policy Paper No. 7, 2014.

Ali, M., O. H. Fjeldstad, and I. H. Sjursen. . "To Pay or Not to Pay? Citizens' Attitudes Toward Taxation in Kenya, Tanzania, Uganda, and South Africa." *World Development* 64 (2014): 828–842.

Ani, G. T. . "Effects of Ease of Doing Business to Economic Growth Among Selected Countries in Asia." *Asia Pacific Journals of Multidisciplinary Research* 3.5 (2015).

Bonga, W. G. . "An Empirical Investigation of the Nature of Corruption in Zimbabwe." Doctorate Thesis, Atlantic International University, Honolulu, Hawaii, 2014.

Carter, A., and A. Cebreiro. "Africa's Tax System: A Survey OECD Observer." OECD Centre for Tax Policy and Administration, 2011.

Charalambous, L. "Trade Barriers Hindering African Growth." *Global Tax News*, 2012. https://www.taxnews.com/news/Trade_Barriers_Hindering_African_Growth____53899.html

Economic Times. "Ease of Doing Business." 2018. https://economictimes.indiatimes.com/definition/ease-of-doing-business

Fjeldstad, O.-H. "Taxation for Development: Myths, Facts and Challenges for African Countries." TFESSD Conference 2011, Chr. Michelsen Institute & International Centre for Tax and Development, Oslo, 2011.

Ghosh, Gargee. "Why Taxes Will Be Central to Africa's Development." *World Economic Forum*, 2016.

Haidar, J. I. "The Impact of Business Regulatory Reforms on Economic Growth." *Journal of the Japanese and International Economies* 26 (2012): 285–307.

Hsiao, C. 2003. *Analysis of Panel Data*, 2nd ed. Cambridge: Cambridge University Press.

International Finance Corporation, World Bank. 2012. Doing Business in the Arab World: Doing Business in a More Transparent World.

Isbell, Thomas. "Tax Compliance: Africans Affirm Civic Duty but Lack Trust in Tax Department." *Afro Barometer Policy Paper No.* 43, 2017.

Jahnsen, Kari, and Kyle Pomerleau. "Corporate Income Tax Rates around the World." *Tax Foundation*, 2017. https://taxfoundation.org/corporate-income-tax-rates-around-the-world-2017/

Kamal, Baher, and Fareed Mahdy. "Africa Launches Largest Trading Block with 620 Million Consumers." *International Press Service*, 2016. http://www.ipsnews.net/2016/02/africa-launches-largest-trading-block-with-620-million-consumers/

Kasongo, K. B. Foreign Direct Investment in Sub Saharan Africa Countries: Does the Business Regulation Matter? Lessons from DR Congo, Seoul National University, 2013.

Laporte, B., C. De Quatrebarbes, and Y. Bouterige. "Mining Taxation in Africa: The Gold Mining Industry in 14 Countries from 1980 to 2015." Études et Documents, No. 13, CERDI, 2017.

Mahuni, K., and W. G. Bonga. . "Nexus between Doing Business Indicators and Foreign Direct Investment for Zimbabwe: A Time Series Analysis." *Dynamic Research Journals' Journal of Economics and Finance* 2.2 (2017): 1–8.

Marek, H. "The Doing Business Indicators, Economic Growth and Regulatory Reform." *Policy Research Working Paper*, 6176, 2012. ©World Bank, Washington, DC. https://openknowledge.worldbank.org/handle/10986/12020 License: CC BY 3.0 IGO.

Messaoud, B., and Ghak El Z. Tehem. Business Regulations and Economic Growth: What Can Be Explained? *International Strategic Management Review* 2 (2014): 64–78.

Moyo, V. "Modelling the Capital Structure of Manufacturing, Mining and Retail Firms Listed on the Johannesburg Stock Exchange." Doctorate thesis (Financial Management Studies), University of Pretoria, 2013.

Muhumuza, H. "Uganda Just Rolled Out a 5-Cent Daily Tax to Access Social Media. People Aren't Happy." *Time*, July 2, 2018.http://time.com/5328463/uganda-social-media-tax/

Opeyemi, A. A Re-examination of the Twin Deficit Phenomenon in the Nigerian Economy, College of Development Studies, Covenant University, 2012.

Otage, S. "Nile Breweries Shuts Down Plant over Taxes." *Daily Monitor*, July 9 2018.http://www.monitor.co.ug/News/National/Nile-Breweries-plant-taxes-Chibuku-opaque-beer-SABMiller/688334-4653158-mr5wkhz/index.html

PwC South Africa. "Africa Tax Survey." 2018. https://www.pwc.co.za/en/publications/pwc-africa-tax-survey.html

Song, H., and S. F. Witt, *Tourism Demand Modelling and Forecasting: Modern Econometric Approaches*. Pergamum, and Cambridge, 2000.

UNCTAD Report. "FDI to Africa Rises in 1999, But Continent Must Become Bigger Market Player." 2000. http://unctad.org/en/pages/PressReleaseArchive.aspx?ReferenceDocId=2713

Wahl, I., B. Kastlunger, and E. Kirchler. "Trust in Authorities and Power to Enforce Tax Compliance: An Empirical Analysis of the 'Slippery Slope Framework.'" *Law & Policy* 32.4 (2010): 383–406.

Wooldridge, J. 2009. *Introductory Econometrics*, *A Modern Approach*, 5th Edition. Michigan State University.

World Bank. 2016. "Africa's Unexplored Potential of Trade in Services." http://www.worldbank.org/en/news/feature/2016/08/04/africas-unexploredpotential-of-trade-in-services

World Economic Forum. *The Global Competitiveness Report 2014–2015*.

· 7 ·

LAYING THE FOUNDATION, GOING FORWARD

For any continent to attain sustainable, inclusive and shared development which cascades to all its inhabitants, the foundation upon which this takes place has to be firm and solid. Africa is struggling to keep pace with the rest of the world, which has been the greater part of discussions of this volume. The continent is overwhelmed with huge opportunities, which if fully harnessed it will never remain the same. It will turn into a jewel which will be a marvel to the rest of the world.

Amidst the sea of debilitating challenges which keep on hammering relentlessly the hapless continent, Africa cannot afford to sit back, relax and watch in awe as others proceed in the right direction. Africa too has to wake up from her deep slumber and move forward. At what pace then should she move? Making baby steps in the right direction is better than galloping in the wrong direction. Certain things have to be made right by the continent. Whilst some efforts are laudable to also do the correct things by the continent, many at times mistakes have been made. The net effect of some mistakes has been to stifle progress, hampering sustainable development.

For instance, industrial clusters which we shall discuss in greater detail shortly have been tried and are continuously being tried in some pockets of the continent. Few of them have made regional let alone global impact, hence most are barely visible. In places where attempts at clustering has been made, half-baked strategies have been very common, consequently giving not so convincing results. In contrast in developed and emerging economies, where they have been properly executed, they have been catalysts of massive growth and development of various regions in the concerned countries. Industrial clusters have driven value addition and a surge of exports, at the same time spurring competitiveness of the concerned countries. Africa still lacks this. Those of Africa have been lacking the proper ingredients, making them of little use in catalysing development. As we shall note in the coming discussions on industrial clusters, very few countries of the continent subscribe to the global body of clusters, TCI which helps in cluster best practices as membership statistics will show. In contrast, countries which have registered phenomenal economic transformation work closely with this global cluster networking organization. Thus we can say that without active participation on the global platform not much is expected out of Africa with respect to industrial clusters. So are industrial clusters of importance to the continent? We shall see how they have been used to front load massive development in other countries.

On the other hand, Africa continuously clamours for investment flows from across the globe. The model of investment is gradually changing the world over. That model which fosters sustainable development still lacks in Africa so as to fully address current development woes of the continent. Does the continent have the clout to negotiate for win-win deals which have a generational impact as opposed to fly by night arrangements which not only impose a burden to the present but also future generations? Some investments the continent has received from abroad have not been sustainable. For example extractive sectors such as mining, oil have had many foreign companies participating in the continent depleting the precious resources without adequate compensation to locals and the environment. On the other hand, the growing influence of China on Africa with its numerous deals was scrutinised in depth in Chapter 4. There is a likelihood of Africa facing more problems in future as China closes in on the continent. It is not Africa alone, but other countries as well have higher chances of landing in trouble as they absorb China's deals.

The Prime Minister of Malaysia, Mr. Mahathir Mohamad in a speech recently warned against a situation in which powerful countries were taking advantage of poor countries. In his words, he firmly avowed that, "We do not want a situation where there is a new version of colonialism happening because poor countries are unable to compete with rich countries."

(ABC News, 2018). He has been critical of a number of infrastructure projects mainly from China which have potential to plunge Malaysia into huge debt. A number of African states fell into this pit due to China's opaque deals with the weak states of the continent as we have explored in Chapter 4. Mr. Mahathir Mohamad emphasized that even if it is "free trade" it still has to be "fair trade." As we pointed earlier, Africa is still in a cesspool of poverty. How then do we crawl out of the big hole? In this section we discuss four key areas which can help Africa set herself on a sustainable path to develop.

Rolling Out the "Red Tape" and Rolling on the "Red Carpet"

Africa has to be ready to do business not only with itself but also with the rest of the world. The current state of readiness of the continent presently does not promote much of its attractiveness, despite plenty of existing opportunities. In the previous chapter we showed that doing business in Africa currently faces a number of impediments in areas such as taxation, mobility across national boundaries etc.

World Bank (2016) in an article titled "Africa's Unexplored Potential of Trade in Services" moots a number of strategies to at least reduce barriers around areas of taxation and mobility with respect to Africa, in the process red tape is rolled out:

- Improving cross-border trade by simplifying border procedures, limiting the number of agencies at the border and increasing the professionalism of officials, supporting traders' associations, improving the flow of information on market opportunities, and assisting in the spread of new technologies such as cross-border mobile banking that improve access to finance;
- Removing a range of non-tariff barriers to trade, such as restrictive rules of origin, import and export bans, and onerous and costly import and export licensing procedures; and,
- Reforming regulations and immigration rules that limit the substantial potential for cross-border trade and investment in services.

In Chapter 6, corruption was also shown to be an impediment to doing business in the continent. To show that corruption is slowly crippling sustainable development of the continent, the African Union in a recent summit set its 2018 theme as "*Winning the Fight against Corruption: A Sustainable Path to Africa's Transformation*." From the theme we can infer that the continent is at war with corruption and corruption seems to be advancing and gaining ground. The more ground corruption covers and keeps on winning, then development keeps on stalling for the continent.

To substantiate the theme, during the same summit, in an address President Buhari of Nigeria declared corruption as one of the "greatest evils of our time." This shows that corruption is still deeply rooted in the continent. Unless Africa fights back strongly, corruption will keep on pummelling the feeble continent with lethal jabs. This brings us to the question—are the continent's weapons sharp enough to win the fight?

What to Do with the Corruption?

Successfully reducing corruption is ultimately a matter of political will on the part of governments in the continent, combined with strong institutions of governance that exercise effective checks and balances, systems that ensure transparency and accountability to citizens, and clear sanctions for those who engage in corrupt behaviour (USAID, 2005: v). While the above statement seems feasible, it requires governments to walk the talk. African governments have for long stated their motive to address corruption, but this objective has never been achieved. Successive governments have only used the quest to address corruption as a trump card to gain majority for nomination into office. After being elected into office, it's the same old story. Nothing much is achieved, yet the solution to end corruption rests on the will of the politicians. What has been noticed in Africa, is the involvement of new leadership in new corruption deals and/or dealing with petty corruption yet grand corruption which poses greatest threats to economic development continue unabated. Anti-corruption programs and taskforces have been developed, however, their ability to enforce laws is questionable. The institutions together with the judicial systems have failed to separate themselves from politics. The case of the Philippines (taking an example out of Africa) under President Benigno Aquino III shows how fighting corruption can succeed in enhancing investment and growth, buoying presidential popularity and improving a country's international ratings (Klitgaard, 2015: 7).

Formation of regional blocs in Africa has aided on reducing corruption, as it has been part of the agenda among objectives. However, African states have failed to control each other to avoid serious violations of stipulated standards as gazette in the agreements. Blocs also have failed to implement everything on the agreement, with some economies lagging behind on implementation. Some leaders have also joined hands to protect each other even on matters that do not need such partnerships but only for their individual benefits. Such has been seen in elections, civil wars, corruption and human rights violations.

An axiom of corruption studies is that real change rarely happens in the absence of committed and motivated political leadership (USAID, 2005:4). Fighting corruption is no easy task. It calls for multifaceted strategies targeting political, economic, legal, administrative social and moral aspects of the ill (Lumumba, 2014). Long-term approaches are required with great consistency to address corruption. Other authorities postulate that fighting corruption is mostly about fun addressing poor governance rather than catching the crooks. Servant leadership is expected from politicians in order to tackle corruption. So if corruption is not decisively fought, it will continue fighting against the systems of the continent.

The AU Convention to Prevent and Combat Corruption (AUCPCC) set-up has given Africa an opportunity to speed up the curbing of corruption. It is a shared roadmap for countries to implement governance and anti-corruption policies and systems on both national and regional levels. Strong provisions are contained in AUCPCC that help in resolving corruption challenges across the continent for the longer term. According to African Union Advisory Board on Corruption (AUABC), the AUCPCC is a fundamental instrument with provisions that can resolve the corruption challenge on the continent. The AUCPCC was adopted in 2003, and strong entry was made in 2006. The resolution of the AUCPCC is only feasible if the provisions are adopted and implemented nationally by individual countries. To date, only 38 of 54 member states ratified the AUCPCC, and for those that have ratified they have not reported progress on implementation.

Plugging infrastructure gaps should also come as a priority for Africa to roll on the red carpet so that it appears as a destination of choice for investment. Current state of infrastructure has allowed regional blocs to have efficacy problems in trade facilitation and mobility across borders making doing business costly. Aspiration 2 of Agenda 2063 (2015:5), with respect to infrastructure in the continent inspires hope:

> By 2063, the necessary infrastructure will be in place to support Africa's accelerated integration and growth, technological transformation, trade and development. This will include high-speed railway networks, roads, shipping lines, sea and air transport, as well as well-developed ICT and the digital economy. A Pan-African High Speed

Train Network will connect all the major cities/capitals of the continent, with adjacent highways and pipelines for gas, oil, water, as well as ICT Broadband cables and other infrastructure. This will be a catalyst for manufacturing, skills development, technology, research and development, integration and intra-African trade, investments and tourism.

The envisaged path to infrastructure by the continent is commendable. This will in turn help to drive industrial clusters sustainably towards broader industrialization of the greater continent. However, the question remains will the individual countries walk the talk? Will they commit themselves to this noble cause? Only time will tell.

Change of mind sets and attitudes by individuals towards the vice of corruption is also very critical for the continent to win the fight against corruption. Mind set change was also reiterated during the AU summit by Mr Buhari. If individuals and eventually countries can change attitudes towards this ill, problems like "goat mentality" we looked at as part of Afrocentric barriers will be substantially reduced. Political will we looked at earlier becomes key in helping people change mind sets up until the continent as a whole.

Impact Investment, Beyond Traditional Investment

The traditional investment model has largely focused on exploitation of natural resources which the continent is endowed with. Sadly, Africa of the 21st century still has massive investment deficits when compared to other continents across the globe. Whilst the continent exhibits encouraging potential in numerous sectors and subsectors as we indicated in Chapter 1 due to a number of comparative advantages, real investments with positive impacts have often been elusive to the continent. Grinding poverty is still the order of the day in most countries, challenges such as energy deficits, unemployment, environmental degradation, financial exclusion etc. are still prevalent in the continent.

To make matters worse who will risk investing in a continent drowning in cancerous corruption as Chapter 3 has shown? More so, with regional blocs and their respective challenges examined in Chapter 5, can the continent entice serious investors? Chief among the obstacles in the regional groupings being both the quality and quantity of infrastructure currently available in the respective blocs. Furthermore, much of Africa is not so ready to work with other continents owing to difficult business environments explored in

Chapter 6. Empirical evidence in the chapter showed that aspects such as getting credit, getting electricity, enforcing contracts are among major stumbling blocks when it comes to doing business with most countries in the continent. In addition, trading across borders has proven to be difficult due to diversity of the countries. This has caused them to have varying pieces of legislations, diverse business cultures, mobility restrictions etc. which often escalate the cost of doing business across national frontiers, hence even intra Africa trade is currently weak. Due to all this, the continent will find it difficult to dovetail into global value chains which are increasingly becoming intricate.

The above is not to imply that Africa is receiving virtually nil investment flows, but in some instances the few investment flows have given the continent problems. For instance in this era where climate change has become a topical issue, some companies have exploited the environment of Africa causing much harm which will burden not only the present but future generations as well. Furthermore, at a time when other continents are becoming richer due to massive investments in global trade, perpetual poverty in Africa, particularly income poverty is still a major challenge afflicting mostly vulnerable groups such as the youth and women. This vicious cycle has to be broken, of which having abundant impact investment projects across the continent can be a powerful tool of intervention. There is a need to rethink on the current models of investment obtaining in most states in the continent. Impact investment provides a much better alternative given the numerous challenges the continent has. In this section, we examine how emphasis on impact investment as a development vehicle has a potential to steer Africa's numerous immature economies towards a path of sustainable development beyond the traditional investment model.

Impact Investment and Africa

There is no conventional definition of the term impact investment. Whilst the definition is still widely debated, (UNDP 2016), the concept according to Global Impact Investment Network (GIIN) is concerned with investments made into companies, organizations which aim to generate a measurable social and environmental impact alongside a financial return. Similarly, Investopedia (2018) views the concept as;

> Investing that aims to generate specific beneficial social or environmental effects in addition to financial gain. Impact investing is a subset of socially responsible investing (SRI), but while the definition of socially responsible investing encompasses

avoidance of harm, impact investing actively seeks to make a positive impact by investing, for example, in non-profits that benefit the community or in clean technology enterprise.

The two definitions imply that beyond merely making profits, there is an important component to the concept–that is making a positive impact through bequeathing good societal aspects like clean and efficient environments free of ills like pollution, depletion of finite resources, clean energy, healthy populations etc. Thrust is on impact which transforms people's lives.

Impact investment can be done by individuals, pension funds, institutions etc. Renowned impact investors include, Bridges Ventures, Bill and Melinda Gates, JP Morgan, Gatsby Charitable Foundation, insurance and asset management companies such as AXA Group among others. For instance AXA Group in 2013 committed 150 million euros so as to start impact investments. The target sectors being, climate change, health and longevity as well as poverty, Spotlight on the market report (2014). Impact investments aim at maximising profits as well as maximising impact on welfare of people.

According to United Nations Development Program (UNDP, 2016) impact investment is differentiated from other forms investment by the following three key principles:

- The expectation of a financial return: impact investors expect to earn a financial return on the capital invested, below the prevailing market rate, at the market rate or even above it.
- The intention to tackle social or environmental challenges (i.e., the impact or intentionality): in addition to a financial return, impact investors aim to achieve a positive impact on society and/or the environment.
- A commitment to measuring and reporting against the intended social and environmental impact: impact investors commit to measure performance using standardized metrics.

The concept of impact investment is prominent in emerging markets and developed countries which has seen also development of related concepts such as Social Impact Bonds in countries such as, UK, Australia, US, Netherlands etc., largely aiming at making the greatest impact on societies. A 2014 Spotlight on the market report, shows that of $46 billion impact investments carried out, 30% were in developed countries whereas 70% were carried out in emerging economies. Impact investment is a fairly new and exciting concept which if properly executed can bring tremendous results for the continent.

For developing continents like Africa, a lot of work needs to be done so as for impact investment to also take centre stage in various policy platforms for the greater benefit of the continent. Engaging renowned global impact investors will also be instrumental for the success of impact investment projects in the continent through creating impact investment marketplaces which are visible. The concept should be understood and embraced as it has allowed other continents to move well. At this juncture, we pose an important question, is there evidence to support that Africa needs impact investment?

The impact investment industry has grown in leaps and bounds in most developed continents. Awareness and understanding of the immense benefits which come with fully embracing the concept still lacks in Africa as we shall note. One way of addressing Africa's Incomplete Cycles of Development is emphasizing much on impact investment as a key strategy, given that it endeavours to create great impact on welfare of people than only financial returns which is mostly the thrust of traditional investment. A thorough exegesis of impact investment in this section will allow a deeper understanding on the concept. In addition, it will increase awareness and appreciation across numerous policy platforms, to prove that there is overwhelming demand for impact investment in the continent.

Impact investment is integral to progress of the continent towards a trajectory of sustainable development as summarised by Severino and Baraton (2013: 3):

> By nurturing companies targeting unsatisfied demand for basic needs or by accelerating innovation, impact investing can precisely help African economies to address development challenges. For instance, local generic medicine producers allow the sale of drugs at lower prices than if they were imported and contribute to improved health outcomes. Impact investment also contributes to sustainable development by fostering environmental, social and governance practices in local firms. Respecting international standards can improve local companies' competitiveness and minimize negative externalities that spring from firms' activities.

Africa has full potential for impact investment industry to thrive due to its overwhelming poverty levels which has seen millions of inhabitants choking in a sea of deprivation and despair as shown below by Keeler (2015:5):

In Africa, high poverty rates mean that investors can have an impact by investing in a broad range of companies that:

- Engage the mass market as customers or suppliers
- Create quality jobs
- Are run by economically excluded people
- Have strong ESG or sustainability policies, or
- Are focused on high impact before commercial returns

The burgeoning masses of impoverished people will make up the *demand side* in the impact investment model. We will explore two key populations in this section i.e. women and the youth as they make up most of the poor in the continent. The continent over the years has witnessed a steady growth of wealthy individuals, celebrities, Development Finance Institutions (DFIs), Microfinance Institutions (MFIs) etc. To complete our impact investment model, this clique of high net worth people and organizations will then make up the *supply side*, thus enhancing chances of success of the concept.

The continent has a youthful population comprising of millennials who are tech savvy and are driving innovation so as to solve some of the problems in the continent. This generation is the future and hope for transformation of the continent. Impact investment will therefore facilitate promotion and growth of innovative enterprises, (UNDP, 2016). Sadly, this generation has not had much of opportunities as observed by Severino and Baraton (2013):

> Despite rapid economic growth, the creation of economic and social opportunities for the younger generation remains a crucial challenge for African governments. Indeed, the employment-to-population ratio has remained virtually constant over the last 20 years (from 59 percent in 1991 to 60 percent in 2011).

Besides having abundant youths who live in poverty in the continent, women are also a vulnerable segment of the population in the continent who if targeted by impact investments, the impact will be phenomenal. Women bear burden especially of climate change in Africa. According to World Health Organisation (WHO, 2010) seminal paper, women play multiple roles in families, so this poses extra burdens to them in cases of climate change. Women Environment and Development Organisation (WEDO, 2007) contends also that the majority of the world's poor are women and are vulnerable to climate change, which also worsens gender gaps. Impact investments will then target women by capacitating them so that they have access to strategic resources such as water and energy.

A notable proposal in the African continent which has potential to empower women is the "50 Million Women Speak" grant facility amounting to USD 9.8 million by Africa Development Bank (AfDB). The facility targets urban and rural women entrepreneurs in the continent, set to run for three years. The facility was scheduled to start in 2017. It intends to address challenges faced by women such as lack of collateral, weak property rights etc. (AFDB, 2016). This pro women oriented initiative is spot on and will have a huge impact if fully embraced.

Globally, climate change, is rearing its ugly head. Africa as a continent is worst affected. Evidence of climate change, is plenty in the continent. United Nations Environmental Programme (UNEP, 2014) gives evidence on melting of glaciers of Africa located in East Africa. This is largely attributable to climate change. This is being observed in four countries, i.e., Tanzania which has mount Kilimanjaro, mount Kenya in Kenya and mount Ruwenzori shared by Uganda and Democratic Republic of Congo. Livelihoods of about 1.5 million people who survive directly or indirectly on Kilimanjaro are gradually getting affected. Impact investments targeting empowering these vulnerable communities with apparatus of resilience to this effect of climate change will be most appropriate.

Impact investment is a feasible model in contemporary Africa due to prevalence of Small and Medium Enterprises (SMEs) in most countries in the continent. Kenya is composed of 75% SMEs. Most of these have no collateral. Micro financing becomes a critical vehicle of financing. Fully capacitating them will be instrumental for developing the middle class in the continent. This will facilitate ownership by locals of means of production as noted by Severino and Baraton (2013) through having impact investments:

> Impact investment may also allow Africa to ultimately own its corporations. There is a risk that Africa's current economic model will result in foreign businesses dominating the supply of goods to its domestic market, as well as the continent's exports to the outside world, be they Chinese, European, American or Indian.

The words of Severino and Baraton echo almost similar sentiments with the concern raised by Malaysia's Prime Minister which we encountered earlier on, especially on China's overtures on poor and weak states. Moreover if Africa is able to own its own corporations, this will help the continent to be able to finance its own development initiatives through local mobilization of resources. This dovetails with one of Agenda 2063's Africa's need to own and finance its own development.

Related to the above, is the fact that manufacturing sector is still in its nascent stages in the continent. In some instances it is even declining,

Africa Development Bank (2013) cited in Severino and Baraton (2013: 2) highlights this:

> Manufacturing industries remain very small in Africa, representing only 10 percent of its GDP—a share that declined by around 1 percentage point between 2006 and 2011.3 Indeed, manufactured goods represent only 23.5 percent of sub-Saharan exports, against 83.5 percent in Asia. African economies also have a very low level of diversification.

There is need for Public Private Partnerships (PPPs) in provision of critical enablers such as infrastructure. We explored how there are still infrastructure gaps in the continent. Impact investment will be critical in complimenting existing initiatives. Around 2013, Africa was in need of an estimated USD 390 billion in infrastructure in the sector of energy over the medium term, Severino and Baraton (2013). A model of a provision of such critical enablers can be best through exploring of PPPs given that most national governments are hamstrung to go it alone in the continent.

Impact investment is the future of modern world given the ever changing global environment and challenges which keep on calling for better strategies. There is serious need for socially and environmentally responsible business practices to allow for generation of profits and at the same time things like the environment being preserved and promotion of general welfare of people. Given the nature of problems explored in the early chapters of this book, it is easier in the continent to get unscrupulous foreign investors, in most cases they mostly care for profits at the expense of societies they operate in. Most companies will plough back less in their communities despite reaping huge gains.

In Zimbabwe, the government introduced a noble initiative termed Community Share Ownership schemes in 2015. With this program, the idea was that firms were supposed to make financial contributions from part of their profits which went towards development of communities they operated in. Projects such as roads, clinics, schools, self-help projects etc. would then be supported through this fund. Thus the idea would be to create maximum possible impact from the investment.

The initiative was born out of the realization that for some communities in particular mining towns, once a mineral is depleted and the investor relocates elsewhere, the town which was subsisting mostly on the now exhausted mineral will plunge into chaos. Besides the mineral being exhausted, it could be due to falling global demand with time of the mineral being extracted. Due to viability problems the respective investor may decide to wind up operations. In the two scenarios, the mining town slowly degenerates into a ghost town. With little or no economic activities to fall back on, inhabitants of such towns are plunged into poverty of unprecedented levels. If only impact investment had been embraced as a model for investment people's lives could have been better.

An example from mining of the commodity asbestos from Zimbabwe will help us illustrate how impact investment has been lacking and the accompanying problem. Two mines Mashaba and Shabani Mines are situated in two different provinces in Zimbabwe and less than 100 kilometres apart. For a long time the two mines were responsible for asbestos production. During peak periods in the 1990s, the companies used to command huge workforce and serviced the export market such as South Africa with asbestos. The two mines during glory days also used to be famed for churning reputable sports personalities which have even represented Zimbabwe at various levels internationally. Gradually, demand for asbestos has been falling, due to health concerns around the product. This coupled with several operational challenges resulted in the two mines shutting down. Consequently communities depending on them were plunged into chaos. Mashaba Mine is the hardest hit with virtually little economic activity taking place following the collapse of mining operations. The town has deteriorated to a pale shadow of its former self, with most of its populace unemployed. If only models similar to Community Share Ownership schemes had been mooted earlier, the story could have been different for the two towns.

Challenges in Implementing Impact Investment in Africa

In light of the above, are impact investments feasible in Africa? Can the impact industry grow in the continent so as to leverage sustainable growth and development? According to a UNDP (2016) report, there is lack of absorptive capacity for large investments in developing countries for impact investments to materialise. Thus availability of feasible projects remains a key issue in most developing countries. This is also corroborated by Keeler (2015:3) who notes that:

Many companies cited low return on investment/commercial viability and partnerships with communities as top challenges to growth. This reflects the high cost of doing business in Africa, which is amplified for businesses that engage with poor communities and work in remote rural areas.

Lack of appropriate knowledge to operationalize impact investments is another key challenge for impact investment in the continent. For most countries in the continent the concept of impact investments may not be readily understood, making its implementation a challenge. Common problems according to UNDP (2016), may have to do with for example taking into account different understanding of the financial risks and intended impact between a global investment committee and a local community. Such confusion can derail successful implementation of noble impact investment initiatives. To further complicate the problem of information availability is the lack of local networks to inform on impact investment. Existence of these will help to link up with global networks. Further, these help in stimulating awareness through debates, policy tools, methodologies etc. on how best the continent can also implement the concept. The networks can also help in consistent reporting on impact investment activities which helps in correct information dissemination.

Restrictive business environments of Africa are still a challenge and a threat to sustainably front load development for the continent. We observed in Chapter 6, how these environments hamper success in regional blocs and doing business in general as shown in Chapter 5. The same business environments make impact investments not easy as observed by Keeler (2015: 5):

> But Africa's challenging business environment means that returns are more constrained in relation to impact goals:
>
> - At the small-cap level and for many high-impact social enterprises, many investors are only able to return capital at cost
> - Mid-cap companies, and those where impact is defined loosely as job creation, serving mass market customers or ESG standards, often produce market rates of return; but some would argue that this low level of impact is indistinct from traditional investing.

Similarly, Severino and Baraton (2013:2–3) support Keeler's view on business environments of the continent by touching on a wide range of issues:

> Infrastructure gaps and a difficult business climate have exacerbated direct and indirect costs for African companies. Frequent electricity shortages, high transportation costs, the lack of financing and bribes are key challenges. African companies lose about 13 percent of their working time because of selective power cuts, compared with only 1 percent for Asian companies. Transportation costs are more than double those in East Asia. Labor costs are higher than in other regions at the same level of GDP: Southeast Asia labor costs are 40 percent lower than in Africa.

We highlighted in Chapter 6, the problems with doing business in the continent in an empirical study of twenty six nations. Africa is therefore in need of a raft of measures so as to attract meaningful impact investment projects which can transform the continent. Regulatory environments in the continent have to be fine-tuned to allow for this. In addition, offering of fiscal incentives such as tax cuts and subsidies will be useful in luring potential impact investments. Taxes for instance remain high in the continent constraining businesses as observed by Severino and Baraton (2013: 4):

> Taxation is often a problem for private equity. African tax systems vary considerably, but more and more countries heavily tax profits on equity when investors exit. This is especially a problem in the absence of a taxation treaty between investor and investee countries; double and excessive taxation occurs in these cases and represents an obvious constraint for investors.

According to Spotlight on the market (2014), a survey carried on effectiveness of government policies in driving impact investment, policies such as tax cuts and subsidies ranked top in promoting impact investments. The report further states that in the UK in 2014 for example a 30 % tax relief was introduced for social investments. Later, the government also launched the Social Stock Exchange which features companies engaged in visible impact investments. In short, government will be instrumental in creating a policy environment which instils confidence among impact investors. The view on taxes as a fiscal incentive for impact investments is also shared by Dalberg Group of Advisors in a (2011) report.

Another challenge is lack of national governments support in promotion of impact investment initiatives in the continent. This may be due to lack of appreciation on the part of governments on the importance of impact investments. Governments in developed countries such as the US directly spearhead initiatives to broaden embracing of impact investments to steer robust growth and development. Here is a summary of these from Spotlight on the market report (2014) with respect to the US as of 2013:

In 2013, the Obama Administration launched the National Impact Initiative (NII) to expand the use of impact investing as an element of the Administration's strategies for economic growth and global development. As part of the NII, the US Small Business Administration (SBA) announced a new round of solicitation for the Small Business Investment Company (SBIC) Early Stage Investment Fund that will increase the amount available for investment from USD 150mm to USD 200mm annually.

The above example about the US government on its efforts to promote impact investment in the country shows the critical enabling role a government should play. For impact investments to result in huge and positive impact, there has to be a buy in from government. This is an important cue for African countries so as to realise significant gains of impact investments.

This far we have seen from the above the concept of impact investment how it has the potential to transform Africa, just like it is helping other continents. The concept is being practised sporadically across the continent. Regions such as East and West Africa are notable examples of success stories of implementation. For instance, countries like Kenya, Uganda, Tanzania, Ethiopia have most impact investments in East Africa, GIIN (2015). Despite this, the concept remains under practiced in most parts of the continent, as development linked problems in the continent continue to mount.

Impact investment industry has massive potential to flourish in the continent. Sectors such as energy, infrastructure, water and sanitation, urbanization, SMEs can be explored through impact investments leading to transformation of lives of inhabitants of the continent. Who then should initiate impact investments for the continent? We believe that impact investment initiatives which are driven from within have a potential to last longer and also to exert greatest impact. Locally driven initiatives will imply local ownership and better visibility of programs. Moreover, preinvestment support is easier for locals than for foreign players who at times face too much restrictions.

Some impact investment models currently practiced in the continent such as in agriculture, nutrition, water and sanitation sectors etc. are largely driven from outside. This is not bad. However, more still can be done. There is need for continuity, which then will drive sustainability. We pointed earlier how affluence is growing steadily among local individuals, institutions etc. These should be at the forefront of initiating impact investments. What they need greatest is appropriate knowledge and global networking. In addition, they can then come up with consortiums of local impact investors, in the process they are able to impact the continent greatly towards sustainable development.

Industrial Cluster Strategy: Embracing Globalised and Outward Looking Models, Towards Industrialisation of Africa

Developed nations and emerging economies have made strides in buttressing economic growth and sustainable development through execution of properly organised industrial clusters. Clusters are well known for their ability to reduce costs, enabling research and development, increased productivity among other advantages. Sadly, Africa lags behind in the phenomena of industrial clusters. We have shown how the continent also lags in other respects in Chapter 1 compared to the rest of the world. Empirical studies on the concept of clusters have shown a strong link between organised industrial cluster activity and economic growth and development.

The view of this section is to encourage a rethink by Africa on how it is currently implementing industrial clusters. This allows her to reconfigure current cluster initiatives in line with global best practices. Basing on our experience and knowledge about the continent, we discovered that the phenomena of clusters in Africa is not given seriousness as in other parts of the world. Partly, it can be due to the ignorance of the immense benefits which can be derived from having clusters which are properly modelled. Furthermore, the concept is often misunderstood as a result it is then not properly implemented. What we may call "industrial clusters" in Africa, we discovered may not be worthy to be called such when compared with international best practises of successful models. Most often the impact of our clusters has been small to leverage sustainable development.

Factors prohibiting implementation of organised industrial clusters in Africa will also be explored. Case studies to look at successful clusters which have made a global impact will wind up discussions in this section as well as what Africa should do so as to also develop better clusters.

Industrial Cluster Concept

Industrial clusters are defined as a group of specialized small and medium sized firms which are domiciled in a particular geographical area.On the other hand, they can be further defined as a group of firms located in the same geographic area, such as an industrial district, town, small region where there are significant number of firms specialising in producing inputs for and manufacturing the same type of good.

Further, industrial clusters can also be defined as a geographically proximate group of interconnected companies and associated institutions in a particular field linked by communalities and complementarities (Porter, 1998:199). On the other hand, OECD (2009) defines clusters as a network of closely related enterprises for production and added value and strategic alliance among main actors including universities, research organisations, knowledge service providers, brokers and consumers.

Industrial clusters were firstly embraced by Western European and North American countries, Ketels and Memedovic (2009). As time went on emerging economies began to adopt clusters as a model for economic development. The table below gives a sample of notable clusters which have had a global impact. Examples of successful global industrial clusters include South Korea's automobile manufacturing, Pakistan surgical tools manufacturing etc.

How then do industrial clusters develop? Ketels and Memedovic (2009) maintain that well organised clusters develop overtime. Further, they state that there is no single cluster model. They can develop where there are SMEs, from which the rest builds on them. On the other hand they argue that clusters can develop where there is a successful institution e.g., a university or a big company. This leads to attraction of other companies for instance the biotech cluster of North Carolina which developed from within a network of universities.

There is general consensus that the concept of industrial clusters dates back to the works of Alfred Marshall (Andersen and Opsal, 2010; Ismalina, 2010; Thompson, 2005; Boja, 2011). According to Andersen and Opsal (2010) the concept of clusters can traced to foundations laid by authorities such as Marshall (1920) and Weber (1929). They contend that Marshall studied how industrial districts of England evolved overtime. During the time, Marshall observed three main reasons as to why firms located at one place; specialisation, labour pooling and knowledge spill overs.

The concept of clusters was later advanced by Porter and Krugman others in the 1990s, according to Korea Industrial Complex Corporation (KICOX) 2015 handbook. According to Andersen and Opsal (2010) works by Porter brought more understanding and appreciation of the concept of clusters than the traditional held view. This was captured in his book, "The Competitive Advantage of Nations" which features the Diamond theory. In the concept, emphasis is put on the need for cluster networking of various stakeholders e.g., suppliers, firms, institutions etc. Their synergies create competition and innovation, which in turn enhances competitiveness of a cluster helping enhancing economic performance. The importance of networking is also supported by Ketels and Memedovic (2009) they term it collaboration.

Having proper industrial clusters can create massive economic benefits for a country and spur its competitiveness on the global arena. The benefits come in several dimensions. Clusters enable higher productivity. Companies can operate with a higher efficiency, drawing on more specialised assets and suppliers with shorter reaction times than when working alone (Porter, 1998).

- Companies and research institutions can build connections to better learn and innovate, as tacit information and knowledge are best developed and exchanged locally (OECD, 2001; Porter, 2001).Thus proper cluster framework allows for networking, which facilitates cross pollination of vital information.
- Muranda et al. (2014) note the significance of the concept of clusters. They argue that they enable growth of industries which is a prerequisite for economic growth. This according to them is enabled through technological and skills transfer effects.
- Thompson (2005) gives two crucial points on importance of clusters. She argues that clusters help in boosting export performance of a country. According to her, Sialkot, the Pakistan cluster of surgical instruments produced output amounting to $122 million between 1995–96.On the other hand, the Brazil, Sinos Valley footwear cluster produced $200 million in exports in 1993. Another benefit of clusters according to Thompson are what she calls the "positive externalities" associated with clusters. In summary these include numerous advantages such as market access, productivity, specialisation and reduction of transaction costs.
- Clusters are an essential strategy for economic development. Clusters are an essential tool for competitiveness of an economy which allows also to foster balanced regional development. This is enabled by having each region to focus on the economic area it is well positioned on.

Sustainable take off of industrial clusters in Africa is still being impinged by a number of factors. The following are some key factors which still make formulation of proper industrial clusters in Africa difficult. Unless these and some other factors are dealt with seriously, the continent will never reap huge benefits which come with proper clustering.

- In most countries in Africa present industrial cluster initiatives lack adequate resources e.g. funds, infrastructure etc. That's when the role of government becomes particularly important in availing of budgetary support to cluster initiatives in the economy. The cluster can then be weaned off from government funding with the passage of time, as member subscriptions can now sustain the cluster. Government should play a facilitatory role in clusters in as far as resource provision is concerned and enacting policies which help in ensuring that comparative advantage is enhanced.

- Presence of too small, largely SME driven and fragmented cluster activity in parts of Africa. Presently, cluster activity is dominant in traditional sectors such as such as furniture and handicraft however, these are not growing much. For instance, a survey carried in Zimbabwe by FINSCOPE in 2012 on the SMEs sector reflects a number of problems embedded in this sector. The research found out that 71.6 % of the businesses are individually owned and with no employees. Those into the medium category with 30/40–70 employees were only 0.7 %. The research also identified that only 15 % SMEs were registered/unlicensed, the rest are informal. FINSCOPE showed also that most SMEs operate at residential premises, about 39%. Thus the SMEs sector cannot be relied upon entirely to be an engine for sustainable industrial cluster activity.
- Weak networking and absence of strong institutions to link and drive cluster activities dominates in economies of the continent. Despite numerous universities, colleges, trade associations companies and research centres dotted across the continent, their linkages and collaborations remains weak, making it difficult for robust cluster activity to take place.
- Inadequate requisite knowledge on industrial clusters is prevalent in the Africa. Industrial clusters though it might sound as a simple concept, this has subjected them to being misunderstood. To come up with proper clusters a profound knowledge of the concept is required. This enables dissemination of correct information about the concept, formulation and execution of correct strategies. For instance training of cluster practitioners becomes particularly important. For instance a country like Zimbabwe is strategically located in relation to other member countries in the SADC regional trading block, with adequate knowledge a transport and logistics cluster could be considered. Furthermore a national ports authority could also be mulled so as to coordinate all infrastructure projects for the country.
- General lack of marketability and attractiveness of present cluster activities in most parts of the continent.Given the random nature of current cluster activity at present, they generally lack appeal to be able to attract serious international investors, funding, resources etc. what Ketals et al. (2003) term the "Greta-Garbo" effect. Overally, this makes it difficult to formulate robust cluster models which can neatly dovetail into the global value chains.

- Failure of cluster initiatives to be complimented by other policies areas such as foreign direct investment comes in as a shortcoming of present cluster initiatives in the continent. Empirical studies have shown that investment policies (FDI), regional SMEs policies and Research and Development (R&D) policies, are crucial for cluster activities. The Global Cluster Survey of 2003 revealed that those countries with successful clusters, the aforementioned policies were strongly upheld than those without.
- Inadequate competition within industrial clusters contributes to poor cluster activity in Africa. Presently, given the nature of the clusters, level of competition is very low and weak. The net effect has been slow growth of clusters in most parts of the continent, low efficiency, lack of creativity and new products.
- Absence of affiliation to global benchmarking organisations such as The Cluster Initiative (TCI) network. This makes it difficult to bench mark local cluster activity with best practices. TCI is a platform which allows for interactions and interface of countries seriously into cluster models.
- An observation of most African countries will reflect dominance of traditional, static and subsistence level cluster activity which barely go beyond the subsistence level. Subsistence cluster activity has little emphasis on the growth and export orientation, making it difficult for the countries in the continent to dovetail into the global value chain. Furthermore, this sector has low innovation. In terms of value, the realised output has small value to make very meaningful contributions to the economy. The Global Cluster Survey of 2003, identified more than 500 cluster initiatives globally. It noted a number of findings, key among them being that most progressive clusters were in areas inclined towards high technology sectors e.g., telecommunications, automotive, pharmaceuticals etc. It was also noted that government national policy towards promotion of science and innovation was also important.

To show the importance of science in modern clusters a look at dominant clusters of Countries such as South Korea have attained tremendous milestones in this respect. Regions such Seoul digital complex, Banwol and Sihwa, Namdong, Gumi Changwon, Ulsan and Mipo, Gwangju High –Tech have clusters hugely anchored on science and technology. Most output produced is high value including petrochemicals, electronics, automobiles, ship building, automobile parts among others. In all these, the resulting exports are of high value.

From the preceding discussions, we have shown what industrial clusters are and how they have been instrumental in the growth and development of most successful countries. African countries have a number of challenges to fully formulate industrial clusters which can have a global impact. Most challenges share in common with issues highlighted in a number of sections in this volume. We now want to look at cluster success stories from a few countries. Our emphasis is on how each cluster developed and the factors explaining the success of the respective cluster. So we have seen that Africa desperately needs proper industrial clusters. The continent can still achieve its industrialization dream as espoused in the African Union Agenda 2063. What then should Africa do to come up with better cluster models befitting 21st century economies? The strategies to this will wrap up discussions in this subsection, let us briefly examine only three successful cluster stories, from South Korea, Canada and South Africa.

- Seoul Digital Industrial Complex in South Korea. According to KICOX (2015), the cluster was founded in 1964 in the capital city of South Korea. Is one of the major projects initiated by Korea, as a thrust to promote export led growth. The cluster falls under the Information and technology industry. It also includes clustered activity on electronics, textiles and apparels. A number of factors motivated growth of the sector. Key factor to its establishment was availability of a large piece of state land which allowed building of factories at affordable costs. The cluster is strategically located in the capital city of the country, which allowed accessibility to other key support services e.g. financial, consultancy etc. The cluster was enabled by concise planning. The modernisation plan of 1997 allowed improvement of the cluster. Infrastructure and institutions e.g. roads, convenience facilities, universities and research centres were put in place.Industry academia collaboration was also enabled. Networking within the broader cluster model was enabled, leading to success.
- Waterloo, Canada ICT cluster. According to Wolfe (2009), the cluster was formed around 1970s. The starting point according Wolfe (2009) for the development of this cluster was Waterloo University. Initially, the cluster focused on computing and software. Later on it has diversified its ICT products ranging from robotics, biotech, automobiles and financial services. According to Wolfe (2009), Waterloo University, was instrumental in developing a practical technical knowledge bridging the gap between theory and actual practice in industry. This was

fostered by massive collaboration between the university and the industrial community in the region which was enabled by the Waterloo Plan put in place. As a result a robust cluster model was created and ranks as one of the best in North America.

Wolfe (2009) points to a number of factors explaining success of this cluster. The university served as an innovation hub which constantly churned a supply of professionals with hands on experience. Industry academia collaboration also fostered creation of a robust platform for networking. Another factor was the role played by business associations e.g., Canada Technical Triangle, Waterloo Regional Prosperity Council etc. in offering support services. In the fold also were SMEs, they formed synergies with large companies. Lastly another important factor was the general entrepreneurial culture of the region, this enabled regional cohesion towards the same goal.

- Textiles and Apparel cluster in South Africa. According to Chadda et al. (2009), much of textile and apparel activity is mainly concentrated in Western Cape, Durban and Gauteng provinces. The cluster started around the 1930s, specialising in blankets, rugs and sheets. It ventured into industrial textiles, clothing and later on synthetic fibres. Despite numerous challenges, chief of them being price competition from low cost Chinese and Taiwanese products, the sector has remained resilient. Western Cape province is largely the main hub of textiles and apparels. It contributes 35 % of South Africa's textiles exports. A number of factors have been responsible for this cluster's resilience. The cluster is located where there is geographic proximity to retail chains. Both provincial and national government has contributed to the success too. For instance at initial stages, government maintained tariffs which were high enough to protect the sector, gradually liberalising.

In 2004, collaboration of key stakeholders was fostered through The Cape Clothing and Textile (CCTC) initiative. It brought together universities, design firms, retailers, government among other players. This allowed creativity which ensured skills and quality upgrade. Thus despite price competition faced in the sector, South Africa is able to service the high end European markets due to high quality textiles and apparels. Gelvenor Textiles is one such success story to come out of South Africa which commands 50% global market share for parachute fabrics through specialising in technical textiles.

From the few case studies explored above, we can deduce that a strong positive relationship exists between most of the countries with organised industrial cluster activity and economic growth. If properly executed, clusters go a long way in improving competitiveness of an economy, acts as a source of sustained economic growth, increased GDP etc. Robust cluster models go a long way in defining a nation, through creation of powerful and dynamic synergies in the economy. Global brands such as Huawei, Kia, Samsung, Apple, Toshiba, Kodak, originate from countries where organised industrial cluster activity is the hallmark.

From the discussions, much work has to be put by African economies if they hope of any chances of formulating competitive industrial clusters. Most problems developing countries share are similar. The following section explores some factors African economies should consider in their quest to come up with organized clusters. Whilst, the list is not exhaustive, the few points we examine are essential;

TCI membership. According to TCI Network website TCI is defined as "…a network of persons and organisations with the common objective of making their regions and clusters more competitive." The organisation has membership throughout the world. It was founded in 1998 with its clear vision being to "be a leading global network of professionals and organisations active in cluster based economic development." Its broad mission is to "support the effective use of cluster based economic development approaches as tools to raise the competitiveness and innovative capacity of firms, regions and countries." In most cases most of these economies with substantial membership are doing fairly well in with the exception of a few cases though in terms of economic growth. We briefly look at TCI 2016 membership statistics for a sample of countries. South Africa 4; Uganda 10; Burkina Faso 1; Egypt 1; Senegal 7; Nigeria 1; South Korea 12; Germany 36 and Australia 26. From the statistics, participation of African countries is low, implying that the issue of well organised industrial clusters is still not treated seriously on the basis of membership figures we have just shown.

Being a member of TCI network comes with a lot of benefits. TCI helps in expert advice on cluster mapping so as to identify workable networking in the economy. Further it provides an opportunity for study tours among members which is vital for information sharing. Hosting of TCI conferences is also enabled among members to allow for visibility of their cluster activities as well as mentoring of cluster practitioners.

Hard and soft infrastructure. Both hard and soft infrastructure is vital for properly organised cluster activity. Aspects such as roads, rail systems internet connectivity, electricity, water cost and availability, financial systems and markets are crucial for cluster programmes. Availability of these affects cost of doing business. In Chapter 5 we emphasized too how infrastructure deficits have also frustrated integration efforts in different regional blocs. Ketels and Memedovic (2009) corroborate this view. They opine that an economy will advance economically, "if it creates an overall business environment that is more supportive to cluster development." Good infrastructure will create a necessary environment for nurturing of proper industrial clusters.

Moving towards science oriented education. Appropriate education in an economy is crucial in cluster programmes. An empirical study by Andersen and Opsal (2010) on the Norway offshore industry showed science education was particularly important for cluster programs of Norway as it is innovation oriented. In their research, they showed also that what was important was not the number of higher education institutions (for Norway case), rather what is important is to invest on enhancing quality of current institutions. As such it is imperative for African countries to model their education systems to focus more on science, this makes them competitive in high knowledge sectors.

Collaboration of key stakeholders. Meaningful cluster activity requires collaboration of various stakeholders, this has been reflected for instance in the success of cluster initiatives in South Korea, Canada etc. Figure 7.1 shows some of the main players which are crucial for clusters programs to take-off.

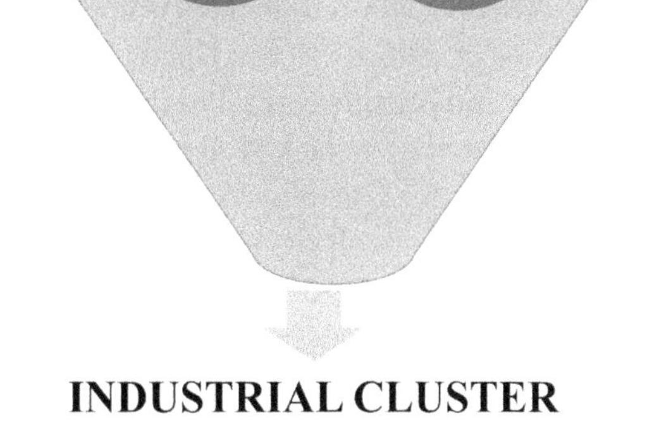

Figure 7.1. Key industrial cluster stakeholders.

From the diagram, stakeholders such as the government, universities, vocational centres etc. have to come together to come up with a heathier cluster model. This collaboration is depicted as a funnel in the illustration above. Thus the cluster concept is a broader concept requiring bringing in of diverse skills to feed into the overall success of the programme. In particular more should be done to encourage industry academia collaborations, Andersen and Opsal (2010). Collaborations allows for depth and intensive networking. An example of collaborations of various stakeholders is the Innovation Network of Denmark. This is spearheaded by the ministry of higher education and science. Its thrust is to foster innovation, collaboration, growth and internationalisation for the purpose of aiding businesses in Denmark. To date more than 22 innovation networks in 9 different professional fields have been created ranging from ICT, energy, transport etc.

Commitment to the industrial cluster programs. Success of a cluster programmes requires overall commitment of all stakeholders towards realistic targets. A common risk factor of failure of clusters according to OECD is to have a cluster policy which is vague with expectations which outweighs resource availability, what it terms "wishful thinking cluster" framework, which becomes nothing but a "field of dreams."

Development from Below

This book so far has discussed developed which is top down and spearhead by states and governments. Scott (1998) has showed that macro-level approaches to development have failed to address challenges and issues that people face in their everyday lives. Writing on macro-level and state-driven development processes, Scott (1998) clearly showed that the statist development processes involve collectivization that often is not in line with everyday realities. A case in point for in Africa was the Ujamaa in Tanzania where the state took central planning and became central in the development processes. This approach was top-down that it lacked grassroots buy-in and support. Furthermore, the state is involved in development projects that facilitate consolidation of power. In essence, all development initiatives by the state involve strengthening control over citizens. Development processes aid a phenomenon Scott (1998) calls *legibility*, and what Foucault calls *governmentality* (see Foucault, 2012; Scott 1998). There realizations have triggered different ways of thinking about development and ways of realizing. There have been calls for development from below as it has been recognized to benefit people and communities directly. In this section we discuss ways of promoting development from below.

Development from below can be achieved by focusing on activities that ordinary people engage in to strengthen their livelihoods and achieve self-sufficiency. By bolstering what ordinary people are already doing, states and NGOs can contribute meaningfully to improving the lives of those people. This is part of development from below as the initiatives and the activities involved have their origin from the ordinary people. In such situations, NGOs and states come in on terms of the ordinary people. This approach to development places *humans* the centre of development processes and initiatives. The aim here is not to develop GNPs and GDPs but to strengthen activities and processes that focus on human who are supposed to be the intended beneficiaries of any development process. This ideas forms the core of what Keith Hart (2010) calls *the human economy*. Growing the economy must not be for its own sake but to improve the lives of human. Positive growth in the economy must all be channelled to raise the standards of living.

There are a number of ways that have been identified to promote development from below. The first way is identify, capacitate and strengthen meso-level institutions that have access to ordinary people in their everyday lives. Meso-level institutions such as religious organizations, housing cooperatives, Stokvel and credit rotation clubs and local community organisations are some examples of institutions that have direct link to ordinary people. Meso-level institutions have been ignored in development processes yet they have direct access to people or are formed by the ordinary people themselves (Powers, 2015). These institutions have the means to reach out to ordinary people whom the state often misses. Furthermore, meso-level organizations have the ability to link ordinary people to macro-level institutions such as the state, banks and international organizations involved in development processes. The linkages allow for a holistic development process linked from the bottom to the state and NGOs. Theodore Powers (2015) illustrates ways in which meso-level organizations managed to link local concerns to national issues. The linkages opened doors for the democratization of the AIDS policy in South Africa.

A number of scholars have documented the role of churches, for example, in development process. Bompani (2010) notes that in South Africa, African Initiated Churches promote development initiatives through teachings that encourage monogamous marriage, faithfulness and limits drinking of alcoholic beverages (see also Maxwell, 2006). Bompani (2010) notes that the teaching partly contributes to the fight against the spread of HIV and AIDS. The contributions may be localized and low level but have an impact on members. if fighting against new HIV infection, then AIC are making contributions from their end. Apart from spearheading behavioural changes, AIC are vehicles for ordinary people develop social capital and relations that they will depend on it times of need. Social capital is a form of empowerment and resource which the poor can bank on.

As we have discussed in Chapter 4, local religious organizations are slowly venturing into social development through programmes that encourage construction of infrastructure, creating employment, capacitating members to be financially literate. It is of importance to know that current strands of Christianity has become acceptable to educated and wealthy members. Linking the economically stables with the poor and marginalized allows the latter to be assisted. Furthermore, the increase in charity activities and social engagement positively impacts society and communities. Piecemeal they may seem, but their impact on conditions of most Africans.

This chapter discussed possible solutions and the first steps that need to be taken and addressed in order for the continent to develop. These are some of the strategies that need to be considered carefully in order for African nations to meaningfully increase the standards of living for citizens. These strategies are not prescribed, nations must pick the best strategy that impacts most on its citizens.

References

ABC News. "Malaysia's Mahathir Mohamad Warns Against 'New Colonialism' During China Visit." 2018. Retrieved 23 October 2018. https://www.abc.net.au/news/2018-08-21/mahathir-says-china-will-sympathise-with-malaysia-problems/10145750

Andersen, C. E., and T. Opsal. Knowledge Based Innovation and the Benefits of Clustering: A Study of Norwegian Offshore Industry. *B1 Norwegian School of Management*, 2010.

Boja, C. *Clusters Models, Factors and Characteristics*. International Journal of Economic Practices and Theories, Academy of Economic Studies - Bucharest, Romania, 1(1): 34-43, 2011.

Bompani, B. Religion and Development from Below: Independent Christianity in South Africa. *Journal of Religion in Africa* 40.3 (2010): 307–330.

Chadda, Anmol, Qahir Dhanani, Ryutaro Murotani, Fode Ndiaye, and Ruth Kamukama. "Textiles and Apparel Cluster in South Africa." 2009. https://www.isc.hbs.edu/resources/courses/moc-course-at-harvard/Documents/pdf/student-projects/SouthAfrica_Textiles_2009.pdf

Dalberg Group of Advisors. "Impact Investing in West Africa." April 2011. https://assets.rockefellerfoundation.org/app/uploads/20150610104900/Impact-Investing-in-West-Africa.pdf

Eliason, A., R. Howse, and M. Trebilcock. *The Regulation of International Trade*, 4th Ed. London and New York: Routledge, 2013.

FinScope MSME Survey Report for Zimbabwe. 2012.

Foucault, Michel. *On the Government of the Living: Lecturers at the College De France 1979–1980*. Translated by Graham Burchell and edited by Michel Senellart. Hampshire: Palgrave Macmillan, 2012.

Global Impact Investment Network. The Landscape for Impact Investment in Africa. 2015. https://thegiin.org/research/publication/westafricareport

Hart, K. "Informal Economy." In *The Human Economy*. Edited by K. Hart, J. Laville, and A. Cattani. Cambridge: Polity Press, 2010. 142–153.

Industrial Complex Clusters in Korea: Achievements and Challenges, Korea Industrial Complex Corporation, 2015.

Ismalina, P. . "An Integrated Analysis of Socioeconomic Structures and Actors in Indonesia Industrial Clusters." *University of Groningen*, 2010. https://www.rug.nl/research/portal/files/10465073/00_titlecon.pdf

Keeler, R. "Impact Investing in Africa: Performance Insights from the IDAS Africa Portfolio." *KPMG*, April 2015. www.assets.kpmg.com/content/dam/kpmg/ke/pdf/idas/thought-leaderships/kpmg-impact-investing-april.pdf

Ketels, C. H. M., and O. Memedovic. "From Clusters to Cluster-Based Economic Development." *Int. J. Technological Learning, Innovation and Development* 1. 3 (2009): 375–392.

Klitgaard, R. *Addressing Corruption Together*. OECD, 2015.

Lumumba P.L.O. *Corruption: The Bane of Africa*, in "Corruption in Africa a Threat to Justice and Sustainable Peace," Globethics.net International Secretariat, Switzerland, 2014.

Marshall, A. Principles of Economics, 8th Edition, London: Macmillan, 1920.

Maxwell, D. *African Gifts of the Spirit: Pentecostalism and the Rise of Zimbabwean Transnational Religious Movement*. Harare: Weaver Press, 2006.

Morgan, J. "Spotlight on the Market Report." 2014. Accessed 17 October 2018 https://thegiin.org/assets/documents/pub/2014MarketSpotlight.PDF

Muponda, G. *Nurturing Latent Entrepreneurship and the Growth of Small firms in Zimbabwe*. Harare: University of Zimbabwe, 2012.

Muranda Z, Kamoyo M., and F. Mavhima, "Cluster Approach to Microenterprise Development: A Comparative Study of Clustered and Isolated Wooden Furniture Enterprise in Zimbabwe." *Journal of Sustainable Development in Africa* 16. 5 (2014).

Porter, M. E. *Clusters and the New Economics of Competition*. Harvard Business Review, 1998.

Porter, M. E. *Clusters of Innovation: Regional Foundations of U.S. Competitiveness*. Washington, D.C.: Council on Competitiveness, 2001.

Powers, T. "Negotiating State and Market: The South African HIV/AIDS Movements and Social Change." In *Economy For and Against Democracy*. Edited by K. Hart. New York and Oxford: Berghahn Books, 2015.

OECD. *Clusters, Innovation and Entrepreneurship*. Edited by J. Potter, and G. Miranda. OECD Publications, 2009.

Scott, J. C. *Seeing Like a State: How Certain Schemes to Improve the Human Condition Have Failed*. New Haven: Yale University Press, 1998.

Severino, Michel J., and P. Baraton. "A New Economic Path for Sub-Saharan African Countries through Private Impact Equity." 2013. www.brookings.edu/wp-content/uploads/2016/06/2013-BBR-Sub-Saharan-Africa-Private-Impact-Equity-Version-2.pdf

Thompson, M. T. "Essays on Cooperation in Developing Countries Industrial Clusters." University of Maryland, College Park, 2005.

A. Weber. Uber Den Standord Der Industrien, Tubigen, 1909. (English Translation by C. J. Freidrich, Alfred Weber's Theory of Location of Industries; Chicago University Press, 1929.)

Wolfe, D. A. *Universities and The Powering of Clusters*. Toronto, University of Toronto Press.2009.

World Bank. "Africa's Unexplored Potential of Trade in Services." 2016. http://www.worldbank.org/en/news/feature/2016/08/04/africas-unexploredpotential-

· 8 ·

CONCLUSION

Realising a Future for Africa

How best can we characterise the current pathetic state of Africa as a continent regarding sustainable development? Candid assessment can reveal that Africa is akin to a *giant*. A giant which however cannot be propped by mosquito limbs sustainably. The continent is a "giant" in the sense that it houses immense potential in terms of human and material endowments which however require immense nurturing so as to leapfrog the continent towards a path of sustainable growth. This potential remains heavily untapped and underutilised. The burden of poverty still weighs heavily on the shoulders of the inhabitants of the continent at a time when other nations have advanced tremendously.

The "mosquito limbs" by and large can be paralleled to the few comparative advantages which include the underutilised resources and present weaknesses and challenges the continent still exhibits, as explored largely in Chapters 3, 4, 5 and 6. These conditions as they presently appear cannot fully buttress a momentum good enough to leverage meaningful transformation of the continent towards a sustainable path like we witness today in most developed continents. Logically, supporting a giant on mosquito limbs cannot be expected to last for long. The limbs will easily give in under the sheer weight of the giant. More often, the continent has shown visible signs of progress here and there, only for the momentum to fizzle away. For instance during blissful times when prices of commodities such as oil are firm, it will be good news for most countries which are oil rich dotted across the continent including Algeria, Angola, Nigeria to mention just a few. When however prices go down south given the nature of the vulnerable economies in the continent, there is always pandemonium and chaos as economies crumble under the adverse pressure exerted by the broader unforgiving global economy.

In the midst of challenges examined in the greater part of this book, *Africa's Incomplete Cycles of Development*, there is still hope for the continent. Plenty of it! What are the possible sources of hope in pursuit of sustainable and shared development? The rest of the world has advanced, Africa still assumes a mediocre position in many aspects which has been our preoccupation of discussions in Chapter 1.

Is Aid the source of hope for Africa? Moyo (2009) strongly objects this, as it has proven to foster corruption in most parts of the continent. Billions in Aid have been poured into the continent, but much of it has gone down the drain. On the other hand, Collier (2007) does not see Aid of much use as an intervention required by bottom billion states to which Africa is a subset as it has its own challenges. To Collier (2007) Aid alone cannot rescue bottom billion countries much since it has tended to be too politicised as an instrument of intervention.

Acemoglu and Robinson (2012) also observe that aid is marred with challenges as a tool to develop poor countries. They give an example of Afghanistan where UN tried to help the country through pouring aid, but much of it was wasted due to costs incurred by NGOs administering it as well as *corruption* in general in the overall distribution of the aid. Much of the African continent is submerged in a deep sea of cancerous corruption as we noted in Chapter 3. Our empirical analysis in Chapter 4 further collaborates the view that corruption among other factors remains a serious challenge increasing cost of doing business in the continent. Unless drastic measures are executed to bring it to a halt, resources will continue to be siphoned out of the continent through this ill.

Can it be military intervention? Since decolonization of the continent from the late 1950s, the greater part of Africa is now enjoying a modicum of peace and stability as witnessed by decrease in the number of coups coupled by increasing elections which have allowed civilian governments to rule. Even if coups may be experienced here and there in some parts of the continent, they may not be as vicious as in the "decade of coups" era we explained in Chapter 4. We explained further in Chapter 4, how a "smarter" version of coups is gradually gaining traction in the continent in the form of manipulation of constitutions. Here and there although violence and internal clashes occasionally erupt in some countries for instance Ethiopia, Nigeria etc. However terrorism is becoming a fresh challenge for the continent, this still contributes significantly to instability as shown in Chapter 3. Countries such as Mali, Cameroon, Nigeria, Tunisia, Kenya frequently face terror threats, disturbing sustainable progress despite plenty of potential exhibited by these nations.

How about international trade? It is a powerful tool to uplift economies from poverty. Africa is benefitting, but much gains are accruing to more advanced countries. Advanced countries are much more prepared in terms of infrastructure, trade openness and policy environments so as to absorb as much gains from international trade. On the contrary, the myriad of challenges haunting Africa in the respective economic blocs highlighted in Chapter 5 partially reflect that Africa is not very ready for business, significant mountains still have to be moved if the continent relishes any hopes of being taken seriously by the rest of the world. Africa resembles a closed economy due to challenges still besetting it.

In most forums, Africa yearns to be treated as an equal partner than taking a mediocre position-this stance is laudable. However, to fully achieve this status, Africa should work harder so as to match blow for blow with other successful continents. We partly explained this under Chapter 4 when we explored key African barriers in the present time where we implored the need by the continent to also sweat.

In line with the above, our analysis in Chapter 6 on ease of doing business also supports Chapter 5 which examines several specific benchmarks on the numerous regional blocs found in the continent by pinpointing that the business landscape of the continent still has significant sticky issues which need urgent attention. Trade coupled with global migration have created challenges. Collier (2007: 175) summarises this when he writes about impoverished countries which he call the "bottom billion," to which the majority of Africa currently belongs:

> Trade is more likely to lock them into natural resource dependence than to open new opportunities, and the international mobility of capital and skilled workers is more

likely to bleed them of their scanty capital and talent than to provide an engine of growth.

Collier's observation has been vindicated. Trade has for over long time trapped Africa in overdependence on natural resources with their associated challenges captured in Chapter 5. Furthermore, we showed in the same chapter that state of dependency of Africa on primary commodities averages 80%–100%, a very disturbing statistic when comparing with other continents. The dependency of Africa is in key commodities like oil, minerals among others, mostly in their raw form. With these, the continent cannot effectively compete to claim a strategic position on the global stage. Our observation on trade should not be misconstrued to imply that we are advocate for an Africa which does not trade, but a continent should be better prepared to absorb meaningful gains from this global phenomena by having high value products. Value addition and beneficiation should be the way to go for the continent!

Will the development woes of the continent end now that China is deepening its friendship with the continent? China is gradually becoming a darling to most African states. At some point a country such as Zimbabwe adopted a Look East Policy following a spate of sour relations with the West. China was among the "friendly" countries the country wanted to look forward to in terms of fresh lines of credit and other interventions. In Chapter 4 we gave an overview of how China has related with African countries. To the reader interested in China Africa relations, the following are seven key questions worthy pondering over when analysing closely the relationship between China and African states in recent times.

- Now that China continues with her overtures to the continent, can the continent now fully take-off towards a path of sustainable development which it has failed to do over so many years?
- Is China the long awaited messiah for Africa to deliver its masses out of the cesspool of poverty?
- Can China be fully trusted to ensure that the continent catches up with the rest of the world?
- Is China honest in its dealings with Africa?
- The relationship between China and Africa is increasingly becoming fodder for discussion and analysis in numerous platforms. So is the future of the Africa in the hands of China?
- Most African states have challenges in upholding human rights, a component of development. Will association with China improve this?

- Is China not taking back with its left hand what it has given with its right hand to Africa?

There are alternatives contemporary Africa can pursue so as to salvage a development momentum which can be sustained. However, the dynamics of challenges Africa face today are quite different from Africa of the days gone by. The Africa of today is a free Africa, free from foreign dominion. In spite of this, it is joined to the rest of the world due to globalization. This phenomena has created complex networks in the politics and economics of the present unlike the past. In all this, Africa has to remain relevant.

In this book, *Africa's Incomplete Cycles of Development* we focused on tracing the development journey Africa is still travelling. The path to sustainable development is thus infested with a lot of challenges, such that at any given time it is difficult for the journey to be completed. If only the journey could be completed, then we would have a continent which is at par with other developed continents, a continent full of hope. Africa could be a continent with countries which are able to sustain themselves comfortably with minimum assistance from outside countries. Furthermore the continent will be in a position to outreach to other countries with Official Development Assistance (ODA), as well as from a perennial beggar of aid to an aid benefactor.

The greater part of this book has showed that Africa is still failing to realise her full potential to develop at each and every phase of its journey to better herself, hence we talk of Africa's incomplete cycles of development. Our thesis of incomplete cycles of development helps us to show that at different stages along the development path by Africa, the foundations will be shaky such that they cannot be relied upon for real transformation of the continent

From this book, Africa's Incomplete Cycles of Development, there are number of lessons that are worth recalling. African states need to re-orient their economies in such a way that their entry into the global economic system produces dividends which catapult the continent out of mediocrity. Africa already has numerous comparative advantages on the global platform. Africa provides most of the raw materials needed by corporates in the global North. Value addition and beneficiation of these which can be enhanced through proper 21st century industrial cluster models, which are competitive becomes an imperative. What matters nowadays for modern economies is '"value," as global trade is fast becoming dematerialised.

Policy somersaulting and ideological zig zagging need to be addressed in the continent due to their adverse effects on economies and people. Policy shifts are ad hoc, hence at times good policies fail to be followed up. Africa's dependence on external funders and its bid to be part of the global community limits African states to come up with home-grown solutions to poverty, poor economic performances and sustainable development.

As we highlighted in the main text, new development goals and agendas are set before most African states have satisfied the previous ones, the shift from MDGs to SDGs is one example. In support of this Shizha and Makuvaza (2017) with respect to the pillar of education, lament that before most countries in Sub Saharan Africa have been able to provide educational programs in light of the MDGs framework, the UN has since put in place SDGs which span till 2023. Africa still lags behind.

Furthermore, there is need to remove barriers that stifle African states from maintaining a momentum of progress and advancement in the present. There are various facets to development that we highlighted. Most African states are still lagging behind in most aspects whilst not so convincing efforts are being made to address this worrying status quo. There is need for post-colonial states to systematically come up with blueprints that allow them to monitor and evaluate their efforts on improving the conditions of its citizenry and maintain the gains realized in national economies. At the same time walking the talk on the blueprints will allow the continent to progress sustainably, for instance Agenda 2063 is feasible if all the conferencing and talk shows are hammered into practical actions. Moreover, all facets of development must be prioritised to avoid the Beijing model of economic successes without liberties. Africa still needs to create conditions that allow citizens to have unfettered choices and freedoms that enhance lives.

Related to the above we have seen in Chapter 2 the three cycles of development of countries in the continent. The key to also unlocking the development potential of the broader continent arguably lies in real and not current cosmetic transformation of most of countries in the second cycle. In Chapter 3, we explored the importance of seeing the light and sharing it with the rest. Thus there is plenty of light hidden in the second cycle group of countries. If only their lamps could be switched on and be elevated, the greater continent will shine with dazzling beauty.

We reiterate again that there is hope for Africa--plenty of it. There has to be a paradigm shift in the mind set and approaches to development in the continent. Completing the cycles of development is very much feasible so as to realise a future for Africa. The continent is still a global giant with a lot still to offer in terms of sustainable development and real transformation, although a lot has been stolen from her. Hence, if Africa's time is not now, then when?

INDEX

A

B

C

D

N

O

P

R

S

T

U

www.ingramcontent.com/pod-product-compliance
Ingram Content Group UK Ltd.
Pitfield, Milton Keynes, MK11 3LW, UK
UKHW021838100926
8556IPUK00004B/423

9 781433 168215